A History of
The Catholic Press Association
1911-1968

by

Sister Mary Lonan Reilly, OSF

The Scarecrow Press, Inc.
Metuchen, N.J. 1971

ISBN 0-8108-0389-5

Library of Congress Catalog Card Number 75-152543

For B. P. Reilly--
father, friend, teacher, and critic

Preface

Until the recent past, many historians have limited their investigations to those directly concerned with politics and diplomacy. As a result many economic, social, cultural, and intellectual areas of our history are still to be researched. One such large sector is that of the history of the Catholic Church in the United States in all its various aspects. A particular phase of this field that has remained generally unexplored over the years is that of the Catholic Press.

Nothing of substance has been published since the early 1930's when Father Paul Foik of Notre Dame completed Pioneer Catholic Journalism and a Franciscan, Apollinaris W. Baumgartner, published Catholic Journalism: A Study of its Development in the United States, 1789-1930. The present work is the first full-length study of the principal association of the American Catholic Press in the twentieth century, the Catholic Press Association. This organization emerged in 1911 through the concerted efforts of a few dedicated Catholic editors and has continued to grow over the years. Since 1920 the group (composed of both laymen and clergy) has worked closely with the Press Department of NCWC (recently reorganized under USCC). It has met annually to discuss problems relating to its field of journalism and has been a unifying agency for its members. Moreover, the CPA has consistently been concerned with topics of current happenings. These have been discussed at Association meetings and have occupied a prominent position in publications of the member journals.

According to the Catholic Press Directory for 1969-1970, there are now in the United States 141 Catholic newspapers and 290 Catholic magazines with a combined circulation of 25,599,766. The most important of these publications hold CPA membership; therefore, it is hoped that this study of the Association with its proceedings and problems may throw some light on the place of the Catholic Press in this century and encourage additional research in the area of the American Catholic Press.

In tracing the history of the Association it seemed expedient to examine the beginnings and early years in chronological order. Once the period of maturity was reached, however, the CPA's activities were so similar from year to year that a topical approach was used. The work does not pretend to be the full and complete history of the fifty-seven years of the organization's existence. Rather, I have tried to establish how the CPA came into being, its changing interests over the years, the evolution of the organizational structure, and cooperative efforts with other groups.

Because the CPA did not have a national headquarters until 1950, records covering the first forty years of its history are far from complete. Some early leaders did donate their correspondence and printed proceedings to the central office and some material can be found in private collections, but many papers, unfortunately, were destroyed either by the owners themselves or by their descendants. Also, the CPA in the early years was inconsistent in printing minutes of board meetings and proceedings of its annual conventions. Two factors seem to account for this: financial conditions at the time and the calibre of Association leadership. Member publications, and especially host papers, usually devoted space to the general conventions as did NC Releases and the NCWC organ under various titles from 1920-1953.

The work itself would never have been undertaken had not Francis P. Clark, Head of the Microfilm Department in Memorial Library at the University of Notre Dame, introduced me to the CPA and opened to me his personal file of Catholic Press materials collected over a number of years. He has also been a helpful critic and a willing source of information during the months that the work has been in progress.

Furthermore, the fact that a history has been completed is due to the encouragement of Dr. Philip Gleason, Associate Professor of History at Notre Dame, who directed it in dissertation form and gave extensive time and attention to it despite his many other duties. His suggestions were invaluable, his patience unending, and his scholarship inspiring.

CPA officers Msgr. Terrence McMahon, Joseph A. Gelin, Msgr. J. G. Hanley, and Rev. Louis Miller were cooperative, enthusiastic, and generous with their time and contributions. Executive Director James A. Doyle and his staff at the central office (especially Eileen Nugent and Peggy Casey) not only allowed me to research the files there during a period of several weeks, but also answered numerous enquiries both in interviews and letters.

Msgr. Francis T. Hurley, Assistant General Secretary of USCC, made the files of that office available to me. Episcopal Chairman Clarence G. Issenmann and Assistant Chairman James P. Shannon, NC Director Floyd Anderson, the entire Press Department staff, and the Press Department librarians under the able direction of Miss Kathryn Creveling were all most helpful. Father John Shellam and his capable assistant James Ward made my brief investigation of The American Catholic Historical Society Collections in Philadelphia most worthwhile. Father John Reedy, CSC, editor of Ave Maria, and his secretary Anne Gapczynski were always available and ready to supply missing data. Mrs. Helen Daly of Richmond not only opened her late husband's files but also her home and her heart to me in true Virginian hospitality.

Alexander J. Wey, George A. Pflaum, Jr., Henry Gonner, the Diocese of Erie, and Our Sunday Visitor all sent files of manuscripts and printed materials. Archivists Thomas T. McAvoy, CSC, of Notre Dame and Raphael N. Hamilton, SJ, of Marquette were gracious and of much assistance as were Father Michael Donovan of the Columbus Chancery, Mike Collins of the Columbus Times, and reference librarians at Notre Dame, Catholic University, Fordham, Marquette, and Ohio Dominican (Columbus).

Personal interviews with Jeremiah O'Sullivan, James F. Kane, Edward Walsh, David Host, Joseph A. Breig, Humphrey E. Desmond, Msgr. John S. Randall, Charles McNeill, William Holub, and Thomas Stritch were very profitable. Correspondence with Father Paul Bussard, Brother Lawrence Gonner, Mrs. Mary E. Howard, Frank A. Hall, Patrick Scanlan, and Thomas J. Carroll added interesting personal insights. Many other editors and publishers, past and present CPA members, former Episcopal Chairmen, diocesan officials, and staff members of CPA publications whose names are too numerous to list supplied incidental facts or verified information from their files and memories.

Finally, the members of my religious community, my family, my fellow graduate students, and other personal friends supplied constant support and encouragement during the years devoted to this history. To them, too, I am most grateful.

Table of Contents

List of Abbreviations

A. Collections

ADC	Archives, Diocese of Columbus, Ohio.
ADE	Archives, Diocese of Erie, Pennsylvania.
AMF	Ave Maria Files.
AUND	Archives of the University of Notre Dame.
CC	Personal collection of Francis P. Clark, Notre Dame.
CPA	Catholic Press Association Files, CPA Central Office, New York City.
DC	John J. Daly personal papers in possession of Mrs. Helen Daly, Richmond, Virginia.
HC	Personal collection of Msgr. J. G. Hanley, Kingston, Ontario.
NCCB	Files in the office of the General Secretary of NCCB-USCC, Washington, D.C. Formerly NCWC.
OSV	Our Sunday Visitor, Huntington, Indiana.
PC	Personal collection of George A. Pflaum, Jr., Dayton, Ohio.
PDF	Press Department Files (NCWC-USCC), Washington, D.C.
WC	Personal collection of Alexander J. Wey, Cleveland, Ohio.

B. Official Association Records

Program... [year]

Abbreviated Report...[year]

Minutes...[year]

Proceedings...[year]

Resume...[year]

Synopsis...[year]

Transcipt...[year]

Yearbook...[year]

"Minutes, Board...[date]"

"Minutes, Officers...[date]"

(Individual titles of all these records vary from year to year. Likewise, such records appeared from time to time, and for some years official convention reports were not published.)

C. Publications

Bulletin — National Catholic Welfare Council/Conference Bulletin (1919-1930)

Review — N.C.W.C. Review (1930-1932)

CA — Catholic Action, NCWC publication which followed the Bulletin and Review (1932-1953)

CJ — Catholic Journalist, house organ of the CPA since 1945

CJN — Catholic Journalist Newsletter, supplement to Catholic Journalist since August, 1963

D. Organizations

ABC — Audit Bureau of Circulation

ACP — Associated Church Press

ACPA — American Catholic Press Association

AF of CS — American Federation of Catholic Societies

CAP — Catholic Associated Press

CCC	Civilian Conservation Corps
CCS	Community Counselling Service
CFN	Catholic Family Newspapers
CJSF	Catholic Journalism Scholarship Fund
CNAB	Catholic Newspaper Advertising Bureau
CNR	Catholic Newspaper Representatives
CPA	Catholic Press Association
CSPA	Catholic School Press Association
IUCP	International Union of the Catholic Press
NCCB	National Conference of Catholic Bishops
NCWC	National Catholic Welfare Council/ Conference
NODL	National Organization for Decent Literature
NRA	National Recovery Act
SRDS	Standard Rate and Data Service
ULAPC	Union Latinoamerica de Prensa Catolica
UN	United Nations
USCC	United States Catholic Conference
WPB	War Production Board

Chapter I

Genesis of the CPA

As a prelude to the study of any organization, it is necessary to examine the climate in which it originated and to determine the reasons for its formation. The Catholic Press Association, which began its corporate existence in 1911, was an outgrowth of conditions existing since the early history of the United States. It was inevitable that groups professing various faiths would be attracted to a country in which there was no established religion and equally unsurprising that once there they would use the press as a means of reinforcing their doctrines and explaining their beliefs. In early American history Catholics were few and, at best, only tolerated. Most secular papers felt no obligation to promote their cause or even to give them an unbiased hearing, but Catholics were neither wealthy nor numerous enough to support their own publications, and their position was too precarious to risk jeopardizing by overt action.[1]

It was not until June 5, 1822, then, that John England, the first bishop of Charleston, South Carolina, established The United States Catholic Miscellany which is ordinarily considered the earliest genuine Catholic journal in this country. Experienced as an editor in his native Ireland, Bishop England had attempted to explain Catholicism to Americans through the pages of the secular press. Soon, however, he realized the need for an independent organ as an antidote to the public newspapers which often printed misrepresentations of the Catholic faith and calumnies against the Church.[2]

American Catholics of England's day were still but an insignificant minority, numbering no more than 200,000 in a total population of 8,000,000.[3] But by 1830 the great European migrations had begun; this massive population movement added hundreds of thousands of faithful to the American Church and profoundly changed its character. Concerned with the spiritual needs of these newcomers, the Catholic hierarchy recognized the importance of a religious press. Although most of the bishops failed to follow England's example in personally establishing a paper, they welcomed the independent Catholic papers that began to emerge. In the Pastoral Letter of 1837 issued at the close of the Third Provincial Council of Baltimore, the bishops exhorted the clergy and the faithful alike to give more support to these journals "which though not officially sanctioned by us, still are most useful to explain our tenets, to defend our rights and to vindicate our conduct."[4]

By this time the nativist movement was in full swing; in addition to verbal and printed accusations, acts of violence were perpetrated against Catholics and their institutions. In reaction to these outrages, a number of Catholic weeklies sprang up to counteract the Protestant charges by presenting the true doctrines of the Catholic faith.[5] But the bigotry of their fellow Americans also tended to undermine the self-respect of the Catholic minority and to create a defensive attitude which lingered in Catholic journalism until very recent times.

When the Civil War broke out the population of the United States had grown to almost 27,000,000, and immigration had increased the Catholic ranks to over 3,000,000. More than twenty Catholic periodicals were being published, all but four of them in the English language.[6] Meeting soon after the conflict ended, the bishops again touched on matters of the press in the Pastoral Letter of 1866. Designating lack of finances as the major cause of the shortcomings of the Catholic journals of the day, the bishops once more urged the faithful to support these publications. They noted, however, that a misapprehension had arisen regarding episcopal approbation and made it clear that the contents of such papers did not necessarily have the sanction of the local bishop or present his personal views.[7]

Continuing immigration after the Civil War brought waves of Irish and German Catholics through the 1880's when a new surge from Eastern Europe over-shadowed them. When the Third Plenary Council met in Baltimore in 1884, the Catholic population numbered over 7,000,000 and comprised about one-seventh of the total population. The Bishops' Pastoral that year recommended that each Catholic home receive at least one Catholic periodical of good repute.[8] The reminder was timely for numerous "Catholic" journals were being published by that date. There had been no ecclesiastical supervision of the press; in some instances where two or more papers were competing for readers within the same districts, controversies arose between the competing editors. Foreign language publications were common, and though better managed than the English journals, they were sometimes divisive insofar as they appealed to nationalistic elements.[9]

Not only the hierarchy but also a number of Catholic lay journalists were coming to the realization that lack of coordination in the Catholic Press dissipated its energies and weakened the American Catholic community at a time when unity was essential to meet a new wave of nativist bigotry. Before 1880 a Catholic Press convention had been suggested,[10] and during that decade a few journalists kept the idea alive.[11] This desire for unity and the belief that it could be furthered through organization was but a reflection of the social milieu of the times. During the late nineteenth century Americans joined associations and societies in large numbers, and Catholics, quite naturally, formed special organizations of their own.[12]

In earlier years Catholics had affiliated with societies established along devotional, fraternal, and benevolent lines. Irish immigrants had incorporated the Ancient Order of Hibernians in 1836, and within a decade the first American conference of the Society of St. Vincent dePaul was functioning in St. Louis. In 1855 German-American Catholics had organized the Central-Verein, and 1869 saw the formation of the Irish Catholic Benevolent Union. However, these societies tended to be parochial and ethnic in character, and it was only in the last quarter of the century that Catholics attempted to forge national organizations or cross ethnic lines in professional associations as a means of achieving Catholic unity. Among the advocates of such organizations were Catholic editors and publicists many of whom were laymen. It is not surprising, then, that these efforts at unification usually included discussion of the Catholic Press and even provisions for a special association for those working in that area.

The unification movements, however, were initiated by the older societies and often reflected an increased interest in lay activity. By the late 1870's both the Central-Verein and the Irish Catholic Benevolent Union were taking a greater interest in affairs of national scope. By this time, too, there was talk of establishing a National Catholic Union similar to organizations in several European countries or of convoking a Catholic Lay Congress for the purpose of discussing such matters as free schools, libraries, the press, a Catholic university, and social conditions. During the Third Plenary Council, Bishop John J. Keane advocated lay participation "in the non-theological aspects of the Church," and recommended that the laity join Catholic societies. The Pastoral issued after the meeting referred to the suspect secret societies of the day and incorporated Keane's recommendation.[13] But this encouragement from the hierarchy was really unnecessary. The Knights of Columbus had begun in 1882, and in 1885 the Irish Union and the German Central-Verein met at the same time in Brooklyn and urged unity among Catholics. A year later the Knights of St. John organized, and the Germans began a series of national congresses that were to continue almost to the end of the century.[14] When the bishops decided to meet in Baltimore in 1889 to commemorate the centenary of the founding of the American hierarchy, advocates of a Catholic Congress viewed this occasion as an ideal time to inaugurate that movement.

Under the leadership of Henry F. Brownson, who had attended a European Catholic Congress, and William J. Onahan, a well known Chicago layman, plans were laid and preparations begun. The majority of the outstanding lay Catholics of the day greeted the project with enthusiasm. But several bishops opposed it because they feared that a mass meeting of the laity would only arouse animosity among Protestants. Finally, through the intercession of John Ireland, the liberal Archbishop of St. Paul, Minnesota, James Cardinal Gibbons agreed that if properly supervised, a lay congress could do no harm. An episcopal commission was named, and those chosen to read papers at the Congress submitted them in advance. The program did not provide for discussion of the papers presented, and the bishops distributed the cards of admission.[15] The delegates met for two days in November "to counsel and deliberate upon subjects and affairs of common Catholic interest, and for the mutual social benefits to be derived from the intercourse and opportunities afforded by such a meeting."[16] Encouraged by the addresses which touched on many aspects of lay activity, the delegates voted to convene a second time in the city designated to host the approaching World's Fair. In a final address to the Congress, Archbishop Ireland praised the laity and enjoined them to go back to their homes and do great things.[17]

When plans for the Congress were being formulated, members of the Catholic Press were at first overlooked. Cardinal Gibbons himself finally insisted that this group be included; the late invitation resulted in some ruffled feelings but eventually the Congress Committee asked George Dering Wolff, editor of the Catholic Standard in Philadelphia, to give a paper on "The Catholic Periodical Press."[18] Wolff defined a Catholic paper as one "which sets forth and defends the doctrines of the church, narrates the progress of the church at home and abroad, and is ready to submit in all things to the authority of the church." He called on Catholic editors to "cherish the spirit of fraternal unity" and maintained that an "energetic Catholic associate [sic] press agency" must be established so that Catholic papers would have the proper facilities for obtaining news. The Congress heeded the editor's words. Among the resolutions adopted at the end of the meeting was one anticipating not only a Catholic associated press agency but also daily Catholic newspapers in the large cities and recommending that Catholics give better support to existing periodicals.[19]

In addition to Wolff's address, another development touching on the Catholic Press culminated in Baltimore. Brownson and Onahan had begun their correspondence with notable laymen in February of 1889. It was August, however, before Catholic journalists received their belated invitations. In the interim L. W. Reilly, an editor from Columbus, Ohio, had sent out a circular to members of the press calling for a convention of Catholic editors in Baltimore during the Congress. Commenting on this action after the Congress Committee had announced plans for a paper on the press, Maurice Francis Egan, a former newspaperman teaching at Notre Dame, contended that even though a plank had been dislodged from Reilly's platform, editors should still make some effort "to cultivate fellow-feeling" and to force the "unscrupulous advertising agents to be honest." Egan asserted that "not more than four" of the existing papers had "any real vitality," and he intimated that if Catholic editors neglected to unite, there would soon be no Catholic papers at all.[20]

The proposed convention was not held during the Catholic Congress. Nevertheless, a group of editors and business managers who attended the gathering met informally in the Hotel Rennert on November 10 with representatives of twenty-six journals present. Although the group named Father F. W. Graham of the Catholic Tribune as chairman and Condé B. Pallen of the Church Progress as secretary, the only definite action taken was to set a date and place for the proposed convention--the first Wednesday in May in Cincinnati.[21] Under date of April 15, 1890, Father Graham and Mr. Pallen sent out a joint letter to editors and business managers of the Catholic Press inviting them to participate in discussing "such measures as might be of benefit to the Catholic press of this country..."[22]

The convention met in Cincinnati on May 7 at the Dennison House. The temporary officers of the November gathering conducted the meetings which were attended by representatives of fourteen papers. Pallen read numerous letters of regret from editors unable to attend but interested in this effort to promote unity and fraternal feeling within the Catholic Press. After the convention voted to establish a permanent Catholic Press Association, a committee was named to draw up a constitution and to submit a slate of officers for the new organization. The name chosen was The Catholic Press Association of the United States, and the members were to be editors or business managers. Dues, five dollars annually in advance, were to be paid by the publication. Regular meetings were scheduled for the first Wednesday in May, and the object of the group was "to promote a closer union, in a truly Christian spirit, of those engaged in Catholic Journalism, to elevate the tone of Catholic newspapers and periodicals, and to promote the general interests of the Catholic Press." After the members had voted to adopt the constitution, they enthusiastically approved the officers named by the committee: President, Condé Pallen; Vice President, Father J. H. Conway (Courier, Ogdensburg, N. Y.); Treasurer, Father Graham; and Secretary, James Delaney (Catholic Youth, Brooklyn).

At a session the next morning the editors agreed to send local news items to the secretary for distribution to other Association papers. An executive committee composed of the officers and three additional elected members was authorized to arrange for foreign correspondents, to investigate the possibility of establishing a Catholic advertising agency, and to prepare and distribute a circular to editors and publishers explaining the new association. Before adjourning, the convention adopted a resolution thanking the German-Catholic Press Society, represented at the meeting by Anthony Dittrich of Der Wahrheitsfreund of Cincinnati, for its interest and support and scheduled the next meeting for the first Wednesday in May of 1891 in New York City.[23]

Many years later Dr. Thomas Hart recalled that the first news dispatch sent out by the new Catholic Press Association was published during the week of June 1, 1890, and was a report of an interview with Cardinal Gibbons concerning the organization of the Catholic Press.[24] Apparently news dispatches that first year were sparse; announcements of the 1891 meeting appearing in March declared that the prime purpose of the May convention would be the establishment of a "bureau of correspondence" to provide channels for both foreign and domestic news.[25]

The New York meeting convened in Xavier Hall at the College of the Jesuits on May 6 with more than forty publications represented. President Pallen reviewed the objectives of the Association and told the delegates that the purpose of this particular meeting was to form a Catholic associated press with foreign correspondents, to "weed out dead beats" (subscribers who were in arrears), and to establish a purchasing bureau for quantity buying. The convention adopted reports favoring incorporation of the Association; employment of correspondents in Rome, Paris, London, and Berlin; the establishment of an advertising bureau; and the setting up of a purchasing agency. On Thursday, Father Patrick Cronin addressed the convention on the "Editorial Page," W. J. O'Brien discussed the "News Page," and Milton E. Smith talked about "Advertising." In the election of officers Condé Pallen and James Delaney retained their positions as president and secretary. Father Cronin became vice president and Patrick Donahoe, treasurer. The convention also sent a cablegram asking the Holy Father's blessing and selected Washington, D. C., as the site of the 1892 meeting.[26] At a public meeting on Thursday evening presided over by Archbishop Michael A. Corrigan, Pallen told the audience of the action taken by the convention and Father Cronin spoke on "A Powerful Catholic Press." Other addresses and selections by the Protectory Band completed the program.[27]

The news service planned by this convention had a brief existence. The members for a time received letters from Rome and London as well as some domestic news items.[28] The service soon failed, however, because several editors who had agreed to take it neglected to pay for it, and Pallen had to make up the difference of more than three hundred dollars.[29] Perhaps for this reason the 1892 convention was cancelled; at any rate, there is no record that it met as scheduled. However, a few of the editors joined the Paulist

Fathers in their January Apostolate of the Press Convention in New York City. At this meeting Daniel A. Rudd, the Negro editor of the Cincinnati Catholic Tribune who had been a member of the Committee on Organization for the Baltimore Congress and had attended the 1889 and 1890 press meetings, presented a paper as did William F. Markoe of the recently organized Catholic Truth Society. A spirited discussion on Catholic newspapers ensued when Miss Katherine E. Conway of the Boston Pilot argued that to be an effective Apostolate the Catholic Press must be "conducted on sound business principles."[30]

During the early 1890's preparations were made for the next Catholic Congress. A Committee on Future Congresses had been named at the 1889 meeting, and it was planned that another Congress would meet in 1892.[31] When the World's Fair (Columbian Exposition), was announced for Chicago in 1893, however, the date was shifted to coincide with the Fair. In the interim, differences had arisen among the hierarchy over a number of matters. Perhaps the most bitter was the school controversy touched off in 1890 by a speech of Archbishop Ireland in which he seemingly gave approval to state-supported schools. Ireland even began having doubts about the feasibility of a Congress, and Cardinal Gibbons remained quite opposed to the idea. Enthusiasm among the laity had abated somewhat also, but several groups began planning to hold meetings of their organizations during the Columbian Catholic Congress.[32]

Among these was the Catholic Press Association. In mid-August of 1893 the Catholic Citizen carried a brief notice of the coming convention reporting that an informal meeting would be held and that "distinguished prelates" would address the group. The editor noted: "We think we may say that a very representative attendance is already assured." Two weeks later the Citizen printed the proposed program for the meeting listing as one of the papers Miss Conway's address delivered to the Apostolate of the Press meeting. Among the two laymen and three priests scheduled for other talks were Condé Pallen and Father Patrick Cronin.[33] The convention met in the Art Palace on Wednesday, September 6, with thirty-five papers represented. Although both the president and vice president of the 1891 meeting were in attendance, Father David S. Phelan of the Western Watchman (St. Louis) presided as temporary chairman, and F. B. Sharon of the Iowa Catholic Messenger served as temporary secretary. There was some support to retain Father Phelan as president but because he had been involved in the recent ecclesiastical controversies, the group elected instead Father A. P. Doyle of the Catholic World. Father Phelan was named vice president and Thomas A. Connelly of the Catholic Universe (Cleveland), secretary. Assigned papers were read, the organization declared itself a permanent one, and the convention drew up resolutions supporting the Holy Father and condemning character attacks in the columns of Catholic papers. [34] Reports of the meeting made no reference to any "distinguished prelates," but Cardinal Gibbons did send the convention a note expressing regret that he was unable to accept the invitation to address the group, commending the editors, and giving them advice concerning the spirit of unity that should exist among them and on their role of service to the Church. [35]

There is no record that the group met again. This may have been due to a financial recession that had begun even before the Congress met (September 4-9, 1893), and continued through 1896. Also, the lay Catholic movement had lost momentum. Leadership was wanting, and no other national Catholic Congress ever convened. [36] Furthermore, controversies among the hierarchy had continued. In addition to differences over the schools and secret societies, the bishops were divided in their support of the Catholic University which had opened in 1889. The Lucerne Memorial of 1890-1891 alleging the loss of faith of American Catholics and asking for stronger representation of various nationality groups in the hierarchy had added cleavages along ethnic lines, and the establishment of the Apostolic Delegation in 1893 caused further frustration. This disunity among Church leaders in turn tended to discourage initiative and activity of the laity. [37]

Although the editors apparently did not meet during these years, they sometimes exchanged views in the pages of Catholic publications. L. W. Reilly started such a controversy in 1894 when an article by him entitled "The Weak Points of the Catholic Press" appeared in The American Ecclesiastical Review. Reilly deplored the fact that Catholic papers were "business enterprises of laymen" rather than "official publications." He declared that for that reason the clergy was inattentive to the needs of the Catholic Press, the laity felt no obligation to support the publications, and non-Catholics had little reason to respect them. Reilly went on to enumerate poverty, incompetent editors, personal vagaries, involvement in politics, the "absence of concord of opinion," and the use of undesirable advertising as the major weaknesses of the Catholic Press of his day.[38]

In May The Review published several replies to Reilly. Condé Pallen, although "admitting the substantial accuracy" of the earlier article, contended that the weak points must be measured in relation to the times and surroundings. He suggested that the secular papers had so influenced the American reading public that Catholic editors felt impelled to follow the form and content of the secular organs. Recommending that the first step toward advancement was limitation of the number of Catholic journals, Pallen argued against making the Catholic Press official since a journal would then become "the mouthpiece of the Bishop--a mere printed vicar-general."[39]

Other replies pointed out that Catholics were not convinced that their press was "necessary and feasible," that capital was insufficient, and that papers were too often parochial, tied to nationalistic issues, and lacking in attention to the "everyday life and thought of the people." It was noted, too, that some journals of the day designated as "Catholic" were really instruments through which the Catholic name and the Catholic faith were weakened.[40]

In January of 1901 Humphrey J. Desmond, editor of the Catholic Citizen in Milwaukee, devoted several columns to a discussion of the future of the American Catholic Press. He spoke of the poor circulation of Catholic publications, the apathy of most of the readers, and the general lack of enthusiasm within the Catholic Press itself. Desmond also sent out an inquiry to a number of prominent editors soliciting their opinions on whether it would be profitable to hold a convention and on the possibility of forming a Catholic Press syndicate. L. W. Reilly, who was by then editor of the Pittsburgh Observer, labeled the discussion "a beating of the air--time and talk wasted," and he repeated his earlier arguments for ecclesiastical control.[41] Other journalists vetoed the idea of a convention "because of the strain of antipathy between the clerical editors and the lay...," questioned that any benefits would result from such a meeting, and expressed pessimism about the entire American Catholic Press. Although some were "unable to perceive any fruits of former gatherings of this sort," other editors were openly enthusiastic about attempting affiliation again and were eager that a syndicate be formed. Even though the New York and Chicago meetings had not given "much encouragement to further efforts," one editor thought that the ends to be obtained were worth another try. Father Doyle not only supported the plan but suggested that the meeting be held in New York City. He promised that he would "arrange for all the detail" including procuring a hall and obtaining "ecclesiastical commendation." Summarizing the exchange, Desmond declared: "When, as a result of a good deal of preliminary discussion, Catholic editors and publishers are prepared to formulate some practical purposes, a press convention may wisely be held."[42]

Another movement reaching a climax in the same year had some effect on the decision of the editors to forego a convention at the time. Catholic Unions and the Congresses had not succeeded in permanently uniting the laity, and it is apparent now that such attempts at unity were premature. As the century drew to a close, however, controversies within the hierarchy subsided following the apostolic letter Testem Benevolentiae on January 22, 1899, which settled the so-called "Americanist heresy."[43] Catholic numbers had reached almost 12,000,000 in a total population of approximately 67,000,000. Nonetheless, bigotry continued with frequent attacks against the Church and its activities. The administration of the territories acquired following the Spanish-American War seemed to Catholics to be overly secular in tone. Obviously, there was need of social and civic unity among Catholics of the day,[44] and those who had been for some time advocating a national federation of all the existing Catholic societies now discussed the idea at length in the Catholic Press as well as in private correspondence. Endorsed by Bishops James McFaul of Trenton, New Jersey, and Sebastian Messmer of Green Bay, Wisconsin, the first convention of the new federation finally convened in Cincinnati December 10-12, 1901.[45] Perhaps because the Catholic Press in general had favored the federation movement, the national convention of the American Federation of Catholic Societies at this 1901 meeting and again the following year adopted resolutions pledging support of the Catholic Press. Furthermore, in 1903 the AF of CS not only repeated this gesture but also extended a special invitation to editors and journalists to attend its future conventions.[46]

The Catholic Press had grown tremendously so that by 1900 over two hundred fifty journals were being issued in the various languages of the immigrants as well as in English.[47] The preceding years had witnessed the formation of various syndicates and press associations founded by the secular papers, and in 1905 an attempt was made to establish a Catholic news syndicate. Accepting the proposal made by Dr. Hart, several professors at the Catholic University and various other Catholic laymen of Washington, formed a Catholic Associated Press. The group intended to supply Catholic publications "with short articles, discussing social, economic, educational and other subjects."[48] The first article furnished by C. A. P. appeared early in October, but the project was short-lived. Within two weeks the University administration circulated a letter lamenting the fact that Catholic University letter-heads had been used for communications issued by the Catholic Associated Press and denying any connection with the project.[49] This action apparently terminated the venture but not the desire for cooperative efforts.

The national enthusiasm for organizing had continued and, indeed, even increased in the early years of the new century, and various Catholic groups had obtained permanency.[50] Many continued along devotional and fraternal lines, but a number of these were nationwide. Especially noteworthy was the action of teachers and administrators who in 1904 organized the first of a number of Catholic professional organizations, the National Catholic Educational Association. The outstanding achievement along national lines was the American Federation of Catholic Societies, but there were other notable cooperative efforts by Catholics. In 1905 the Catholic Church Extension Society for the home missions had been established, and two years later the first volume of the <u>Catholic Encyclopedia</u> was published.[51]

During these years Dr. Hart continued to dream of a Catholic news agency and of a press convention. In 1908, agitated by what he considered an oversight on the part of the National Catholic Educational Association which had just concluded its convention in Cincinnati without offering a resolution in support of the Catholic Press, the Ohio editor acted on impulse. Several journalists had attended the N. C. E. A. meeting; Hart called them together on Saturday July 25 for a press meeting in the Gibson House.[52] This group organized the American Catholic Press Association and named Dr. Hart president. The new association listed as its objectives the promotion of "educational, literary, news and business interests of the papers concerned, and . . . a closer fraternity among Catholic editors." A second meeting was scheduled for September 12 in Buffalo.[53]

In mid-August, John F. Byrnes, secretary of the A. C. P. A., sent out a circular letter extending an invitation to all Catholic editors and business managers to attend the Buffalo meeting. Informing prospective members that the group planned to organize news and advertising agencies, he noted that costs included a ten dollar initiation fee plus monthly dues of one dollar. The secretary enclosed another letter written by Dr. Hart explaining the purpose of the organization, listing the officers, and inviting all to join in the movement.[54] By this time reports of the July meeting had spread across the country and had elicited varied responses. Dr. Hart printed some of these in the Telegraph and commented on others. One editor questioned the "secrecy" of the July meeting, and others resented the fact that the association had been formed without their knowledge and aid. Some, on a more positive plane, lamented the fault-finding and asked for the "earnest cooperation of all."[55]

Even though there had been such a long period of continued emphasis on unity and cooperation, the majority of the journalists were not yet ready to place the common welfare of the Catholic Press above their own private enterprises. When the September meeting convened, only eleven papers had representatives in Buffalo although several others did send letters expressing interest in the association. Discussion centered on the proposed news and advertising agencies and on ways and means of perfecting the organization, and the group tentatively agreed to meet again in Chicago in January. Resolutions were adopted requesting advertisers to consider the medium of the Catholic Press and inviting all Catholic societies to pledge their support of businesses who so advertised. They also asked the hierarchy and the clergy to encourage the laity to patronize their publications and to release "strictly Catholic news" to the Catholic Press. Finally, the A. C. P. A. resolved to "encourage Catholic writers and foster Catholic literature."[56] Although some of the Catholic societies endorsed these resolutions, and Byrnes resigned from the Columbian so that he might devote more of his time and attention to the new association, the American Catholic Press Association failed to gain momentum. A few sporadic press releases carrying the by-line of the A. C. P. A. appeared until early November, and then this organization, like its predecessors, vanished into oblivion.[57]

Notes

1. An excellent brief history of Catholics in America is John Tracy Ellis, American Catholicism, 2nd ed. (Chicago, 1969). Chapter II, pp. 41-83, discusses "Catholics as Citizens" from 1790 to 1852.

2. Paul J. Foik, CSC, Pioneer Catholic Journalism (New York, 1930), Chapter XII, passim. The Miscellany, although suspended occasionally for want of funds, continued for forty years, until the outbreak of the Civil War. The Bishop's sister, Johanna, not only spent her small fortune in helping England meet the financial needs of the diocese but also had much influence on the paper until her untimely death in 1827.

3. Population figures used in this chapter are taken from Gerald Shaughnessy, MM, Has the Immigrant Kept the Faith? (New York, 1925), pp. 113-196. Ellis, op. cit., fn. 2, states that this book "is the best general work on Catholic population figures."

4. Rev. Peter Guilday, The National Pastorals of the American Hierarchy (1792-1919) (Washington, D. C., 1923), pp. 114-115.

5. Apollinaris W. Baumgartner, OFM, Cap., Catholic Journalism: A Study of its Development in the United States, 1789-1930 (New York, 1931), p. 12.

6. Metropolitan Catholic Almanac and Laity's Directory for the United States (Baltimore, 1860), pp. 267-268. The four foreign language publications were weeklies; one of them was in French and the other three were in German.

7. Guilday, op. cit., pp. 213-214.

8. Ibid., p. 252.

9. Baumgartner, op. cit., pp. 32-37.

10. An editorial in the Catholic Citizen (Milwaukee), August 12, 1911, stated: "Prior to 1880, there was a widely advocated movement for the holding of a Catholic press convention." The editor attributed the movement to the "editor of a defunct Catholic paper (The

Catholic Advocate of Louisville)," and claimed that he had once seen "a bundle of correspondence on the subject [which]... bore many notable authographs." No names nor other historical data were given. The I. C. B. U. Journal (Philadelphia), February, 1878, carried an editorial on a Catholic Press Association being promoted by the Catholic Mirror (Baltimore). After commenting on the advantages of such an organization, the editor added: "So, even if it is an old idea let the meeting be held."

11. For example, the Catholic Telegraph (Cincinnati), September 23, 1886, noted that "The union of all Catholic newspapers into an association for certain well defined purposes... has lately been mooted both in public and private." The writer gave the establishment of a news service and "advantageous relations with subscribers" as two goals of such a group.

12. Thomas T. McAvoy, CSC, "The Catholic Minority after the Americanist Controversy, 1899-1917: A Survey," Review of Politics, XXI (January, 1959), p. 62.

13. For a general discussion of the lay movement see: Sister M. Adele Francis Gorman, OSF, "Evolution of Catholic Lay Leadership," Historical Records and Studies, L, pp. 132-36. Bishop Keane's recommendation is on pp. 135-36. The first advocate of the Catholic Congress was probably the great convert Paulist, Father Hecker. See: [Isaac P. Hecker], "Shall We Have a Catholic Congress?" Catholic World, VIII (November, 1868), 224-28.

14. For an account of the Brooklyn meeting see: J. Philip Gleason, "Not German or Irish so Much as Catholic," Social Justic Review, LI (March, 1959), 384-385. The meetings of the German Catholics continued through 1898. This from Aaron I. Abell, American Catholicism and Social Action: A Search for Social Justice, 1865-1950 (Notre Dame, Indiana, 1960), p. 100. The press was one of the subjects discussed at the 1886 meeting, and the Catholic German-American Press Society came into being on September 7, 1887. At a meeting in Cincinnati the following year, Nicholas Gonner, Sr., the president, reported that sixteen publications had joined the society. See: "Regarding the Short-Lived Cath. G. A. Press Society," Central

Blatt and Social Justice, XXIV (January, 1932), 324. The article neglected to mention the life span of the Society. A representative attended an 1890 Catholic Press meeting, but this writer found no later reference to the group.

15. Daniel Callahan, The Mind of the Catholic Layman (New York, 1963), pp. 65-70. Brownson was the son of the convert-publicist, Orestes. Bishop Ireland was chairman of the commission of bishops. See also: Sister M. Adele Francis, OSF, "Lay Activity and the Catholic Congresses of 1889 and 1893," Records of the American Catholic Historical Society of Philadelphia, LXXIV (March, 1963), pp. 3-23.

16. Official Report of the Proceedings of the Catholic Congress held at Baltimore, Md., November 11th and 12th, 1889 (Detroit, 1889), Introduction, p. vi. Onahan wrote this. The book was published by William H. Hughes, one of the editors who met in Baltimore.

17. Ibid., pp. 187-188.

18. Sister M. Adele Francis, op. cit., pp. 7-8, discusses this oversight.

19. Wolff's address is in the published Report, op. cit., pp. 81-97. The resolutions are on p. 130.

20. Maurice Francis Egan, "The Proposed Convention of Catholic Editors," Ave Maria, XXIX (August 24, 1889), 181-182. Apparently Reilly and Egan were not named as delegates to the Congress by their Ordinaries as their names do not appear in the List of Delegates in the published Record.

21. Catholic Tribune (St. Joseph, Missouri), November 23, 1889. This account names William J. O'Brien of the Baltimore Catholic Mirror as the editor who called the meeting. Pallen's paper was in St. Louis. The date may be questioned. This Tribune notice gives November 19 as does Thomas F. Meehan, "The Press Association Harks Back a Half Century," America, LXI (June 24, 1939), 244. Meehan claimed in this article that only he and Thomas P. Hart survived of the original participants. They may well have been there as the printed Record lists them as in attendance

at the Congress. However, the Tribune article which enumerated papers and representatives included neither. Also, Meehan gave the meeting date as "Sunday, November 19." The Congress met on Monday and Tuesday, November 11-12, which would preclude that date as a Sunday. Furthermore, it seems unlikely that so many editors would have had enough time and money available to remain in Baltimore for an entire week. Meehan admitted: "I do not remember any of the particular details of what was done, nor does Doctor Hart, as he confessed in a note some time ago."

22. The letter was printed in the Catholic Citizen, May 3, 1890. It, too, gave November 10, 1889, as the date of the informal meeting.

23. Pittsburgh Catholic, May 10 and Catholic Tribune, May 17, 1890, printed complete reports of the convention including the constitution. Shorter reports were found in the Catholic Columbian (Columbus, Ohio), May 10, Catholic Citizen, May 24, and Catholic Telegraph, May 8 and May 15, 1890. None of these included the the names of the three additional board members. As Dittrich represented seventeen German Catholic papers, the Telegraph gave the number of papers represented as thirty-one.

24. Catholic Tribune, July 11, 1936. This was an NC Release. Contemporary notices, however, do not list Hart as in attendance at this meeting either. He was practicing medicine and contributing occasional editorials to the Telegraph until he took over the editorial duties of that paper in 1898 according to a brief history of the Telegraph which appeared in the centenary issue of the Catholic Cincinnati Times Star, April 25, 1940.

25. Catholic Tribune, March 14, 1891. Also, Catholic Citizen, May 9, 1891, said that was the main business at the meeting that week.

26. For reports of the 1891 meeting see: Pittsburgh Catholic, May 14, Catholic Columbian, May 16, Catholic Citizen, May 16, and Catholic Telegraph, May 14. The last named account was written by one of the few women active in the Catholic Press at the time,

Miss Mary M. Meline, and makes interesting reading. Miss Meline commented on how cold it was in the hall during the first session. She also noted that the matter of approving a charter caused a long debate but that "Mr. Griffin of Philadelphia, was the only one who opposed the idea and he seemed to do so more as an occasion for talk than for any good reason." She asserted that "A lively discussion was the order of the day, a discussion, the calm waters of which were frequently crisped into wavelets of wit and sarcasm,..."

27. Catholic News (New York), May 10, 1891.

28. Dr. Hart noted this in the NC Release printed in Catholic Tribune, July 11, 1936.

29. [Martin I. J. Griffin], "Catholic Press Association," American Catholic Historical Researches, XXIX (January, 1912), p. 70 commented on this. Without mentioning any names, L. W. Reilly, "The Weak Points of the Catholic Press," The American Ecclesiastical Review, X (February, 1894), 119-120 told of an attempt to form a Catholic Press Syndicate. It ended in failure because editors failed to pay for it. This was quite probably the 1891 service.

30. Catholic Tribune, January 16, 1892. See also the published report: The Convention of The Apostolate of the Press held in Columbus Hall, New York City, January 6th and 7th, 1892 (New York, n.d.). Miss Conway's address, "Mending Old Roads and Making New Ones," is on pp. 76-85.

31. Official Report of the Proceedings of the Catholic Congress held at Baltimore, Md., November 11th and 12th, 1889 (Detroit, 1889), Introduction, ix-x.

32. Sister M. Adele Francis, op. cit., pp. 14-19.

33. Catholic Citizen, August 12 and August 26, 1893.

34. Accounts of the 1893 meeting can be found in Catholic Citizen and Church News (D. C.), on September 16, 1893.

35. New World (Chicago), September 23, 1893, printed the

Cardinal's letter.

36. Sister M. Adele Francis, op. cit., pp. 21-23.

37. Rev. Peter Guilday, "The Church in the United States (1870-1920): A Retrospect of Fifty Years," Catholic Historical Review, VI (January, 1921), 533-547 contains a brief account of the period by a contemporary.

38. Reilly, op. cit., pp. 117-125, passim.

39. Condé Pallen, "The Independence of the Catholic Press," The American Ecclesiastical Review, X (May, 1894), 329-342.

40. Others replying were: John Talbot Smith, "Partisan Politics in the Catholic Press," 343-349; Maurice Francis Egan, "The Need of the Catholic Press," 349-357; and "The Catholic Press and Episcopal Authority," 358-368. This last article was unsigned, but it was probably by the editor, the Rev. H. J. Heuser of Overbrook.

41. Pittsburgh Observer, January 3, 1901.

42. Father Doyle's comments were in the Catholic Citizen, January 12, 1901. Other columns appeared on January 5 and 19. A summary of the exchanges appeared in The Review, VII (February 28, 1901), 385-386. Arthur Preuss, The Review editor, did not favor a convention.

43. For the complete story see Thomas T. McAvoy, CSC, The Americanist Heresy in Roman Catholicism, 1895-1900 (Notre Dame, 1963). See also: Callahan, op. cit., pp. 70-75. One of the editors who answered Desmond in the 1901 enquiry had given the proposed federation as a reason for not calling an editors' convention. See: Catholic Citizen, January 19, 1901.

44. A good discussion of Catholic unity can be found in Thomas T. McAvoy, CSC, "The Background of American Catholic Unity," The American Ecclesiastical Review, CLV (December, 1966), 384-392.

45. Gorman, op. cit., pp. 153-156.

46. Abell, op. cit., p. 133 noted the favorable attitude of the press. References to the press can be found in: Proceedings of the American Federation of Catholic Societies (1st, 2nd, and 3rd conventions). Microfilm, AUND. This friendly relationship was to continue throughout the life span of the Federation which held its last convention in 1917. For the history of the group see: Sister M. Adele Francis Gorman, OSF, "Federation of Catholic Societies in the United States, 1870-1920" (Unpublished Ph. D. Dissertation, Department of History, University of Notre Dame, 1962).

47. M. H. Wiltzius and Co., Official Directory (Milwaukee, 1900), pp. 568-572 lists existing journals. Some notion of the extent of the press can be found by noting that there were approximately 80 English, 30 German, 10 French, and 10 Polish weeklies plus various others in less prominent languages and numerous journals appearing at other intervals.

48. The intent of the group was explained in: Catholic Press Association of the U. S., I am The Catholic Press (n. p., 1946), p. 15. WC. The Catholic Telegraph, October 5, 1905, identified some of the contributors as Professor J. C. Monaghan, The V. Rev. Drs. Pace and Shahan, and The Rev. Drs. Shields and Kerby.

49. The Catholic Telegraph, October 5, 1905, carried the first article and identified it as such. The letter from the University administration appeared in the Pittsburgh Catholic, October 26, 1905.

50. Ellis, op. cit., p. 139 noted that Americans of the twentieth century have had a "national passion for organization,... To this trend the Catholics were no exception,... "

51. The 1937 Franciscan Almanac (Paterson, N. J., 1937), pp. 446-447 lists the founding dates for a number of Catholic organizations. For the story of the Catholic Encyclopedia, see Paul H. Linehan, "The Catholic Encyclopedia" in Vol. IV of Catholic Builders of the Nation (Boston, 1923).

52. Joseph Kneip, "Dr. Hart of Cincinnati," Catholic Press Annual '63, p. 16. Only five papers were represented.

53. Catholic Telegraph, July 30, 1908. Other officers were: Secretary, John F. Byrnes (Columbian and Western Catholic, Chicago); Treasurer, William A. King (Catholic Union and Times, Buffalo); Vice President and Chairman of the Executive Board, William H. Hughes (Michigan Catholic, Detroit); Secretary of the Executive Board, Samuel Byrne (Pittsburgh Observer).

54. Both letters, dated August 15, 1908, are in CC.

55. Catholic Telegraph, August 13, August 27, and September 3, 1908, contained the comments.

56. Ibid., September 17, 1908. The January meeting never materialized as the organization was defunct by then.

57. Dr. Hart in the Catholic Telegraph, October 1, 1908, printed a letter from the St. Louis Federation congratulating the new association and endorsing the resolutions. Byrnes' action was reported in the same paper on October 29, 1908. The Catholic Telegraph carried articles with an ACPA by-line from September 17 through November 5, 1908.

Chapter II

Early Years of the CPA (1911-1919)

It might seem that after so many unsuccessful efforts, Catholic editors and publishers would have despaired of ever forming a professional association. And, indeed, The Catholic Citizen of Milwaukee sounded a pessimistic note in an editorial remark concerning still another press meeting scheduled for August 24-25 of 1911. "[It] will be the fourth such sporadic getting together, in the last twenty years. No single practical step has ever come from these gatherings."[1] The majority of Catholic journalists, however, took a brighter view of things. Most of them shared the opinion expressed by the Bulletin of the American Federation of Catholic Societies which predicted that "the first successful conference or convention" of Catholic editors was about to take place.[2]

Although the editors of non-English-language newspapers were accidentally overlooked by those sending out the invitations,[3] at least thirty-seven publications sent representatives to the organizational meeting held at the Chittenden Hotel in Columbus, Ohio, just after the close of the annual convention of the American Federation of Catholic Societies.[4] The delegates to the press convention were a fairly representative group including in their number a half-dozen women, almost two dozen priests, and more than thirty laymen. The convention booklet, printed and distributed through the courtesy of the Providence Visitor, exhorted each of these delegates to strive for "the greatest possible results from the meeting."[5] The Visitor also provided the temporary chairman of the gathering, Edward J. Cooney, who had been the prime mover in organizing the convention.[6]

Cooney opened the meeting by outlining the aims and purposes which a professional association of Catholic journalists could pursue: publicizing news of Catholic interest, combatting the evil influence of some sectors of the secular press, securing national advertising for their own papers, and agitating against higher postal rates for newspapers.[7] James T. Carroll of the local Catholic Columbian then welcomed the journalists, and James J. Hartley, Bishop of Columbus, demonstrated his support not only by blessing the efforts of the journalists but also by contributing five hundred dollars to the yet-unorganized Catholic Press Association. In gratitude, the convention unanimously elected Bishop Hartley honorary president--a position he was to hold until his death in 1944.[8]

The convention turned to serious business with a paper on "An Associated Catholic Press" delivered by the Reverend Peter E. Blessing also of the Visitor. After reviewing the need for an association, the deficiences of present publications, and the demands of the Catholic readers, Father Blessing concluded:

> The question before this assembly is whether through association we can achieve that which for us, as units, is impossible. Throughout the length and breadth of the land there is resounding a clarion call from an interested and intelligent laity for greater knowledge of what the Church is doing and the reason why she is persecuted. They want facts and their interpretation. The world is girded with the means of information and in every place there are to be found men well equipped to find and send to us the truth. Are we big and broad enough to join forces to take advantage of these modern means that lie within our reach?[9]

The paper was referred to a committee on organization chaired by Nicholas Gonner of Dubuque, Iowa. Later recommendations from this committee were based largely on Father Blessing's suggestions.

As part of the discussion of a news syndicate, Gonner explained the International Telegraph Agency, commonly referred to as the "Juta," which was in the process of being organized in Europe to distribute news to Catholic papers. Twenty-nine delegates pledged that their publications would each contribute at least one hundred dollars to the foundation of the "Juta."[10]

Several speakers on Thursday presented papers on advertising, and that evening the Reverend David J. Toomey of the Pilot in Boston discussed "A Real Catholic Press."

Noting the dangers to the faith inherent in the daily secular press, Father Toomey emphasized the responsibility of the Catholic editor in upholding the cause of the Church: "The manifest Catholic interest should be the special care of the editorial page. The Catholic viewpoint, not the editor's personal opinion, should be the only one given on topics of the hour." The following day the convention featured papers on circulation and advertising problems, but returned to themes of broader interest with an address on "The Relation of Literature to a Catholic Newspaper" by Dr. Thomas O'Hagan of the New World of Chicago. O'Hagan declared that "In the last analysis, the Catholic journal is the greatest factor in our country for the promotion of Catholic literature, and through the medium of Catholic literature for the propagation of Catholic truth."[11]

During the closing session the Catholic Press Association was organized. The purposes set forth in the new constitution were "the gathering and dissemination of correct information throughout the world; the spread of Catholic truth; the promotion of Catholic literature, and to further the interests of all Catholic publications."[12] Fellow Catholic publishers were invited to join; the membership fee was set at ten dollars, paid in advance. The government of the new association was vested in a Board of Directors composed of a president, vice president, secretary, treasurer, and three additional directors to be chosen by plurality vote at the annual convention each year. Officers were unsalaried except for the treasurer who was to receive ten dollars per year. Three special bureaus, each to be governed by a five member board of directors, were established: the News Bureau to gather and disseminate "correct information on topics of current interest both in this and other countries"; the Literature Bureau to encourage Catholic authors and promote Catholic literature; and the Advertising Bureau whose aim was to be "the exploitation of Catholic publications as a medium of advertising."[13] The indefatigable Cooney was the obvious choice as first president of the CPA. After the other offices were filled, and a cablegram sent to Rome carrying the Association's "greetings of undying fidelity to the Holy Father and humbly ask [-ing] his blessing upon the new organization,"[14] the convention ended with the decision to meet the following year in Louisville, Kentucky, in conjunction with the AF of CS.

At last a permanent Catholic press association had been born. Many of those present at that historic meeting must have murmured a fervent "Amen" as they read a press release shortly thereafter which affirmed that "... the association, organized under such favorable auspices, promises well for the future and success of the Catholic press in the United States and Canada."[15] Within a few months, however, President Cooney was sending out "An Official Circular to the Members of the Catholic Press Association" --plainly marked "not for publication"--in which he enumerated the difficulties that had already arisen. First of all, the "Juta" movement had collapsed. A circular sent out to five hundred eighteen Catholic publications soliciting affiliation with this service netted only twenty-one subscribers. In the meantime the "Juta" itself had disbanded leaving the CPA's News Bureau without a suitable means of gathering and distributing news. The Association's Advertising Bureau had likewise encountered difficulties. Cooney himself was chairman of this Bureau, and he reported that plans were at last underway to obtain national advertising through united action. Aiding Cooney in formulating a plan which the president expected to present at the Louisville convention was Louis N. Hammerling of New York who had been especially successful in organizing the foreign-language newspapers for the same purpose.

On a more positive plane, the president noted that the CPA was represented on a committee to meet with the Postmaster General concerning second class postal rates. He also announced that the first story sent out by the Literature Bureau had been well received by the member publications. Ending his communique on an optimistic note, Cooney exhorted:

> ... let us urge all the members of the Association to remain loyal and do what they can to interest those publications not affiliated, in order that we may have a rousing convention in Louisville. It will take the three Bureaus several months to get their plans into shape. There is a great deal to be done before any definite action can be announced. We ask the members to be patient and there is no doubt that we will yet become an organization of wonderful strength and influence.[16]

As August, 1912, approached, CPA enthusiasts were anxious to make the second meeting a success. The convention notice, signed by all the officers, recalled the previous year's gathering and admitted:

> ...when the notices were sent out for the first meeting several papers eligible for membership were over-looked, and acting under the advice of the Apostolic Delegate, now Cardinal Falconio, we take this means of extending you and all editors and publishers of Catholic papers an invitation to send representatives to the convention..[17]

Although approximately fifty publications were represented in Louisville, the actual attendance was smaller than the previous year. One editor accounted for the decline in geographical terms rather than attributing it to lack of interest explaining:

> The majority of our Catholic publications are insufficiently manned and it is difficult for either an editor or a manager to absent himself from his office for even two days and it would have taken several days longer than this period for many of the Catholic journalists, those on either coast to attend the convention.[18]

Some who did manage to absent themselves from their newspaper offices were benignly described by the Reverend Dr. J. H. Cotter in the Buffalo Union and Times a few weeks later:

> ...Dr. Roche, of Toronto, the lines of whose face so strongly resemble Cardinal Logue's, reminded us of his presence in his watchfulness of procedures; Dr. Warren Currier, self-possessed and thoughtful, illuminated debate; then there was the old guard, Dr. Hart, impetuous and chivalrous, Mr. Hughes, gentle, forceful and kind; Father Burke, enthusiastic and scholarly correct; Mr. Gonner, strenuous and progressive,... St. Louis in Louisville, was represented by Mr. Chew, always as calm in his speech as he is profound in his thought,...[19]

These and other delegates heard President Cooney report that the organization had been incorporated in the state of New York under the title of the Catholic Press Association, Inc. Cooney also recounted his efforts to prevent an increase in postal rates. Among other things, he had talked to President Taft and had later received a letter indicating that religious papers would not be included in the increase.[20]

The chairman of the News Bureau, Charles J. Jaegle of the Pittsburgh Observer, gave a lengthy report on the endeavors to procure a news service. To replace the defunct "Juta," he explained that a CPA News Service with Rome had been arranged provided that twenty papers agreed to take the service.

Speaking for the Literature Bureau, Father John J. Burke maintained that limited finances made it necessary for the CPA to establish priorities. Strongly endorsing the plans for a news service, he recommended that available resources be applied to that endeavor and that literary aspects be suspended until the Association became stronger. In a report for the Advertising Bureau, Cooney read a letter to the convention explaining Hammerling's organization of the foreign-language papers and suggesting that the CPA consult him in this regard. Although the members also listened to a Chicago advertising agent present a plan based on unified action and joint rates, the convention declined to approve either proposal.

In attendance at the Kentucky convention in addition to the Honorary Chairman, Bishop Hartley, and the host, Bishop Denis O'Donaghue, were Bishops Sebastian Messmer and Peter J. Muldoon who were in the city for the American Federation of Catholic Societies Convention. The former invited the convention to Milwaukee the following year, and Bishop Muldoon spoke as a representative of the Social Service Bureau of the Federation asking the editors to cooperate in explaining Socialism to American Catholics. A CPA committee met with representatives of the Social Service Bureau, and later reported that the Bureau would furnish a weekly syndicated letter of one thousand to twelve hundred fifty words. In order to procure exclusive control of the newsletters, the CPA contracted for twenty-five letters at the rate of one dollar each per week.

The only public issue on which the convention took a stand followed a request from the National Liberal Immigration League in New York. The convention approved a resolution opposing the Dillingham Bill, then pending in the Senate, and in general protested against further measures to restrict immigration.

The Louisville meeting was described as a "get-down-to-business" affair, and though nothing of great significance had been accomplished, the CPA had attained permanency.

Each year the members assembled: 1913 in Milwaukee, 1914-Detroit, 1915-Toledo, 1916-New York City, 1917-Washington, D. C., and 1918-Chicago. A break occurred only in 1919 when the agenda for the proposed meeting of the American hierarchy announced that the Catholic Press would be discussed at that time.

These formative years found the Association concerned with many matters, some of which were quite commonplace and provincial but others of national import. Because the news service was so vital, discussion of it occurred regularly. At the 1912 convention twenty-three papers had agreed to take the Social Service Newsletter proposed to the group by Bishop Muldoon. As late as October of that year, however, CPA Secretary Claude M. Becker wrote to Father Peter Dietz of the Social Service Bureau: "We have endeavored to get all the papers to sign a contract for the Social Service Letter but up to the present time we have received only twelve contracts."[21] As a result of this delay, the first Newsletter did not go out until January of 1913.[22] Misunderstanding seemed to overshadow the project from the start. The CPA insisted that all applicants for the service must belong to its organization. Some members who had agreed at the convention to take the service arrived home to find that they had acted without authority. Others, despite a signed contract, began to cancel for one reason or another. Some favored the service but could not afford to subscribe to it. Soon members were asking that they be charged only for the letters actually used rather than at the flat rate of one dollar a week as agreed upon. Some even denied that they knew they were to pay for the service and criticized the material received. At least one business manager, finding fault with every aspect of the project, expressed his complaints in a letter to Father Dietz:

> Your apology in the form of a bill for $21.00 for weekly press service gave us a solar plexis [sic] blow. It is the first inkling we ever had that we were to pay for it. Mr. Charles Jaegle, who we believe was President of the C. P. A. last year, wrote us to the effect that we would have to be a member of the Association to get this letter. This is the only monetary consideration that has been called to our attention in regard to same.
>
> Your own personal stuff is excellent, but some of the stuff we have received we have run more out

> of courtesy to your commission than on account of its value as a news feature. There has [sic] also been irregularities in its shipment as we have missed several copies. As we are in the heart of a notorious [sic] bigoted country a dollar means much to us.... We hardly feel that it is fair to us that you should not have notified us that you charge for this service, and we kindly refer the bill back to you for your further consideration.[23]

Fortunately, letters of this type were not frequent, and a few even sympathized with the Social Service Bureau. In his report to the Federation the following summer, the director seemed a bit discouraged. He was over-burdened with work and observed plaintively that he needed as assistant. Nonetheless, he looked forward to better days--the "initial maladjustments" would "no doubt, right themselves in due time."[24]

In 1914 the Social Service Commission attempted to remedy some of the difficulties by offering alternate plans--fifty-two numbers of the Newsletter for the flat rate of twenty-five dollars or one dollar for each letter used.[25] Conditions apparently improved, for in November of 1915 a letter from Jaegle reported to Father Dietz that at the recent convention the Service had been "highly commended," and that he had heard "absolutely no criticism whatever." The chairman of the CPA News Bureau continued: "The majority of our exchanges are using your matter, and it is evident that they think well of it. Keep the good work a going, you are certainly on the right track."[26] In July of 1916, at the request of the Executive Board of the Federation, the Social Service Commission sent out an inquiry asking for opinions concerning the service and received very favorable responses. This first attempt at a Catholic news service continued to the end of the period.[27]

Of course, the Social Service Newsletters treated only one type of news. The leaders of the CPA were much more concerned with a general news service and had arranged for a Roman letter prior to the 1912 meeting. Discussion in 1913 of this service centered on the fact that the correspondent who had been named to the Roman post, L. J. S. Wood, was not a Catholic. Despite this shortcoming, the delegates chose to continue the Roman letter.[28] In a CPA publicity booklet appearing before the 1914 meeting, the officers noted that the journals subscribing to this service found it most profitable, that new journals were joining, and that plans which were under way to establish a domestic news service would be presented at the coming convention. Furthermore, they expected that a foreign bureau would soon be a reality.[29] But when the convention convened, President John Paul Chew revealed that "the majority of the affiliated members did not avail themselves of the news service..." Although Father Burke suggested that a Central News Bureau furnishing a regular weekly service be set up in New York City, the members were content to adopt a tentative plan for a domestic news service. The European War was by this time adding difficulties even for the Roman service. The Continental cables were sometimes blocked thus preventing the controversial Wood from getting his material to the States.[30]

By 1915 the News Bureau had added newsletters from London and Washington. The editors seemed to agree that these as well as the Roman letter were efficient and very helpful. Again, at the behest of Dr. Hart, this convention discussed a domestic service. Hart suggested a "Zone System" with bureaus set up in each zone to collect and send out domestic Catholic news. Although zones were drawn up and cities assigned to each, no further action resulted, and the "Zone System" seems to have died with the convention.[31]

The Jesuit magazine, America, pinpointed one reason for the lack of additional improvements in the news service in an August, 1918, editorial:

> The Catholic Press Association has already done much ... and particularly in developing the news and cable service. Honor and appreciation are due to the men whose foresight brought the organization into being and to the officers who have assumed the burden of carrying out a comprehensive program. One thing alone stands in the way of a splendid achievement of the entire scheme--lack of funds to carry out the plans which have been formulated.[32]

Other CPA members were coming to the same conclusion. One of them, Matthew J. W. Smith of the Denver Register, drew up a plan for a million dollar endowment of the Catholic Press and presented it in the initial paper of the convention that year. At first the members accepted the idea and called for a special Committee on Endowment "to determine the precise objects of an endowment, prepare a plan and suggest what measures, if any, are practicable towards raising an endowment fund." However, this proved to be "too big an idea for the editors of those days," and the proposal was abandoned.[33]

How to procure advertising continued to be a perennial concern. During the earliest years the Advertising Bureau made meagre progress despite Cooney's valiant efforts. At the 1913 session a national advertising plan was presented to the assembly, and both Dr. Condé B. Pallen, associate editor of the Catholic Encyclopedia, and Ambrose Willis from the London Tablet addressed the convention on this subject. Although the delegates expressed much interest in the proposal and discussed the plan fully, it was not adopted.[34] The following year, President Chew brought up the problem again, and "urged that the convention evolve a working plan for the advertising bureau, expressing himself to the effect that it was infinitely better to experiment than to remain inactive even though the experiment be without results." After a lengthy discussion, a tentative plan was drawn up for the establishment of a central advertising agency for the Association.[35] Apparently this idea was not carried out--at least no further mention was made of it. If there was anything a national organization of this type could do to attract large advertising concerns, the means escaped CPA personnel. The pattern sketched above was the one that prevailed all through the early years: an advertising plan was laid before the convention, much discussion followed, and there the matter rested until the next meeting.

The Catholic journalists invariably allotted time in their schedule for matters touching on problems of circulation. Their reasons for being concerned were very valid. During these years even secular papers were losing money, and Catholics seemed to give them more support than they extended to their own publications. Expanding circulation, then, was not only a desirable goal but an absolute necessity if the CPA member publications were to survive. The subject was often discussed informally, and sometimes there was a paper. For example, in 1915, the Reverend Thomas V. Shannon of the Chicago New World outlined "Ways and Means of Securing Subscriptions."[36] In 1917 circulation was featured by a convention, and the Reverend John F. Noll of Our Sunday Visitor aroused a good deal of enthusiasm when he proposed the slogan: "A Catholic paper in every Catholic home." Since, OSV had the largest circulation of any Catholic publication in the United States, Noll's words carried much weight. "He led the formal discussion on circulation, expressing his belief that the Catholic weekly papers in the country, with the assistance of the clergy, could quickly reach heights of circulation still unknown."[37]

Two papers on circulations were presented to the 1918 convention: "How to Increase the Circulation of a Weekly Paper," by Joseph J. Murphy, assistant circulation manager of Colliers' Weekly, and "How to Win the Aid of Educational Institutions," by Mrs. Josephine B. Sullivan Conlon, editor of the Michigan Catholic in Detroit.[38] As these were followed by discussion, they occupied an entire afternoon. Later, a committee was appointed to study circulation ethics, to survey existing practices, to draw up guidelines for Catholic publications in the soliciting of subscriptions, and to suggest remedies for abuses.[39]

Circulation was obviously related to reader interest, and the editors explored many suggestions for increasing their readership. They acknowledged some of the shortcomings of their papers which accounted in part for lack of support, but they also accused the laity of apathy and selfishness. Publicizing the 1914 convention an editorial in America decried the situation:

> Catholic editors do not engage in the publishing business in the hope of making a fortune. But the bare living with which they are satisfied, and the chance which they prize, to further the kingdom of God, will be denied them if people do not interest themselves more actively in the apostolate of the press.[40]

Some felt that the present generation of Catholics had to be taught to support the Catholic Press; hence they advocated a program of education centered in the upper grades of the parochial schools. At the 1915 meeting Mrs. Conlon presented such a plan: at least one-half hour a week set aside for the reading of Catholic papers in the classroom, and a "Catholic Press Day" in the spring.[41] This plan was taken up by the New World, and some of the schools in the Chicago area seem to have adopted the classroom reading program. There were also a few scattered efforts to arouse interest in the Catholic Press, but in general the inertia of indifference prevailed.[42]

Frequently the editors discussed petitioning the hierarchy for a Catholic Press Sunday. The suggestion had come up at the initial meeting,[43] but it was not until 1915 that a formal resolution declared:

> Whereas, since the Catholic Press cannot do efficient work without the cooperation of those in authority over the people, be it Resolved, That the Catholic Press Association respectfully requests the setting aside of one Sunday each year for urging upon the people the importance of Catholic papers in the defense and propagation of faith and morals.[44]

Apparently little came of this gesture, for a 1918 resolution asked "that the officers of the Catholic Press Association be directed at their earliest convenience to memorialize the Hierarchy in behalf of the establishment of a Catholic Press Sunday."[45]

Although other bishops might neglect their cause, Bishop Hartley was an ardent supporter of the newsmen. He seldom failed to attend the conventions, and he sympathized with the editors in the lack of support which they received. He felt that the future of the press would be "just exactly what the children of the Catholic Church [would] make it," and he noted that "Those who are at all familiar with the conditions of the Catholic press know only too well that our Catholic people as a rule do not take very much interest in its progress--nor do they sufficiently understand its importance."[46]

The tendency to reproach the Catholic population for lack of understanding and support came out very strongly in discussions of the need for a Catholic daily. Many considered such a paper highly desirable, but felt that it could never survive because of this apathy. Among the advocates of a Catholic daily were several members of the hierarchy. In 1915 Bishop Joseph Schrembs of Toledo called for Catholic dailies to counteract the evil influences of the secular papers. A strong promoter of the apostolic aspect of the press, Schrembs believed that the daily was the best means of educating and enlightening Catholics.[47] The next year John Cardinal Farley took up the same theme declaring: "I believe and hope for such a publication. It has got to come. I hope to live to see its day myself." There were those who insisted the project was impracticable, but Farley observed that people said the same thing of the

Catholic Encyclopedia which had recently been successfully completed. His words received an enthusiastic hearing, and the Cardinal was "lustily cheered at the conclusion of his address."[48]

Smith of the Register advocated a string of small daily newspapers "dealing mainly with Catholic news and carrying a limited service of secular news." Such papers would be auxiliaries, rather than competitors of the secular press. Even so, they would also fail unless the clergy was united behind the project; as Smith wrote, the plan had to have "pulpit-support."[49] Another faction was certain that support would be forthcoming provided the enterprise could ever get started in the first place. Those saw what a tremendous undertaking it would be. Richard H. Tierney, S. J., editor of America, responding to Bishop Schrembs' 1915 speech, predicted that Catholic dailies would not be feasible for another thirty years. His opinion was respected by at least one Catholic editor because America had aired the question of a Catholic daily at length, and Tierney was very familiar with the subject.[50]

An alternative proposal to a Catholic daily was closer cooperation with secular newspapers. Supporters of this plan agreed with a 1914 speaker that "Most secular journals today record without passion Catholic happenings. Our people form a respectable proportion of nearly every community and their efforts are good material for the daily press."[51] By utilizing the same amount of money needed to underwrite a daily, Catholic news could be inserted in a large number of secular papers thereby making the "daily press Catholic" rather than establishing a "daily Catholic press." In the midst of at least one convention, promoters of this approach discussed a great work being done by a group of ardent Catholic businessmen who had secured, by purchase, control of a secular daily and were using it to present news in an unbiased manner.[52]

Actually, the CPA members were so burdened with the financial problems of their own papers that they gave little serious thought to the establishment of a daily during this period. In 1914 war conditions resulted in an increase in the price of newsprint as well as other print paper. John Paul Chew in his presidential report referred to the increases, and a committee was appointed to investigate the matter and report back to the executive board later in the year. However, no reference was made at the meeting to a combined purchase plan which the CPA officers had mentioned as a goal in a brief booklet circulated by them a few months earlier.[53] In 1918 a session was devoted to topics touching on the financial aspects of a paper. Frank J. Waters, statistician for the Chicago Tribune, presented "The Necessity of a Cost System," while F. W. Harvey, Jr., general manager of Extension talked on "Turning Unused Space into Dollars."[54]

The prospect of higher postal rates was one potential expense item that concerned the Catholic journalists during their first meeting and remained an issue for many years. In 1913 attention was directed to a measure then under study by the Post Office and Post Roads Committee of the United States House of Representatives which anticipated doubling the postage rates on newspapers as a means of eliminating a deficit in the second class category.[55] Hearings on the proposal were prolonged, and it was not until the 1917 Washington meeting that Father Burke, in behalf of the Board of Directors, announced that the measure had been defeated. This was welcome news to the editors who were seldom in possession of sufficient funds. Financial concerns were part of their everyday living and of necessity were in the foreground of their thinking.

Nonetheless, aspects of professionalism received some attention especially toward the end of the formation period. As early as 1915 the convention program included a discussion of the "Editor's Qualifications" under the direction of the versatile Dr. Hart.[56] The following year Stuart P. West of the Associated Advertising Clubs of the World, speaking on "The Presentation of the News," urged "a 'brightening up' of Catholic publications and the getting of points from reporters on secular daily newspapers." At the same session Arthur Benington from the New York World, calling for "sensationalism" in Catholic papers, illustrated his point by presenting to his audience a model staff:

> Imagine a newspaper published today with St. Paul for editor-in-chief; St. Ignatius as managing editor; Hildebrand as editorial writer; St. Thomas Aquinas as political writer; St. Augustine writing 'human interest' stories; St. Peter Damian exposing scandals; Aeneas Silvius Piccolomini as literary editor; a woman's page conducted by St. Theresa; and Archbishop Mundelein of Chicago as business manager--would it be sensational? I rather think

> so! What a circulation it would have! And what a power it would be![57]

In 1918 the Program Committee of the Local Executive Committee under the chairmanship of Simon A. Baldus presented a roster of Chicago newsmen and devoted most of the sessions to various phases of professionalism. A diversity of newspaper problems were discussed by experts in each area including local editors, a cartoonist, writers, managers of subscription campaigns and business departments, and others. Topics varied from "The Vitalized Editorial" treated by Arthur Brisbane of the Herald and Examiner to "Running Down a Rumor" presented in an interesting and humorous manner by Edward Mahoney of the Chicago American. The members also heard, among others, papers on "The Feature Article," "Inside Facts About the Associated Press," "Interviewing Prominent People," and "Political News." The symposium was well received and was described as a "well-rounded and altogether profitable series of events."[58]

Although membership in the CPA was growing steadily throughout this period, the rate of that growth was too slow to satisfy ardent supporters of the Association. John Paul Chew, editor of Church Progress in St. Louis who was elected president to succeed Cooney in 1913, was very active in this regard. The convention announcement sent out by him the following summer contained a special invitation to Catholic publishers to join the group. Accompanying the announcement was a brief pamphlet dealing with the scope and aims of the organization, pointing to the good already achieved by the CPA, and declaring:

> We could not accomplish as much as we have accomplished unless a number of us had coöperated, and had not waited to ask 'What will we get out of it?' We cannot accomplish all that is possible for us, unless all of us coöperate. . . We assure you that by every additional one that coöperates we can do so much more. If all coöperated we would make the Catholic Press Association as efficient and as strong a body in our own field as the Associated Press is in its field. . . We ask you to come and join us in the great cause.[59]

At the convention in Detroit that September (1914), President

Chew reminded the members of the discussion of membership at the meeting of the previous year, told them that he considered that this was a very special concern of his as president, and reported that through his efforts twenty new publications had joined the CPA and several others were considering doing so.[60]

The CPA officers continued active recruitment of new members. Usually the notice of the annual convention included an invitation to non-members similar to that of 1916 which said in part,

> ... an invitation is extended to all Editors, Managers, and Publishers of Catholic Publications. All delegates will be allowed a voice in the convention, but only members in good standing will be allowed a vote.... If you are not a member, come to the convention and see for yourself the benefit of joining the association.[61]

When the 1916 convention met, Chew referred to membership and told the New York City meeting that only about one-half of the Catholic publishers belonged to the CPA. Urging them to procure new members, he pointed especially to the foreign-language press as a fertile field of endeavor.[62] Dr. Hart, who followed Chew as president, continued this activity. The convention circular announcing the 1918 meeting noted: "It is the purpose of the Association to interest many of the foreign language papers in the Catholic Press Association. About ten have already applied for membership."[63] Some success was apparent for when the Chicago convention assembled that August, it had the largest attendance in the CPA's short history. New faces were in evidence, and already some of the pioneers had died. Others, among them Cooney and Father Blessing who had been so very active in the beginning, had turned to other interests, and their names no longer appeared on the lists of convention members.[64]

Structures were changing, too, and in 1916 a revised constitution was part of the convention business. Strangely enough, press notices preceding the meeting made no mention of the proposed constitution, and those reporting on the convention later simply mentioned that the executive committee with Father Burke as chairman presented the document at the New York meeting that year. Obviously there was little or no discussion or controversy as the constitution was presented and adopted at the same session of the second day.[65] The name of the organization was given in the document as the Catholic Press Association of the United States and Canada. Even though the old constitution was completely re-written and enlarged with no section of the 1911 version remaining untouched, comparison of the two reveals no drastic innovations which may well explain the absence of discussion. Unity and mutual help were given as primary purposes of the group, but the original goals of procuring an efficient news service, reducing costs, securing advertising, and promoting Catholic literature were also retained. Although exception was made for foreign-language publications, a membership provision decreed that the first publication to subscribe to a news service in effect thereby obtained a monopoly on the service for that area.

CPA officers were to be elected annually as before, but a majority rather than a plurality vote was now required, and the secret ballot was stipulated. Duties of each of the officers were also specified in the revised form. The News, Advertising, and Literature Bureaus remained with membership on each of the boards reduced from five to three. A quorum for business was set at fifteen members replacing the "one-fifth of the enrolled membership" of the original constitution, but the process of amending remained at a two-thirds vote of convention members.[66] Evidently the Catholic journalists were ordinarily satisfied with things as they were. Five years had intervened before this revision appeared, and only when the Association became dependent on the NCWC News Service did the members succumb, through necessity, to the process of amending.

National affairs were not overlooked by the editors, and each year at least one convention resolution concerned an event appearing in the general news of the day. At the third meeting in Milwaukee, Archbishop Messmer touched on the subject of woman suffrage in connection with the respect that the editors should have for the authority and dogma of the Church. Declaring himself personally against equal rights, he nevertheless contended, "I would not dare to come out positively against the doctrine because here again the Church has not declared." Continuing, the Archbishop told the editors that woman suffrage, a vital question of national importance, must be carefully considered by them in their papers.[67] When overtones of extreme feminism had complicated the issue two years later, a note of warning was sounded against it as well as other radical movements of the day in a resolution adopted by the group:

> Whereas, Since in these days many radical movements dangerous to morality are under way in this country, such as extreme feminism, birth control and similar evils, be it Resolved, that the Catholic Press Association pledges itself to an exposition and refutation of the false principles underlying such movements without impugning on the good faith of those in error.[68]

The 1914 convention expressed its sentiments regarding the Panama-Pacific affair, a controversy of that year.[69] A year later the members pledged the Association to work for world peace as requested by the Holy Father, Benedict XV, and supported "any movement tending to the establishment of peace on the basis of liberty to the inhabitants..." of Mexico which was then in the midst of civil war.[70] When President Wilson and the United States government recognized the Carranza faction shortly after the convention adjourned, the president of the CPA sent an official protest of the action to Wilson. A month later Chew received a reply from an assistant in the State Department quoting the Washington representative of General Carranza who claimed that the Constitutional Government that had been established intended to respect all religious beliefs.[71]

The CPA in 1916 again discussed peace and Pope Benedict's endeavors concerning it. They decided that the individual Catholic editors throughout the country should conduct a campaign advocating that, should a peace commission be set up following the European War then in progress, the Pope should be a member of that body.[72] As the United States had entered the war by the time the editors convened again, a 1917 message to Wilson promised "to support the President in the present national crisis, to work in support of our government for the well being of our country and speedy victory of her arms." Noteworthy, too, in the 1917 convention was Bishop Hartley's address in which he asked that the Catholic papers concentrate on the problems of labor during the ensuing year in an effort to convince working men that the Church had their interests at heart. In response to the Bishop's plea, the delegates set aside a fund to be used to pay for articles explaining Socialism and concerning the Church and labor.[73] It is evident, then, that the Catholic newsmen were interested in both the political and social problems of their day. Perhaps their resolutions carried little weight, but they were made. The editors did take time from their personal publishing problems to be concerned with those affecting their fellowmen.

They also participated in a number of strictly Catholic events. The first of these was suggested to the 1915 convention by Anthony Matre, national secretary of the American Federation, who told of a projected plan for a great "Catholic Week" to be held in one of the larger cities. At this gathering all the large Catholic organizations would come together to participate in a general convention.[74] By the following year the plan had materialized with New York City named as the site much to the delight of the Herald which noted: "It is eminently fitting that the metropolis, with its 1,500,000 Roman Catholics, its hundreds of churches and scores of Catholic charitable and educational institutions and a cardinal of its own, should be the gathering place."[75] Cardinals Farley of New York, James Gibbons of Baltimore, William O'Connell of Boston, and Monsignor Giovanni Bonzano, the Apostolic Delegate, were all in attendance. The CPA delegates were but a tiny fraction of the twenty thousand who poured into the city for the occasion. A magnificent program was held in Madison Square Garden with Cardinal O'Connell giving the main address entitled "Our Country." The patriotism of the Catholics was also evidenced in the adornment of St. Patrick's Cathedral and other church buildings in its vicinity which were elaborately decorated with American flags as well as the Papal emblems.[76]

The following year the convention again was arranged with another event in mind, a Catholic Conference held at the Catholic University that week.[77] And in 1918, two extra-convention attractions added color to the business meetings. In the first place, the local committee (that very active Chicago group) arranged for a Catholic Press Exhibit in the convention headquarters asking member publishers to send one hundred copies of their publications as well as any other materials they wished displayed.[78] The second "extra" was an outgrowth of a short story contest inaugurated the previous year. This was conducted by the Literary Bureau with first prize being the publication of the story chosen, a solid gold medal donated by the ever-faithful Bishop Hartley, and one hundred dollars in cash presented by the CPA. Announcement of the winner was made at a public meeting held at Woods' Theatre following a program of music, readings, and addresses. The judges, all well known in the Catholic literary world, chose as winner "Three Squares a

Day" submitted by Miss Mary Elizabeth Prim of Boston.[79]

By 1918 it was generally agreed that the CPA had come a long way. The Catholic editors and publishers, through their annual meetings, had become acquainted personally one with another, and misunderstandings among them were less evident than had been the case prior to 1911 when editorials had often degenerated into violent harangues against journalistic enemies.[80] Furthermore, as illustrated above, leaders within the organization had grasped, to a degree at least, the importance of competency, of professionalism, and of cooperation with their secular counterparts. The foundations had been secured; hopefully, a constructive period was beginning.

The convention notice appearing in July, 1919, and naming Cincinnati as the place of the meeting stated in a very businesslike manner:

> The sessions will be devoted mainly to the discussion of practical questions; and the members are urgently requested to come prepared to participate in the conferences, which will be devoted to editorial management, business management, news service and circulation.[81]

Before the editors could convene, however, an announcement from the hierarchy proclaimed that the Catholic Press would be one of the principal topics discussed at the national conference to be held in September. Out of deference to the bishops, the executive board of the Catholic Press Association postponed the 1919 session. Whether those officers realized it or not, the CPA had come to the end of an era. Thereafter, it would be closely connected with the Press Department of the newly established NCWC.

Notes

1. The Catholic Citizen (Milwaukee), August 12, 1911.

2. Bulletin of the American Federation of Catholic Societies (Cincinnati and St. Louis), July and August, 1911.

3. "Catholic Press Association of America," America, V (September 2, 1911), 497 refers to this slight as does John J. Burke, CSP, "The Convention of Catholic

Editors," Catholic World, XCIV (October, 1911), 84.

4. For most of this period the CPA continued to choose the convention site and time to coincide with the convention of the AF of CS. The Catholic Columbian (Columbus, Ohio) is credited with suggesting this arrangement. See: Michigan Catholic (Detroit), May 28, 1911.

5. First Annual Convention of the Editors and Managers of the Catholic Publications of the United States and Dominion of Canada (Providence, R. I., n. d.), Foreword. CC.

6. "Catholic Press Association of America," America, V (September 2, 1911), 497; "Ten Minutes with the Managing Editor," Extension Magazine, VI (October, 1911), p. 1; and The New World (Chicago), September 2, 1911, are among those commenting on the work done by Cooney in preparation for the convention.

7. Reported in Catholic Standard and Times (Philadelphia), September 2, 1911.

8. Indiana Catholic, September 1, 1911. Bishop Hartley had shown much interest in the Catholic Columbian from the time that he became bishop of Columbus in 1904. ADC. After Hartley's death, M. Rev. Francis C. Kelley was named honorary president. Following his death in 1948, it was decided that the Episcopal Chairman should hold that title.

9. Ibid. "In physical presence, Msgr. Blessing was a courtly man, tall and erect, handsome, a smile always on the edge of his lips, and his whole manner manifesting those old-fashioned graces that could charm without trying." This from: One Hundred Years St. Michael's Parish, 1859-1959 (Providence, R. I.), no pagination.

10. Michigan Catholic, August 31, 1911, and Catholic Columbian, September 1, 1911. Nicholas Gonner, Sr. had died in 1892. The Gonner referred to in the remainder of the study is Nicholas, Jr.

11. Catholic Standard and Times, September 2, 1911, refers

to both addresses. Father Toomey's view was challenged later by one of the convention participants. See: [Martin I. J. Griffin], "A Real Catholic Press," The American Catholic Historical Researches, XXIX (January, 1912), 36-39. Griffin called for a free press rather than official organs.

12. Constitution of the Catholic Press Association (Providence, R. I.), Article II. CC.

13. Ibid. The governmental structure is treated in Article IV. Griffin also criticized the salary specifications. See: [Martin I. J. Griffin], "Press Association-$10. a Year for Treasurer," The American Catholic Historical Researches, XXIX (July, 1912), 237.

14. Michigan Catholic, August 31, 1911. Other officers chosen were: Vice President, W. A. King (Union and Times, Buffalo); Secretary, Claude M. Becker (Tablet, Brooklyn); Treasurer, Charles J. Jaegle (Pittsburgh Observer); Board of Directors: John J. Burke, CSP (Catholic World, New York); Edward J. Spillane, SJ (America, New York); and James T. Carroll (Catholic Columbian).

15. This was the view of The Catholic Tribune (St. Joseph, Missouri), September 9, 1911.

16. All material in this section is based on the communique itself: "An Official Circular to the Members of the Catholic Press Association," n. p., n. d. CC. For Hammerling's background and questionable activities, see: Robert E. Park, The Immigrant Press and Its Control (New York, 1922), pp. 377 ff.

17. Bulletin of the American Federation of Catholic Societies, July, 1912, was among those printing the notice.

18. Catholic Columbian-Record, August 23, 1912. This was an edition of the Catholic Columbian published briefly for the Indianapolis area.

19. Indiana Catholic, August 30, 1912, reprinted Father Cotter's observations.

20. Proceedings... 1912. All references to the 1912 meeting are based on these Proceedings. A copy of Taft's

letter to Cooney dated July 24, 1912, was provided by Cooney's daughter, Mrs. Mary E. Howard.

21. Becker to Dietz, October 5, 1912. CC.

22. AUND has most of the Social Service Newsletters on microfilm.

23. J. J. Casey (Catholic Register, Kansas City, Missouri) to Dietz, October 25, 1913. CC. Of course, Jaegle was not president but rather treasurer of the Association during these years. Letters concerning the other points mentioned are also among the Dietz Papers in the CC.

24. Rev. Peter E. Dietz, "Report of the Secretary of the Social Service Commission, August, 1912-August, 1913." Microfilm, AUND.

25. Dietz offered this plan in February of 1914. See: Dietz Papers, CC.

26. Jaegle to Dietz, November 8, 1915. CC.

27. Mary Harrita Fox, Peter E. Dietz, Labor Priest (Notre Dame, Indiana, 1953), p. 104 gives the date of the last Newsletter as April 16, 1918.

28. Catholic Standard and Times, August 30, 1913. Wood continued to be the object of criticism after the transfer of the News Service in 1920. Justin McGrath complained that dispatches under Wood's signature were still being received six months after the correspondent had left Rome to head up the Paris bureau of the UP. See: McGrath to Jaegle, March 26, 1920. PDF.

29. The Catholic Press Association (n. p., n. d.), pp. 9-11. CC.

30. Chew's report was found in the Michigan Catholic September 17, 1914. For other convention reports see: Catholic Columbian-Record, September 18, 1914, and Church Progress (St. Louis), September 17, 1914. Interference with the dispatches was reported in Church Progress, August 6, 1914.

31. Michigan Catholic, August 26, 1915.

32. M. O'Brien, "What the Catholic Press Most Needs," America, XIX (August 3, 1918), 399-400.

33. Church Progress, August 22, 1918, reported Smith's plan while the Committee on Endowment was referred to in L. F. Happel, "Echoes from the Catholic Press Convention," America, XIX (September 7, 1918), 523. The reason for not implementing the plan appears in "Memoirs of Monsignor Matthew Smith," Catholic Register (Denver), March 24, 1949.

34. The New World, August 23, 1913.

35. Chew's comment is from Michigan Catholic, September 17, 1914. Reference to the advertising agency is from Church Progress, September 17, 1914.

36. Michigan Catholic, August 26, 1915. L. F. Happel, Associate Editor of The New World, read Father Shannon's paper to the convention.

37. Reported in Church Progress, August 16, 1917.

38. The New World, August 9, 1918, announced these papers.

39. Christian Home and School (Erie, Pennsylvania), August 30, 1918.

40. "Notes and Comments," America, XI (September 12, 1914), 540. A later editorial also referred to this situation: "The Catholic Press Association," America, XV (September 2, 1916), 499.

41. Michigan Catholic, August 26, 1915, reported Mrs. Conlon's plan.

42. The New World, September 3, 10, 17, 1915, carried articles on the plan. An example of other efforts is a supplement to the Winona Courier issued by the Catholic Press Club of Winona, Minnesota, in June, 1916, which listed Catholic newspapers and suggestions of ways to promote the Catholic Press. CC.

43. This was mentioned by [Martin I. J. Griffin], "A Real Catholic Press," The American Catholic Historical Researches, XXIX (January, 1912), 36-39. He chided the editors for being overly deferential toward the

hierarchy.

44. Michigan Catholic, August 26, 1915.

45. Happel, op. cit., 523.

46. Michigan Catholic, September 17, 1914.

47. Ibid., August 26, 1915.

48. Church Progress, August 24, 1916, reported the Cardinal's hope while City World (New York), August 20, 1916, recorded the editors' reactions.

49. Smith's plan was in a letter to the editor, America, XIX (April 13, 1918), 14.

50. Michigan Catholic, August 26, 1915, makes this observation.

51. Ibid., September 24, 1914. However, this group would not have agreed with the conclusions reached by the speaker, Reverend James T. Irwin, who set up as an ideal the establishment of many Catholic dailies.

52. William F. Markoe was such an advocate. See his letters in: America, XIX (August 10, 1918), 429-430, and ibid., XX (December 28, 1918), 292. Happel, "The Catholic Daily Once More," America, XIX (September 14, 1918), 549, refers to the convention discussion.

53. Michigan Catholic, September 17, 1914, noted the price increase. Church Progress, August 16, 1917, records that President Chew told the convention members that the year just past had "been the most trying in the history of American journalism, [and that] many non-Catholic journals had been forced to the wall.. " The Catholic Press Association, op. cit., p. 11, mentioned a central buying plan.

54. The New World, August 9, 1918, listed these as convention topics.

55. Since 1885 the rate on second class mail had been one cent a pound. The secular press was also disturbed by prospects of a raise. See: Edwin Emery, The

History of the American Newspaper Publishers Association (Minneapolis, Minnesota, 1950), pp. 113-114 for discussion.

56. Michigan Catholic, August 15, 1915.

57. Church Progress, August 24, 1916. Catholic Columbian, August 25, 1916, was critical of Benington's view charging that he "judged weeklies altogether from the standpoint of a daily."

58. Church Progress, August 22, 1918, thus labeled it. A list of the topics discussed may be found in a circular sent out by the committee under date of July 29, 1918. CC. A report in the Catholic Review (Baltimore), August 24, 1918, mentioned the Brisbane and Mahoney papers among others.

59. Quotation is from The Catholic Press Association, pp. 8 and 12. The announcement is the "Final Call for Fourth Annual Convention." CC.

60. Michigan Catholic, September 17, 1914.

61. Convention Circular, 1916. CC.

62. Herald (Louisville, Kentucky), August 19, 1916.

63. Catholic Press Association, Convention Circular no. 2, July 8, 1918. CC.

64. Church Progress, August 22, 1918, called the meeting the "most successful" ever held. Father Blessing had turned to parish work in 1916 according to One Hundred Years, op. cit. Cooney left the Visitor in January of 1915 to become "publicity director and general advertising manager" of a Providence department store. See: Providence Visitor, January 1, 1915.

65. Church Progress, August 24, 1916.

66. Discussion of the constitution is based on comparison of copies of the 1911 and 1916 versions both of which are in CC.

67. The quotation is from Michigan Catholic, August 21,

1913. The Catholic Tribune, September 2, 1913 contains the other observation.

68. Michigan Catholic, August 26, 1915.

69. Ibid., September 17, 1914. The delegates contended that one Ernesto Nathan who was officially connected with the Panama Exposition had "villified and insulted their religion" and was thereby "preventing numerous conventions and individuals from attending the said exposition."

70. Ibid., August 26, 1915.

71. Church Progress, November 15, 1915, printed a copy of the letter received by Chew. The CPA president was editor of that paper.

72. Ibid., August 24, 1916.

73. For a report of the 1917 convention see Church Progress, August 16, 1917.

74. Michigan Catholic, August 26, 1915.

75. Herald, August 20, 1916.

76. The Standard Union (Brooklyn) and City Telegraph (New York) for August 20, 1916, carried reports on the "Catholic Week."

77. Church Progress, August 16, 1917.

78. Circular letter from the Local Executive Convention Committee, July 20, 1918. CC.

79. See Catholic Review, August 10 and August 31, 1918. Also "A Short Story Contest," Extension Magazine, XII (April, 1918), p. 1. Judges were Mary Synon, Kathleen Norris, Father Francis J. Finn, John Talbot Smith, and Frank H. Spearman.

80. "The Eighth Annual Convention of the Catholic Press Association...," Extension Magazine, XIII (October, 1918), p. 24.

81. Catholic Tribune, July 5, 1919.

Chapter III

Period of Transition (1920-1930)

An organization commonly known as the NCWC had been constituted more than a year before the September, 1919, meeting of the American hierarchy. Originally the initials stood for the National Catholic War Council, the purpose of which was to co-ordinate the war efforts of American Catholics. Once the war had ended, the hierarchy determined not only to safeguard the interests of Catholics, especially regarding Federal legislation, but to broaden the aims and scope of the Council and give it the element of permanency.[1] One contemporary account characterized the new NCWC as

> ...the National Catholic War Council perpetuated for the greater purposes of peace: the mechanism for applying the teachings of the Catholic Church to the solution of the great problems now confronting society: problems of social reconstruction, of improved education; the struggle with the rising tide of Paganism, and the ever-waxing tyranny of State Autocracy--and many other critical situations.[2]

Seemingly the bishops were thinking along the same lines for the 1919 meeting established five departments covering the major areas of Catholic life: Legislation; Social Service; Education; Press, Publicity, and Literature (soon referred to simply as Press); and Catholic Societies. An Episcopal Chairman headed each department, and an Administrative Committee of seven members functioned in behalf of the hierarchy between the annual meetings.

American Catholics anticipated great things from the post-war NCWC. A CPA member, Benedict Elder of Louisville, summed up their aspirations in an article appearing in the Catholic World shortly before the bishops gathered for their second meeting: "...it is just this coordination, development and use of all Catholic activities and resources,...

that affords the Church in action her unequaled facility for reaching all classes of society with her influence." Noting the progress made by the Administrative Committee in less than a year, Elder confidently expressed the opinion that in the coming meeting "... our leaders with God's blessing, will solidify the results already obtained and remove any lingering doubt that a new era has truly dawned."[3] Perhaps this recently appointed editor of the Louisville Record and CPA enthusiast had been favorably impressed by the Pastoral issued by the hierarchy at the close of the 1919 meeting. The Letter contained a special section on the press and said in part: "The unselfish zeal displayed by Catholic journalists entitles them to a more active support than hitherto has been given ... they are doing what no other agency could accomplish or attempt, in behalf of our homes, societies, and schools."[4]

Furthermore, when William T. Russell, Bishop of Charleston, was named as Episcopal Chairman of the Press Department, he had begun immediately to organize that department. A preliminary survey concluded that an international news gathering and distributing service was of the first importance. As noted in Chapter II, the CPA had already set up a news agency, but lack of finances and personnel stymied its development. After Bishop Russell had formulated a plan, he suggested that the Association members meet in convention so that he might present it to them.[5] Within the week, President Hart had sent out a circular promising editorials and galley proofs of a story on the convention so that more editors would be able to get away from their papers to attend the meeting.[6]

To facilitate meeting with the NCWC officials, the 1920 convention was scheduled for January 23 and 24 in Washington, D. C., where the new Council was establishing its headquarters.[7] Bishop Thomas J. Shahan of the Catholic University addressed the delegates who also heard a paper concerning modern methods of publicity delivered by Don O'Connell of the press bureau of the Friends of Irish Freedom and another entitled "The Reader's Part in Editorial Art," presented by Mrs. W. A. King of the Columbian. The chief work of the convention, however, was the transferring of the CPA News Service Bureau to the NCWC Press Department. Bishop Russell addressed the group on this matter pointing out that his authority came from the bishops and that he was responsible to them. He likened the new NCWC to a living organism and said that the press would be the voice of that whole body. Being an organic part, it was inseparable from the Council. "Its work cannot be handed over to any other organization," he declared. Praising the work done to date by the Catholic editors and especially the CPA, he asked the Association's "fullest cooperation in the plan outlined." Feelings were mixed as the Catholic Review noted: "... although the spirit of approval of the plan was whole-hearted and constant the delegates were keen to scrutinize the details and were resolved that the interests and the prestige of their organization should not suffer."

A committee named to study Bishop Russell's plan recommended that the CPA continue as an independent organization and that at least eight CPA members (including some of the officers) be members of the Council of the Press Department of NCWC. It further advised that the CPA give its News Service over to the NCWC when the latter had established an efficient "set-up" and that a joint committee expedite the transfer. In addition, the committee suggested that the NCWC Press Department assume the financial obligations of the CPA News Service and asked that the new service, whenever possible, give preference to the Catholic Press. After discussion from the floor, the delegates voted unanimously to transfer the News Service. Realizing that amendments would have to be added to the CPA Constitution, the convention named a committee to draw them up.

Most of the changes were minor, but one affecting membership included an element not specified directly in the convention resolutions that was to cause much disturbance in the future. It read: "It will be a condition of subscription for the cable and Washington service, to be provided by the Press Department of the National Catholic Welfare Council or otherwise, that the subscriber have membership in the Catholic Press Association."[8] Evidently the members were serious about looking out for their interests and prestige. Apparently, too, many of them had visions of an easier future. Mrs. King commented in the Columbian of the following week: "The CPA never had brighter or broader outlook. Hitherto it has had, as a body, the actual encouragement of only one Bishop--Rt. Rev. James J. Hartley, DD. Now it is to receive the practical encouragement of all the Hierarchy. This is a great step forward for our nation's Catholic journalism. Watch it grow!" In a more tempered tone the Gonners' Catholic Tribune of the same week observed: "We have fullest confidence in the plans as mapped out by the leaders of our increased means of Catholic news service." The editor asked, however, that Catholics, and particularly those interested in the press, be patient because "It will especially take much MORE time than many of the over-enthusiastic friends of adequate Catholic publicity will be willing to allow, before they can see the world reformed through a properly equipped Catholic news-gathering and distributing service." Following the convention, Bishop Russell reported:

> A full agreement was reached between the Catholic Press Association and the Press Department, and I wish to take advantage of this opportunity to express my gratitude to the Catholic Press Association for its loyal and helpful attitude. I feel that the Catholic Press Association deserves words of the highest praise for its loyal Catholic response to the plans of the Hierarchy. The Association itself has maintained not only its independent existence, but by its affiliation with the larger work will add greatly to its membership and its strength.[9]

The old CPA News Service had no paid personnel. The news had been issued in proof form, the foreign service had been limited to Rome and London, and the fee had been minimal--just sufficient to cover postage and cable costs. The NCWC Press Department planned to improve and enlarge this existing service. Through the efforts of Father John J. Burke, who was instrumental in organizing the entire Council, and who served as its first General Secretary and as supervisor of the News Service, Justin McGrath--an executive in the employ of Hearst Publications--was obtained as Director of the NCWC News Service. His fellow worker and successor as Director characterized McGrath as a gentle, thoughtful person with a good sense of humor, "but particularly aggressive and firm in his work." McGrath was to serve until a few months before his death in May of 1931, and he stamped his personality on the News Service. At his death Father Burke admitted that McGrath had cherished "... a love [for the Catholic Press] that sometimes ran over into a love of a father and irritated others by its paternalism..."[10]

These traits, however, were not to appear until later. McGrath began his task immediately and by mid-summer of 1920 was able to report: "With a blessing from Pope Benedict, the Press and Publicity Department of the National Catholic Welfare Council inaugurated its work during the second week of April by issuing a News Sheet to the Catholic Weekly papers of the United States." He had a staff of four, and forty Catholic papers (as compared to twenty-three in the former CPA system), subscribed to the news sheet and mimeograph service at two dollars per week while twenty-one paid five dollars a week more for the cable service. An editorial sheet was issued gratis each month, and McGrath also sent each member of the hierarchy the weekly news sheet.[11] The Bureau's Exchange Department received twenty-one secular daily papers and sixty Catholic weeklies. Because news was issued on a weekly basis, problems of timeliness and pertinence arose. The Bureau attempted to be to the Catholic Press what the Associated Press, United Press, and Universal Service were to the secular papers, but it concentrated on news that was strictly Catholic or of particular interest to Catholics.[12]

The work was well under way when in the spring of 1922 Rome interfered. A decree issued by the Consistorial Congregation declared that the work of the NCWC was now obsolete and directed that it disband. This was disconcerting to say the least. A letter to Philip R. McDevitt, Bishop of Harrisburg, referred to the incident: "Washington is aghast at the news about the Welfare Council--no one seems to know exactly what it means and the extent of the damage. Even the heads of some of the Departments are kept in the dark. All sorts of theories are of course afloat."[13] It seems that the decree was the result of a semantic problem. The word Council in the title of the organization apparently led the Holy See to believe that the hierarchy was presuming to sit as a permanent body. An editorial written a few years later explained that Rome thought the NCWC was acting as the fifteenth century Council of Basle had done.[14] Fortunately, the Administrative Committee was able to obtain a suspension of the decree. After presenting the facts to the Pope, the Council was permitted to continue its work. To eliminate the misunderstanding, the bishops in their 1923 meeting changed the title from Council to Conference.[15]

In the interim, difficulties concerning the News Service had arisen over the CPA's determination that only members of that organization were eligible for the service. The Press Department accepted this stipulation in 1920 and even sent out a letter stating that "This condition is obligatory under the agreement by which the Catholic Press Association was taken over by the National Catholic Welfare Council."[16] The following year at the national convention Father Burke, speaking for Bishop Russell who was unable to attend, told the delegates:

> To my mind... the work and purpose of the Catholic Press Association and its growth, are more important than ever before. It has its own organization; it has not only that but even the rules and regulations under which the Press Dept. of the N. C. W. C. is run. Every paper that we serve must fulfill the condition of membership in the Catholic Press Association.[17]

But privately, Bishop Russell expressed dissatisfaction with the provision, and Father Burke approved only because he felt that the Press Department would be unable to work with individual papers should refusal of the NCWC to accept the resolution lead the Association to disband in protest. CPA officers had already registered their displeasure; President Claude M. Becker, presenting to the same convention evidence that non-members were receiving the service, had suggested that action be taken.[18]

Father Burke's statement settled the issue temporarily. Nonetheless, the majority of CPA members seemed indifferent toward the service, failed to use it extensively, and even copied materials from other sources without subscribing themselves. McGrath on his part continued to disregard the provision at times, threatened the officers that if the CPA did not give more support to the service the bishops would discontinue it, and chided the editors for being oblivious of the true value of the service.[19] A certain uneasiness existed for several years, and toward the end of the decade circumstances brought the issue to a head.

By the time the 1927 convention met, CPA membership losses were becoming serious. Attendance hit an all-time low with only twelve weekly newspapers represented at the meeting. Fearing that if papers dropping membership were allowed to continue to receive the News Service there would soon be no CPA, the executive board decided on rigid enforcement of the 1921 provision.[20] Membership continued to decline. McGrath, excluded from his usual place on the convention program of 1928, retaliated by having Assistant Director Frank Hall prepare a pamphlet tracing the history and achievements of the News Service.[21] Shortly before the convention met, the True Voice published in Omaha, Nebraska, resigned from the Association, and the CPA executive board instructed McGrath to discontinue sending the News Service to it. The director replied that he did not think that the True Voice came under the ruling quoted from the Constitution. When this letter was read at the September board meeting, the directors again ruled that the Service must be discontinued and "insisted that one of the conditions which must be fulfilled if a paper wishes to receive the News Service is to have membership in the Association."

Preliminary to the general convention session the following May, the executive board met, and "The question of discontinuing the News Service to papers which drop out of the Press Association was then discussed at greath length and from all angles." In behalf of the board, Father E. F. Ferger, vice president that year, read a report on the News Service to the general session. This report asserted: "That many of our papers are dissatisfied with the N. C. W. C. News Service may prove to be no surprise to the Right Reverend Executive Chairman or the Director of the Service." Noting that over the years the CPA had gradually assumed the costs of the News Service until it was then paying three-fourths of the total, the report decried the fact that the CPA had no voice in its operation. It also pointed out the deficiencies of the Service, as well as its arbitrariness, and suggested that an executive board for the NCWC News Service be appointed and that a detailed financial report of the expenditures of the News Service be presented annually at the CPA convention. The paper was discussed at length (to the extent of fifty-four typewritten pages, reports the Yearbook). Then the News Bureau was re-named the News Service Bureau, and Article VI, Section 3, of the Constitution was revised to read:

> The News Service Bureau shall consist of two elective members, of the C. P. A. President and two others, a layman and a priest, for the purpose of exercising, with two representatives of the N. C. W. C. Bureau of Press and Publicity, joint executive and advisory control of the N. C. W. C. News Service in matters of general policy.[22]

Bishop Russell was dead by this time as was his immediate successor, Bishop Louis Walsh of Portland, Maine, who had served from the fall of 1921 until the spring of 1924. Thus, Bishop McDevitt had become Episcopal Chairman in 1924 after the Press Department was firmly established. From the beginning Bishop McDevitt had taken his position seriously. In May of 1925 he attended the CPA convention in St. Louis, and in his address presented to the members seventeen questions concerning the News Service. The purpose behind this was that the Bishop desired "an expression of opinion on the part of the Catholic papers that is frank and clear and definite about the Press Department and the News Service." He maintained that the bishops would like to know if the Service was producing results commensurate with the expense it entailed and, conversely, whether the editors believed that the present News Service was worth the price that they were asked to pay for it. A bit of intrigue on the part of some of the members managed to prevent discussion of the questions on the convention floor. As a result, President Patrick F. Scanlan sent the questions to the members after the convention closed. Although only thirty-three editors from among at least eighty subscribing to the Service responded, these were generally appreciative and even commendatory as shown by the summary published by the Press Department.[23]

In response to the 1929 controversy Bishop McDevitt asked numerous questions and then suggested that pertinent data going back to the 1920 transfer be collected so that he might submit it to the Administrative Committee of the NCWC.[24] Nonetheless, five months later President Anthony Beck in a personal letter to F. P. Kenkel told his friend: "By the way, we have a squabble with Bishop McDevitt and the N. C. W. C. because they insist on giving the service to papers not members of the C. P. A., although they agreed otherwise back in 1921."[25] Two weeks earlier Beck had attended an executive board meeting at which Scanlan, reporting for the News Service Bureau of the CPA, told the directors of a September meeting with the bishop who had contended that the News Service could not be held to the CPA Constitution written nine years before. His reasoning was that "... it would result in a decrease in the annual income and... it was not the prerogative of any organization to say who should and should not get the Service." Bishop McDevitt had called the convention Article "unjust" and reasserted that the NCWC must maintain control of the Service. President Beck was among those who objected to this view agreeing with the majority of the board members that the entire matter must be presented to the 1930 convention.[26]

Before the delegates assembled in Asheville, Bishop McDevitt had resigned because of illness, and it was Hugh C. Boyle, Bishop of Pittsburgh, who addressed the gathering as Episcopal Chairman of the NCWC Press Department. He had taken over the chairmanship only a few weeks earlier and had not been able to meet before the convention with a committee named to present the CPA side of the disagreement. In his address, Bishop Boyle adopted a conciliatory attitude. Although he delivered a point-by-point reply to Father Ferger's report of the previous year, the bishop indicated that it was his desire to see every Catholic publication a member of the CPA so that it could be strengthened and represent a totality of the American Catholic Press.[27] Following the convention, Bishop Boyle reported to Father Burke that the "C. P. A. showed a willingness to adjust the matter in line with the mind of the Bishops."[28]

Nonetheless, the CPA News Service Committee conferring with the Episcopal Chairman in late July remained adamant in the position that the 1920 agreement could be revised only by joint action and charged that the NCWC was simply ignoring it. Bishop Boyle agreed to act temporarily as a buffer between the two groups, but by the time the executive board met in November, he had withdrawn from this position. Therefore, the directors reviewed the entire matter and on the second day of their meeting, having decided that a impasse had been reached, drew up a resolution accusing the NCWC of failing to meet its obligations, severing all relations with the News Service, and recommending that the status of the CPA revert to that existing before 1920.[29] The resolution, of course, did not become effective immediately as it required a majority vote of the membership assembled in convention. In the months intervening between the board meeting and the May convention, some of the directors reconsidered the matter. In addition, Father Burke met with President Elder, advised Bishop Boyle, and in general acted as mediator. McGrath's death occurred just a few days before the 1931 meeting, and the CPA officers gave this as a reason for not presenting the resolution to the general convention.[30]

As a result it was not until the CPA board met in January of 1932 that the matter was finally closed. Father Burke at that time assured the directors that the NCWC desired "the most cordial relations with the C. P. A.," and requested that the resolution be withdrawn. After the issue was discussed for more than two hours, it was agreed that the NCWC would promote CPA membership and the Association cancel the resolution. The directors also appointed two of their members to confer periodically with representatives of the News Service.[31] In late February, letters over Bishop Boyle's signature went out to all News Service subscribers. One, sent to those belonging also to the CPA, referred to the 1920 stipulation and expressed gratitude to these editors for their cooperation and support. The other, addressed to non-members, also mentioned the terms originally agreed upon and urged that these publications join the Association.[32] In April, President Elder informed the members of the "happy ending of the dispute," and a few days before the 1932 convention met, the True Voice once more applied for membership.[33]

This conflict was but one aspect of a general climate of discontent existing not only among CPA members but also among the personnel of the NCWC News Service throughout the entire decade. In his speech to the 1924 convention, Director McGrath upbraided the editors for taking "every opportunity to leave off the credit line of the N. C. W. C. News Service." He often scolded them for their lack of interest in the various services. In private letters to Bishop McDevitt, he referred to the lack of support of the members of the Catholic Press and even mentioned the "personal offensiveness" of some of the editors.[34] In these matters McGrath had a staunch supporter in one of the Bishop's friends, Edward J. Galbally, who also was writing McDevitt about the lack of cooperation on the part of the editors. He suggested that the Chairman "tell [them] plainly that this nagging and carping is ungrateful, unfair, shortsighted and mischievous..." Concerning the director, he continued:

> As an onlooker I see what splendid work he is doing, against odds and for unappreciative editors. ... It is so easy to sit in slippered ease before the fireplace and fault the general's conduct of the war at the front--and it is cowardly, especially from those who should be out there fighting the enemy. 'Sheer treachery!'[35]

The editors on their part found fault with the cable service, the organization's proscription of items other than those of Catholic interest, and the element of standardization that the use of the service gave to the Catholic papers.[36] Some, like the outspoken Arthur Preuss of the Fortnightly

Review condemned not only the News Service but the entire NCWC.[37] Despite these differences, many CPA members did find points to praise regarding the Service. At the 1920 meeting, Charles J. Jaegle, long term treasurer of the Association, asserted: "I believe that this is the day that the most of us who started the Catholic Press Association have looked forward to."[38] In the fall of 1922, an editorial in America remarked how much the Service had done for the Catholic Press in its short existence.[39] Bishop McDevitt's friend, Father Delaunay, CSC, then with the Bengal Missions in India, received the Service and wrote to the bishop: "My admiration grows for the work as each week I see the result of it."[40] About the same time an editorial in the Tablet praised the Service, pointing to the efficient operation of the Press Bureau, and contended "The result is that today Catholic newspapers are more presentable, more readable and accomplishing more good than they ever did before."[41] In a 1924 convention address entitled "How to Make the Best Value of the N. C. W. C. News Service," Vincent dePaul Fitzpatrick noted that the Catholic editors were less appreciative of the Service than outsiders. He pointed specifically to the Methodists and Episcopalians who had recently commented on the excellent coverage of Catholic papers.[42]

Regardless of the perennial expressions of dissatisfaction by individual editors, almost every CPA convention of the decade offered words of praise for the Service. In 1922 and again two years later members showed their appreciation by voluntarily increasing the subscription rate to allow for improvements in the Service.[43] A 1925 resolution stated:

> That the C. P. A. wishes to express its gratitude to the hierarchy of the United States for their generous support, rendered through the National Catholic Welfare Conference, of the Catholic Press. We realize that their aid has been a most effective agency in the improvement of our press, and we renew the pledge of our fullest cooperation and support.[44]

Even during the heated controversy later in the decade there were some words of praise. For example, early in 1927 the subscribers agreed once more to a voluntary raise in rates.[45] The next year President Baldus expressed special thanks to Director McGrath and the News Service for the cooperation given him during the year past.[46] Thus, although the editors were annoyed at the shortcomings of the Service and vocal in expressing their criticism, they usually acknowledged the benefits that had resulted from the change. Perhaps the most conclusive evidence of this is that eighty-four papers received the Service in 1930, compared to only twenty-three ten years earlier. The News Service was sending its subscribers fifty-two thousand words and four columns of pictures a week in contrast to four thousand words in 1920, had increased the number of services to five, and employed fifteen foreign correspondents whereas there were but two in the earlier year.[47]

Moreover, the hierarchy, the Press Department, and the CPA cooperated in initiating a Catholic Press Month during the early years of the decade. CPA conventions had discussed the possibility of a Press Month, or at least an annual Press Sunday, from the first meeting. As noted in Chapter II, the conventions of 1915 and 1918 had passed formal resolutions asking that the hierarchy designate a Catholic Press Sunday. An editorial in *America* in the spring of 1920, calling attention to the fact that such a day was being observed in Spain, noted that the director of the Spanish movement hoped to make it a worldwide event. However, the origins of the Catholic Press Month in the United States are somewhat obscure. Even before the organizational meeting of the CPA, Humphrey J. Desmond, editor of the *Catholic Citizen*, called for a Catholic Press Sunday in October of each year. Becker, CPA president during the first press month campaign, stated in a letter written almost forty years later that 'Nick' Gonner was "responsible for establishing Catholic Press Month, which has grown to such large proportions." On the other hand, the recently published *New Catholic Encyclopedia* states that the idea originated with Father Francis Markert, SVD. Father Markert did write a letter to a Jesuit, P. J. Sontag, in Spain requesting information on the Press *Sunday* held in that country. Likewise, he talked to Bishop Russell about the movement and sent him the materials he had received from his Spanish correspondent. The bishop sent these to Justin McGrath, but when the latter thanked Father Markert for procuring them, he wrote: "Bishop Russell has forwarded to me your letter which accompanied the booklets sent to him on the Press *Month* [italics mine] in Spain."[48]

Although Desmond, Gonner, and Father Markert were all CPA members, it was action taken at the bishops' meeting of 1920 rather than at an Association convention which inaugurated the movement for greater support of the Catholic Press on the part of the American laity. The hierarchy designated March, 1921, as the first national Catholic Press Month and assigned to the Press Department the task of organizing the campaign. Bishop Russell sent a letter to all the bishops and archbishops in the country asking that a sermon on the subject be preached from every pulpit across the land. To explain the movement the Department issued a brochure--Catholics: Do You Know? Pointing out that nearly eighteen of the twenty million Catholics of that day were not reading any Catholic publications, this pamphlet listed Catholic newspapers, magazines, and reviews receiving the News Service and urged that all Catholics support the Press Month. The National Council of Catholic Men and the National Council of Catholic Women volunteered their services, sending out the brochures and letters to Catholic societies throughout the country. To promote the Press Month most dioceses also set up special committees. The slogan chosen was that presented by Father John F. Noll to the 1917 CPA convention--"A Catholic paper in every Catholic home."[49]

At the request of the CPA, Press Month 1922 was changed to February, and again the Press Department published a pamphlet as part of the campaign. The explanation of the Press Month was presented in the form of a dialogue between an editor and a layman in the first section of the booklet while the later pages introduced the personnel of the News Service. The brochure did not sell well; the Press Department lost money on the project, and the campaign in general was disappointing. Therefore, when Linus G. Wey presented a resolution to the CPA convention that year asking that a committee be named "to work out a plan for Catholic Press Month," McGrath had no objections.[50] In 1923 Pope Pius XI issued an Encyclical, Rerum Omnium, devoted to the Catholic Press and designating St. Francis de Sales as its patron. In response to a request of the CPA submitted through the Episcopal Chairman, Bishop Walsh,[51] the United States bishops that fall proclaimed that the Sunday immediately proceeding the feast of St. Francis (January 29) be designated as Catholic Press Sunday and February as Catholic Press Month. The Buffalo convention of 1924 heard Desmond deliver an address: "Oliver Twist and the Catholic Press," in which he commended the hierarchy for fixing a date for Catholic Press Sunday followed by a month devoted to the needs of the Catholic Press and observed that the annual call for such a campaign should continue to come from the Episcopal Chairman. Desmond contended, however, that the Catholic Press itself should devise means of promoting the campaign and should enlist the cooperation of Catholic organizations.[52] The talk was so well received that the convention named a Press Month Committee to draw up "a concrete plan to make Press Month in the United States of practical value to the Catholic periodical publishers."[53]

Following a plan proposed by Simon A. Baldus, this committee decided to compile and distribute through parish committees a million or more copies of a catalogue of Catholic periodicals including those not belonging to the CPA as well as active members. Cooperative membership fee was set at twenty-five dollars, and the National Bureau or Press Month Clearing House was to receive fifty cents of the regular subscription price for each new or renewed subscription received during the Press Month. In August a form letter went out to all Catholic publications asking their cooperation, and some time later a four page leaflet followed. The Press Month Committee secretary, James J. Brady, used the front page to write still another letter to the Catholic publishers asking their cooperation. Noting that sixty periodical publishers had endorsed the plan, he maintained that at least eighty must take part if the catalogue was to materialize. Brady also informed the publishers that several Catholic organizations had already promised their active support. Sample pages of the proposed periodical catalogue which was to contain sixteen to twenty pages in its final form made up the rest of the pamphlet.[54] In October the secretary sent out a final request. Results were disappointing; in March Baldus wrote to his friend Preuss:

> Since last August I have been working day and night, Saturdays, Sundays and holidays, on the Press Month Campaign, the net result of which so far is negligible. There may be improvement in the next few weeks, but I doubt it. After it is all over we will make our report, and it will not be edifying reading. Say nothing about the matter at this time. The experience I have had has been discouraging and disheartening, and in the parlance of the day 'I am through'. Whatever plans may be devised will have to be carried out by others. I have done my share this year.[55]

Baldus had reason to be discouraged. The committee

tee's report to the 1925 convention revealed that most of its efforts had been unsuccessful. The published catalogue was but half the projected size since only about one-fourth of those contacted chose to be listed. Approximately one of every thirty parish priests acknowledged receipt of the catalogue and other literature distributed by the committee, and only seven of the one hundred thirty members of the hierarchy replied. Of the nine leading national societies, six promised cooperation, but when the Press Month Committee distributed eight thousand packages of materials to the various branches, only about one-fourth of the local secretaries acknowledged receipt of the materials even though the Committee had enclosed a post card for this purpose. Although they expected between five and ten thousand subscriptions from this phase of the campaign, the total was only two hundred fifty-eight. Returns from the clergy were equally disappointing. From among the parishes whose pastors had agreed to the plan, the committee selected fifteen in various locations. Of these, six reported turning in a total of 183 1/2 subscriptions. When all returns were tabulated, the committee listed 544 1/4 subscriptions valued at $1229. 43. Therefore, the convention report reluctantly noted that the centralized effort had not succeeded and recommended that in the future each publication should sponsor its own local campaign.[56]

Comments concerning other Catholic Press Months over the decade often expressed disappointment in the results obtained. The blame for the lack of success was sometimes placed at the feet of the clergy. One editor explained: "That failure comes principally from the mistaken idea on the part of pastors that if they preach a good vigorous sermon on the Catholic Press every sinner in the congregation who is not subscribing for a Catholic weekly will immediately do so." He wanted pastors either to canvass the homes of the parish or solicit subscriptions as the people left Church on a Sunday.[57] Others blamed the average Catholic. Reporting on the 1922 campaign an editorial noted: "Again, as was the case a year ago, the great problem is one of dispelling the too general apathy of the great body of American Catholics, and of arousing their personal and practical interest in their own press."[58] The press itself came in for a share of the criticism. A letter to the editor of America written near the end of the decade declared:

The clergy have favored the work from the time of

> its introduction, but the press, with a few exceptions, has not cooperated with the very means that is required to unify and educate the people to active interest in the work. . . . All the talk about Catholic Press Month will be to no purpose if we cannot get the clergy and the press to cooperate in this movement.[59]

The 1925 endeavor showed that none of the three groups was without fault.

Nonetheless, some individual papers profited greatly by the Press Month drives. The editor of the Catholic Register, for example, exclaimed at the close of the first national campaign, "The Press Month was a wonderful success. All that our Catholic papers needed was the support of the clergy and the people." Following the 1924 Press Month campaign in Bishop Russell's diocese of Charleston, the Bulletin of the Catholic Laymen's Association of Georgia announced that the activities had been very beneficial to the Bulletin. More than two hundred subscriptions had been received from Charleston alone and numerous others had come in from other parts of the state.[60]

Besides the annual Press Months, other educational methods begun in the early period continued throughout the decade. In 1924 despite difficulties due to the lack of materials available concerning Catholic journalism, the NCWC Press and Publicity Department drew up a course of study for civic study clubs.[61] The CPA in 1927 and again in 1929 passed resolutions recommending the Catholic Press Hour in the schools. "The Catholic Press Hour in high schools," said President Beck in 1929, "is the logical development of Catholic Press Month and would aid greatly in stimulating interest in our press and in developing circulation." A resolution advocating such Press Hours recommended that the executive board "communicate this resolution to the National Catholic Educational Association."[62] In the last year of this period Benedict Elder who was serving as CPA president was invited to read a paper at the NCEA meeting in New Orleans. In his address entitled "The Value of the Catholic Newspaper to the Catholic School," Elder insisted that ". . . the cause of the Catholic school is the cause of the Catholic paper." Suggesting that the schools give their publicity notices to the Catholic rather than to the secular papers, he pointed out that arrangements could be made for using Catholic papers within the schools, and concluded:

> I trust this is the beginning of an era of collaboration between the Catholic press and the Catholic school, in which both shall realize that as their aim is one their spirit must be one, and every helpfulness possible shall be given one to another.[63]

Basically, the hope of increasing circulation was the underlying motive both for the Press Month campaigns and the educational efforts, and the CPA continued to devote much of its convention time, energy, and funds to matters concerning circulation. To complicate the problem, bogus agencies and unscrupulous solicitors entered the field of religious publications so that the public hesitated to take subscriptions from any agents. Discussing this problem in the Catholic Review just previous to the 1923 convention, the editor expressed hope that the Association would take action against those solicitors who "in their greed for returns, are bringing the blush of shame to many Catholic publications and are putting part of the membership of the Catholic press into disrepute."[64] E. Lester Muller of the Review introduced such a resolution calling for "a definite program of reform." The convention appointed a Vigilance Committee, and in September the bishops at their annual gathering discussed the matter observing that unscrupulous agents and spurious agencies were guilty of many abuses, including the promise of indulgences for subscribing to Catholic papers. The hierarchy condemned these practices and instructed the faithful "never to subscribe to any such projects or buy such periodicals unless a clear announcement be made in the Church, authorizing such agents." The resolution was published in the NCWC Bulletin and sent to all the Catholic papers, but the deception continued.[65]

Little else was done that year, but a new committee named by the Buffalo convention in May of 1924 began action at once. By June 14 it had completed a series of meetings, drawn up a plan, and submitted a report to the executive board. A foreword to the report declared:

> It was the consensus of the Committee that to accomplish any practical results and get to the root of the evils and abuses complained of, it would not be sufficient to merely set forth codes of procedure to be observed by all Catholic publishers, and the agencies or persons employed by them in subscription production, but that it would be likewise necessary to establish more or less

> elaborate machinery to make possible and to insist upon the carrying out of such codes.

The body of the report, after setting forth the objectives of the Committee in great detail, recommended that the Committee be made a permanent standing one and that a Central Bureau with paid personnel be established in Chicago. Furthermore, it drew up plans for the working and financing of this Bureau, demanded that appropriate sanctions be imposed, and suggested legal proceedings be instituted against those who could not be controlled through the machinery of the CPA. The Committee asked for prompt action "to retain the confidence of the Catholic Hierarchy, Clergy and public, and to prove to them that the appointment of this Committee at the Buffalo Convention was not merely an idle gesture."[66] The 1925 convention formally approved the report and renamed the Committee members who immediately went to work implementing their plan. In mid-June, the Central Bureau under the direction of George J. Lillig opened for business in Chicago. Dues were scaled according to the publication's circulation, and several members paid them in advance so that the Committee could get the project started.[67]

The chief work of the Bureau was to be

> ... the investigation of applicants for employment by Catholic publishers as subscription producers and collectors, and the furnishing of results of such investigations to the Catholic publishers employing or contemplating the employment of such parties... [in order] to secure honest and efficient persons for circulation purposes, who will be a credit to the Catholic Publications employing same.

The Central Bureau also arranged to carry out an exchange policy with secular associations of a like nature.[68] In September, Bishop McDevitt reported to the assembled bishops on the activities of the Circulation Committee, received their approval, and then urged the Committee to try to secure the cooperation of all Catholic publications. Accordingly, the Committee distributed copies of Bishop McDevitt's report as well as its own booklet of recommendations to the Catholic publishers, a resume of the Committee's work, and a summary of what it was still attempting.

By the following February another circular letter reported: "The records of the Circulation Committee for the past few months prove conclusively that it is capable of correcting these abuses and in time of putting an end to them entirely if it can but secure the whole-hearted cooperation of all publishers who employ paid agents of any kind." After explaining the advantages of supporting the movement, the secretary invited the publishers to a meeting with the Committee in Chicago near the end of March.[69] At a similar gathering held on December 10, representatives of seventeen Catholic publishers and agencies met to discuss "an equitable and sound commission scale for sales forces for Catholic periodicals." Because only a relatively few Catholic publications employed commissioned sales forces, these seventeen numbered about seventy-five per cent of the total possible. About half of those not present sent word that they "would abide by the decision arrived at...." Therefore, a scale was drawn up and presented to all publishers and circulation agencies for their approval.[70]

The Committee continued its work throughout the period and was actually successful in eliminating irregular agents from the circulation field. In 1928, President Baldus noted that approximately five hundred had been apprehended by that time.[71] In general, the Committee's work was appreciated. Anthony J. Beck, president in 1929, told that year's convention: "If our Association had nothing else to its credit but the achievements of this bureau in recent years, it would have justified its organization eighteen years ago."[72] During the past year seventeen additional periodicals had given their support to the Committee. Several agents had been arrested, prosecuted, and convicted; as these incidents had been well publicized, they had acted as a deterrent to others. The Bureau also reported success in collecting delinquent accounts, a service for which they were charging twenty-five per cent, approximately half of that demanded by commercial agencies. Although the chairman decried the fact that a number of Catholic publishers were still not cooperating--"shirking their duty towards their fellow publishers," as he phrased it--he was convinced the Circulation Committee represented "the most effective means yet devised for accomplishing all that is humanly possible for eradicating abuses and making the Catholic periodical field far more profitable for all engaged in the business."[73]

By the time that the 1930 convention met in Asheville, fifty-four publishers were supporting the Circulation Vigilance Committee. Father Francis P. LeBuffe, Chairman, reported that one thousand sixty-one investigations had been conducted during the year; but since many Catholic schools and other institutions had been victimized by dishonest agents, further work was required. The Committee had devised a seal in red, and the slogan - LOOK FOR THE SEAL - was adopted. After praising the hierarchy and clergy for their support, Father LeBuffe concluded:

> We must not forget our obligation of 'group responsibility'. Nor dare we lose sight of the necessity for continued 'vigilance.' Yet, now, if we will only consolidate our efforts through 'unanimous co-ordination', working each for all and all for each, we may hopefully look forward to achieving our aims, that is, to enhance the prestige of the Catholic Press as a whole and to further improve conditions in the circulation field for all concerned... [74]

Another unit of the CPA that was very active during the 1920's was the Advertising Bureau. In July of 1920, the Bureau hosted a gathering in New York City attended by representatives of fifteen publications. The stated purpose of the meeting was to "take preliminary steps in forming an organization, the object of which would be to secure advertising for Catholic publications represented in the C. P. A." During the morning sessions the participants listened to addresses by advertising experts and to McGrath who presented a plan for a Central Advertising Headquarters. The group adopted resolutions stating that membership in the Audit Bureau of Circulation must precede association in the National Advertising Solicitation Organization of CPA and requesting an appropriation of one thousand dollars from the executive board to be used for propaganda purposes concerning the value of advertising in Catholic publications. [75] When the convention met in 1921, the Bureau had not yet received the money. Charles H. Ridder, chairman, brought this to the attention of the delegates and asked for a resolution placing that amount at the disposal of the Bureau. He mentioned the possibility of procuring an agent to solicit national advertising for the Catholic Press and suggested an audit of circulation figures. "Your Ad [sic] Bureau is capable of doing much good in remedying conditions," he told his fellow editors, "if it is only permitted to act and not just exist for the sake of appearing on the letterhead of the C. P. A."[76] For the time being, however, the Advertising Bureau had to be content with circulating a questionnaire and compiling from it an official list of Catholic publications giving information of interest to advertising agents. The national advertising bureau was abandoned, partly because the bishops were unwilling to advance the funds necessary to get it started.[77]

Following the 1922 convention, however, the Advertising Bureau began soliciting funds to be used in an advertising campaign. In February a NCWC News Service Release announced that thirty-eight publishers had subscribed, representing a combined circulation of two million, and a fund of approximately two thousand dollars had been accumulated to be used in the actual campaign the following month.[78] Part of this money financed the publication of a brochure entitled: Have You Overlooked These Twenty Million Consumers? Declaring, "Here is a chance for the advertiser with vision; the bold adventurous man who can see a possibility before it is demonstrated to him by figures," it stressed that Catholic publications were linked by means of the CPA into a unit--an excellent avenue for a national advertising campaign.[79] After the 1925 convention heard a paper on "Advertising in Catholic Publications," H. P. Pagani of the Advertising Bureau introduced the idea of advertising Catholic papers in the secular dailies. He announced that his committee had one thousand dollars to develop advertising plans, but that they needed fifteen hundred more if all their projects were to be carried out. The Indiana Catholic and Record reported that "Before the session closed, practically all of the $1,500 needed was pledged..." The members seemed optimistic that the Bureau's efforts would bring in the business of the national advertisers.[80]

The Bureau's second pamphlet, A Short and Broad Avenue to 20,000,000 Buyers, announced: "Our effort in this book is to meet the demand for specific, pertinent information on selling fundamentals as supplied by the 228 advertising media comprising the Catholic Press of America."[81] Living standards of Catholic families, size of the Catholic market, and the warm reception that would be accorded the advertisers were all examined. Again an annotated list of Catholic publications was included. The Bureau, in 1928, presented a list of "Advertising Don'ts" to the convention, and these were later sent to all the members of the Association. Touching on matters of accurate circulation figures, type of advertising that should be accepted, promptness in business dealings, and the like, the last

"Don't" summarized the group: "Don't forget that your paper represents the Catholic Press and the Catholic Church."[82] The next year Father Charles J. Mullaly, Chairman of the Advertising Bureau, recommended that an appropriation of one thousand dollars again be made, this time for "publicity advertising." In 1930, noting that nothing had been done regarding his request for funds the year before, Mullaly urged immediate action in this regard. After prolonged discussion the appropriation was made "for propaganda or other purposes." The delegates also recommended "that the bureau adopt a code of ethics and take any other action it may deem necessary to bring conditions up to the standard fixed by the bureau."[83]

Although it was not published by the CPA itself, the Catholic Press Directory, editions of which appeared three times in this period, really served as an adjunct of the Advertising Bureau. Joseph H. Meier, a CPA member who conducted a Chicago agency specializing in Catholic publications, attended the 1922 convention and presented to the members his plan for such a directory. Finding that the secretary of the Association had been collecting data for a similar project, Meier realized that it would not be feasible for him to compete with a CPA publication even though he had planned his version "to include all Catholic papers and periodicals in the United States, and not only the 98 or 99 which are members of the C. P. A." By the following spring the Association had decided not to issue its purposed listing, but Meier was alarmed by the fact that the Press and Publicity Department was compiling a register of Catholic publications. He was having difficulties, too, in getting returns on his questionnaire for the compilation primarily because publishers were reluctant to reveal circulation figures.[84] He had submitted a list of publications to the officials of the CPA who deleted those which in their opinion did not come under the classification of "Catholic" because of their racial or political overtones. The revised list was then sent to all the diocesan chancery officials who likewise scratched publications that they felt did not belong. Meier's original list of more than three hundred was thus trimmed to two hundred fifty-one, and he voluntarily omitted parish monthlies, local fraternal papers, and all but three college publications.[85]

By August of 1923 the Directory was ready. Besides providing relevant data on all the publications listed, the pocket-size volume contained a number of brief articles giv-ung statistics on the Catholic market, reasons for advertising in the Catholic Press, and surveys of the CPA and the NCWC Press Department. About thirty-five Catholic publications supported the Directory by buying advertising space in it.[86] Meier repeated the venture in 1925 and again in 1928. Each time the number of publications listed increased as did the publications and other businesses advertising in it. A flyleaf carried the endorsement of the CPA in 1928, and the convention of that year approved a resolution authorizing Meier "to place in 'The Official Catholic Press Directory' the words (Not Sworn) when circulation figures are presented to him without an A. B. C. certificate or without a sworn statement." The 1930 convention sanctioned still another edition of the Directory "at no expense to the Association," and urged that Meier obtain either A. B. C. or sworn statements for the circulation figures listed.[87]

Each Directory that appeared included but one Catholic daily paper published in the English language--The Daily American Tribune of Dubuque, Iowa. This publication had emerged July 1, 1920, through a gradual evolution of the Catholic Tribune beginning in 1899 as a weekly, continuing from 1915 to 1919 as a semi-weekly, and then becoming a tri-weekly for a little more than a year. The daily was sponsored by the Catholic Printing Company under the guidance of Nicholas Gonner, Jr., who had long been an advocate of a Catholic Press development plan. In an audience with Pope Pius X in 1909, Gonner had spoken of his hope to begin an English Catholic daily. Viewing the field of the Catholic Press as an apostolate, he had visions not only of a daily but of a chain of dailies, and he took advantage of every opportunity to promote the project.[88] At the 1921 convention, Gonner, then vice president of the CPA, chaired a round table discussion on the "Conduct of a Daily Catholic Paper." Not only did he inform the members about The Daily American Tribune, but he also enlightened them about the Catholic dailies in foreign countries. Again in 1922 he made a plea for more Catholic dailies.[89] In the meantime he was negotiating with leading Catholics in St. Louis, Chicago, and Milwaukee concerning the possibility of beginning a Catholic daily in one of those centers. Eventually he settled on Milwaukee and became managing editor of the Herald there. By late November of 1922 he had completed plans to move the Tribune equipment to Milwaukee, but a few days before the actual transfer, Gonner lost his life in an automobile mishap.[90]

Gonner's plan for a chain of dailies died with him, but The Daily American Tribune continued for another twenty years. From the time of its appearance it elicited many commendatory reviews, usually from other advocates of an English Catholic daily. Discussing the first issues, the editor of the Catholic Tribune of St. Joseph, Missouri, held that it "evinces a spirit of enterprise to be admired. Not only does the paper contain all the Catholic news of the day, but ample space is given to current secular events, telegraphic dispatches, a complete market report, etc." The Bulletin from Georgia agreed that the Tribune was "a real newspaper... [that] simply gives a Catholic tone to Catholic news and prints nothing that is anti-Catholic or unfair to the Church..." A Methodist publication was quoted in the Literary Digest as conceding that "... in this matter of a Church daily the Catholics with their accustomed enterprise have scored a victory over the Protestant forces."[91]

Despite the praise, financial support was wanting during much of the period. There was no debt when the daily started, and it actually paid dividends for the first two years. In 1921, however, the postwar depression hit the farming region where it originated, and the subscription price which had been eight dollars per year was reduced to six, resulting in a loss of about fifty thousand dollars annually. Also, in February of that year the Archbishop of Dubuque, James J. Keane, began publishing a diocesan weekly which cut into the circulation in the local area.[92] In 1926 a letter to the editor of America noted that "only about one Catholic family out of one thousand has seen fit to subscribe to this excellent Catholic daily."[93] By this time, however, the paper was better off financially than it had been since its beginning. Beck, who had been editor, wrote of the publishers: "... they are doing a great deal of good. For one thing, they have a following among the young people which no Catholic journal can boast and which is really one of the reasons why the daily has been able to pull through."[94] In the spring of 1927, Charles N. Nenning, who was then acting editor, sent out a circular letter soliciting comments and suggestions concerning the daily. To commemorate the tenth anniversary the editors planned a special edition of the paper which had been renamed the Catholic Daily Tribune in 1929, the year in which it reached its circulation peak.[95]

Over the decade there continued to be much talk about the possibility of other Catholic dailies. Often the Catholic

Press was compared with the Catholic school system, and many agreed with the point of view presented in The Ave Maria: "Without dailies in at least our larger centers of Catholic population, our press will remain as incomplete and truncated as our school system would be if it included only colleges and universities and no grade schools."[96] A few initial attempts were even made in the direction of additional dailies. Justin McGrath as early as 1921 considered buying a Yonkers newspaper to be converted into a Catholic daily. About the same time Dr. Hart was working with Archbishop Henry Moeller in Cincinnati hoping to see the Catholic Telegraph evolve via stages as had The Catholic Tribune. Detroit also was "responding to the idea" of such a project. In 1923 Linus G. Wey submitted a proposal to the convention suggesting that the CPA campaign for funds and subscriptions to finance the "First Five Links in a Chain of Catholic Dailies." But as Thomas F. Meehan observed in discussing a short-lived Catholic daily of the nineteenth century, the basic problem continued to be "the very simple one of the lack of the necessary money to make the venture. Its proportions have grown steadily with the intervening years."[97]

The ideal of a Catholic daily was especially appealing to those who felt that their religious beliefs were misrepresented in secular papers. There was some basis for this feeling in the 1920's, a notoriously intolerant period in American history. To counteract such bias in the secular press, CPA conventions continued to devote attention to matters of national concern, being especially alert to those that touched on religion. In 1921 Miss Mary MacSwiney, whose late brother had been Lord Mayor of Cork and a martyr for Irish freedom, urged the editors not to forget the Irish cause. Although she insisted that the Irish problem was not a religious one, Miss MacSwiney asked that the Catholic Press give special attention to the Irish question.[98] Two years later the aftermath of the war brought another plea to the delegates. The director of the bureau of historical records of the NCWC, Daniel J. Ryan, explained how the press could help to complete the war service records of American Catholics.[99]

By 1924 bigotry was rampant. Both the host bishop, William Turner of Buffalo and Mayor F. X. Schwab of that city, urged the editors to wage open warfare on the Ku-Klux-Klan. A year later a letter from the Catholic Information Bureau in Indianapolis was read to the convention. Established eight months earlier to combat "anti-Catholic legislation and religious prejudice in Indiana," the Indianapolis Bureau offered to place at the disposal of the editors a file of anti-Catholic activities and literature. Another Catholic grievance was aired in the 1924 convention when Father John J. Burke described conditions existing in Haiti, a predominantly Catholic country, then under American occupation. Asserting that the occupying forces were guilty of many unfair discriminations, Burke appealed to the editors to inform themselves and their readers.[100]

The Association also continued its efforts towards promoting Catholic literature and aiding Catholic writers. At its formation, the CPA had provided for a permanent fund to be obtained through $100 Life Memberships. Proceeds from the fund were to be used "to stimulate, encourage and reward Catholic writers and qualified literary and journalistic workers."[101] Although life members were not solicited during the first decade, some literary projects were sponsored, notably the short story contests beginning in 1917. At a meeting of the executive board in January of 1927 the directors discussed the life membership provision, and President Baldus promised to devise some plan to implement it. A few months later, he proposed to the convention the creation of the "Catholic Literary Awards Foundation." Designed to enlarge the Association's promotion of Catholic literary endeavors, the plan was approved unanimously. The entire membership of the CPA was designated as "A Committee of One Hundred"; 500 life memberships was the goal set; and recruiting was to be conducted among the hierarchy, clergy, educational institutions, and prominent layman. Ideally the goal was to be reached within thirty days, and the income from the $50,000 thus collected would not only finance awards in a number of literary categories but also permit the CPA to sponsor contests among high school and college students.[102]

But while the project was hailed as "one of the most forward steps taken by the Association since its organization,"[103] only one hundred twenty life members were enrolled during the year. Two more years of effort netted but eighteen additional life members. While this was disappointing, the CPA was able to sponsor various contests in the latter years of the period.[104]

In general, the decade just closing had been a successful one for the CPA. Although only half the publications listed in the 1928 Catholic Press Directory belonged to the organization, these represented almost two-thirds of the total circulation and an increase in membership of about three dozen in the ten years.[105] The Circulation, Advertising, Press Month, and Literature Committees had been very active. Also, in 1926 the annual meetings had been divided into magazine and newspaper sections and an extra convention day added. Two years later the president could report that the Association had adopted systematic business procedures, and in 1929 an increase in membership dues provided funds enabling the various bureaus to function more efficiently.[106] The Constitution was revised in 1929, and a new set of by-laws adopted the following year.[107] Realizing that there were still many obstacles confronting the Catholic Press, some of the members at times became discouraged. Most of them felt, however, that many advances had been made in the field of Catholic publishing, and at least one asserted that this was

> ... a direct result of the free interchange of ideas which the Association has made possible. The annual conventions are no longer merely occasions for shaking hands and social amenities; some real work is being done; something worthwhile is accomplished every year. In all truth it can be said that the annual conventions are milestones of progress.[108]

Notes

1. William T. Russell, "Confidential Communication to the Archbishops," n. d., but the paper was "the first gun of the N. C. W. C." according to Russell. See: Russell to Burke, July 7, 1921. Both in NCCB.

2. Michael Williams, "The Bishops and Our Press," Catholic World, CXII (March, 1921), 721. Actually, the 1919 NCWC was an entirely new organization. Cooperation was voluntary, and the body was not endowed with legislative powers.

3. Benedict Elder, "'N. C. W. C.'-The Church in Action," Catholic World, CXI (September, 1920), 725, 729. For an official explanation see: M. Rev. Austin Dowling, "The National Catholic Welfare Conference," The Ecclesiastical Review, LXXIX (October, 1928),

337-354.

4. Rev. Peter Guilday, The National Pastorals of the American Hierarchy (Washington, D. C., 1923), p. 291.

5. Reported in Catholic Review (Baltimore), January 3, 1920.

6. Circular letter from Thos. P. Hart, January 10, 1920. CC. Hart managed the old News Service.

7. Data concerning the 1920 convention is from the Catholic Review, January 31, 1920.

8. "Amendments to the Constitution of the Catholic Press Association of the United States and Canada," January 24, 1920. Anticipating that "all Catholic editors and publishers" would belong to the CPA, a 1920 resolution stated: "The distribution of the proposed weekly information sheet [italics mine] shall not be limited to any particular publications." This from Catholic Columbian, January 30, 1920. The membership condition was not entirely removed until the 1954 constitutional revision. Frank A. Hall in a letter to Bishop Thomas K. Gorman, February 17, 1954, traces the history of the stipulation. PDF.

9. Catholic Columbian, January 30, 1920; Catholic Tribune, January 30, 1920. Bishop Russell's view is quoted in: Michael Williams, "The Growth of the Bishops' Press Bureau," America, XXIV (February 26, 1921), 447.

10. This paragraph is based on Frank A. Hall, "Justin McGrath: First Director of NCWC News Service," Catholic Press Annual '62, pp. 38-41, 61-62, passim.

11. Justin McGrath, "The National Catholic Press Bureau," Bulletin, I (June-July, 1920), p. 7.

12. Michael Williams, "The Bishops and Our Press," Catholic World, CXII (March, 1921), 727-728.

13. John B. Delaunay, CSC, to Bishop McDevitt, n. d. McDevitt Papers, AUND. The letter appears to have been written just before Easter, 1922. Another letter from Delaunay dated April 13, 1922, refers to the

same incident.

14. Catholic Herald (St. Louis), June 20, 1926.

15. "National Catholic Welfare Conference," Catholic World, CVIII (November, 1923), 261.

16. Quoted in a letter to the editor of The Fortnightly Review, XXVII (May 15, 1920), 154-155. The author, who signed himself "A Paying Member of the CPA", was much against the restriction. He inquired, "Why should the Bishops' Council identify itself with a private organization that by no means has the monopoly of Catholicity as far as publications are concerned?"

17. Synopsis... 1921, p. 1. CC.

18. The concession was apparently Father Burke's decision. In a letter dated July 7, 1921, Russell told Burke: "I may say that the more I think over it, the less I am inclined to yield to the resolution of the C. P. A. The N. C. W. C. alone must determine what papers will have the benefit of its service." NCCB. The CPA action is recorded in Synopsis... 1921, p. 2. CC.

19. Several letters dating from the fall of 1921 to February of 1924 bring out these issues. CPA presidents, Becker and F. W. Harvey, exchanged comments with McGrath. PDF.

20. S. A. Baldus to McGrath, January 24, 1928. PDF.

21. McGrath's memo for Father Burke, May 9, 1928. PDF.

22. Yearbook... 1929, pp. 15-17, 49-53, and 59. CC.

23. Beck to Preuss, July 19, 1925. CC. Beck maintained that "discussion of all those questions on the floor would get us nowhere." Msgr. Thomas V. Shannon talked McDevitt into the questionnaire approach. Results were issued in The N. C. W. C. News Service. Its Value to the Catholic Press of the United States (Washington, 1925). McDevitt Papers, AUND.

24. Yearbook... 1929, p. 17. CC.

25. Beck to Kenkel, October 18, 1929. CC.

26. <u>Yearbook...1930,</u> pp. 18-20. CC.

27. <u>Ibid.</u>, p. 31.

28. Father Burke made mention of this in a letter to Bishop John T. McNicholas of Cincinnati, May 30, 1930. NCCB.

29. "Minutes, Board...November 22, 1930," pp. 4-6. CPA.

30. Bishop Boyle, McGrath, and President Elder were all less inclined to be conciliatory. See: Boyle to McGrath, February 9, 1931; Burke to Elder, May 19, 1931; and Boyle to Burke, July 8, 1931. NCCB. Also, Elder to Joseph Meier, April 13, 1931; and Hall to McGrath, May 7, 1931. PDF.

31. "Minutes, Board...January 23, 1932," pp. 1-2. PDF. See, too, John J. Burke, "Report on My Attendance at the Meeting of the Executive Board, C. P. A.," NCCB.

32. Copies of both letters are in NCCB. In addition to the <u>True Voice</u> which had started the controversy, only three other publications were involved. This leads one to agree with Bishop Boyle who wrote to Father Burke under date of July 8, 1931, "It has been hinted that there is a lot of hurt vanity back of the conflicts that have arisen." NCCB.

33. Circular: Benedict Elder to all Active Members, April 7, 1932. J. Meier informed Hall of the return of the <u>True Voice</u> in a letter dated May 5, 1932. PDF.

34. McGrath's observation appeared in the <u>Josephinum Weekly,</u> June 7, 1924. References to the editors' lack of interest appear in <u>Yearbook...1928,</u> pp. 37-38; <u>Yearbook...1929,</u> p. 57; and <u>Yearbook...1930,</u> p. 82. CC. Letters to Bishop McDevitt dated May 26 and May 28, 1927, are in McDevitt Papers, AUND.

35. Galbally to McDevitt, September 3, 1925. McDevitt Papers, AUND. Galbally was managing editor of the <u>American Ecclesiastical Review.</u>

36. For examples, see: Catholic Herald, May 24, 1925; George N. Kramer, "Has the Catholic Press Failed?" Catholic World, CXV (August, 1922), 610-622; William C. Murphy, "The Catholic Press," American Mercury, IX (December, 1926), 408. McGrath also mentioned some of the criticisms in his letter to Bishop McDevitt, May 26, 1927. McDevitt Papers, AUND. Also, Yearbook... 1929, p. 50. CC.

37. Preuss to Adolph B. Suess of St. Louis, September 7, 1925. Preuss wrote: "I agree entirely with you as to the flagrant incompetency of the N. C. W. C. News Service and have let Bishop McDevitt know my views; but it will probably do no good. The waste of money will continue until the entire N. C. W. C. is swept into oblivion, where it belongs. Its establishment was a post-war idea, and an unfortunate one at that." Copy of letter in CC.

38. Quoted in Catholic Review (Baltimore), January 31, 1920.

39. "Almost a Century," America, XXVIII (November 11, 1922), 88.

40. Delaunay to McDevitt, December 2, 1924. McDevitt Papers, AUND.

41. Tablet (Brooklyn), August 9, 1924.

42. Josephinum Weekly, June 7, 1924, reported Fitzpatrick's address.

43. Catholic Review, August 5, 1922, mentions the increase of that year; Bulletin, VI (June, 1924), p. 12 reports the 1924 increase.

44. Indiana Catholic and Record, May 22, 1925.

45. Bishop McDevitt, "Address at the Convention of the Catholic Press Association, Savannah, Georgia, May 19, 1927," p. 1 refers to the raise. McDevitt Papers, AUND.

46. Yearbook... 1928, p. 22. CC.

47. "10th Anniversary of the N. C. W. C. News Service," Review, XII (September, 1930), p. 6.

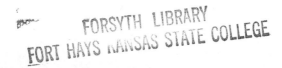

48. "Note and Comment," America, XXIII (May 15, 1920), 95. Desmond's suggestion was reprinted in the Providence Visitor, August 18, 1911, but see also: Humphrey E. Desmond, "Humphrey J. Desmond," Catholic Press Annual '62, p. 57. Becker's statement is in a letter to Gonner's son, Brother Lawrence, January 14, 1960, loaned to the author. The Encyclopedia article appears in V. J. Fecher, "Society of the Divine Word," New Catholic Encyclopedia, IV, 924. The correspondence dates from May 7, through October 11, 1920, and is in CC. See too: Francis Markert, SVD, "How the Catholic Press Month Originated," The Christian Family and Our Missions, XLV (Feb., 1950), pp. 38-39.

49. Catholics: Do You Know? (Washington, D. C., 1921), CC. The special committees were mentioned in "The National Catholic Press Month," Extension Magazine, XV (March, 1921), p. 1; and Noll's slogan was reported in The Catholic Tribune (St. Joseph, Missouri), May 28, 1921.

50. Minutes... 1922, p. 2 tells of the change. The pamphlet was entitled YOU Should Read the Catholic Press WHY? (Washington, D. C., 1922). CC. Wey's resolution appears in Minutes... 1922, p. 11.

51. Minutes... 1923, p. 5 mentions this action. CPA.

52. Desmond's speech was printed in pamphlet form. CPA.

53. This from James J. Brady, Press Month Committee Secretary to "Publisher," August 16, 1924. CC. The same source was used in explaining the plan.

54. James J. Brady, "To the Members of the Catholic Press Association," n. d. CC. It is interesting that there were, according to the 1923 Catholic Press Directory, well over 200 Catholic publications at this time.

55. Baldus to Preuss, March 4, 1925. CC. Although Desmond was the committee chairman, a good share of the work seems to have been done by Baldus and Brady, both of whom were in Chicago.

56. "Report of the Press Month Committee to the Catholic Press Association of the United States and Canada in

Convention assembled," May 10, 1925. CPA.

57. The Catholic Herald (St. Louis), June 8, 1924.

58. Bulletin, III (January, 1922), p. 13.

59. R. M. D., "Promoting the Catholic Press," America, XXXVIII (February 25, 1928), 496.

60. The Catholic Register, April 28, 1921; The Bulletin, February 23, 1924.

61. Josephinum Weekly, June 7, 1924, reported this activity.

62. Yearbook... 1929, pp. 19 and 12. CC.

63. Benedict Elder, "The Value of the Catholic Newspaper to the Catholic School," NCEA Bulletin, XXVII (November, 1930), pp. 391-397.

64. Catholic Review (Baltimore), June 16, 1923.

65. Minutes... 1923, p. 5. CPA. The Catholic Tribune (St. Joseph, Missouri), October 13, 1923, carried the release.

66. Report of the Circulation Committee of the C. P. A. (Chicago, June 14, 1924), passim. CC.

67. Circular letter from Circulation Committee secretary, Giles Strub, OFM, July 2, 1925. CC.

68. Ibid., July 23, 1925. CC.

69. Ibid., October 15, 1925, and February 17, 1926. CC.

70. Ibid., January 4, 1927. CC.

71. Yearbook... 1928, p. 22. However, the Rev. Lewis J. O'Hern, chairman of the Circulation Committee that year, reported at the same meeting that many of these were reentering the field via non-cooperating Catholic publishers. Yearbook... 1928, p. 30. CC.

72. Yearbook... 1929, p. 18. CC.

73. Ibid., pp. 37-40.

74. Yearbook... 1930, pp. 68-76. The name had been changed the year before at the request of the committee. Yearbook... 1929, pp. 40 and 12. Both in CC.

75. "Minutes of the Members of the Catholic Press Association and Subscribers to the National Catholic Welfare Council News Sheet Service held at the Advertising Club of New York, Friday, July 23, 1920," PDF.

76. Synopsis... 1921, p. 3. CC.

77. "Report of the Chairman of the Advertising Bureau, The Rev. Charles J. Mullaly, S. J., Cleveland, Ohio, July 28-29, 1922." See also, McGrath to Fred W. Harvey, Jr., September 28, 1922. Both in PDF.

78. Church Progress, February 1, 1923, carried the release. See: McGrath to Harvey January 13, 1923. PDF.

79. Have You Overlooked These Twenty Million Consumers? passim. CC.

80. For 1925 convention reports see: Church Progress, May 21, 1925; Indiana Catholic and Record, May 22, 1925; and the Catholic Herald, May 24, 1925.

81. A Short and Broad Avenue to 20,000,000 Buyers, p. 1. CC.

82. Yearbook... 1928, p. 60. CC.

83. Yearbook... 1929, pp. 69-71; Yearbook... 1930, pp. 100-103 and 35. CC. Father Mullaly issued still another pamphlet, Are You Reaching These 20,203,702 Buyers? and drew up an advertising code to be presented to the 1931 convention. "Minutes, Board... November 22, 1930." CPA.

84. Meier to Preuss, August 1, 1922, and March 27 and April 15, 1923. CC. This same reluctance to acknowledge circulation figures was referred to in an article in American Mercury a few years later. The author pointed out that only five publications had submitted A. B. C. figures for Ayer's Newspaper Directory of 1926. He alleged that "This curious refusal to

supply advertisers with reliable circulation figures is responsible for the conspicuous absence of national advertising from the greater part of the American Catholic press." He also noted that in Meier's 1925 Directory, 39 of the 264 publications listed "failed to supply any circulation figures at all." See: William C. Murphy, Jr. "The Catholic Press," American Mercury, IX (December, 1926), 400-401.

85. Meier explained the procedure in The Catholic Press Directory (Chicago, 1923), p. 5. The three college publications included held CPA membership.

86. The Catholic Press Directory (Chicago, 1923), passim. An editorial in the Catholic Citizen (Milwaukee), August 25, 1923, noted that 65 weeklies were listed, one less than the number given in the Catholic Directory for 1898. The writer stated, "...the growth of the Catholic press in the last twenty-five years has been in monthlies and devotionals rather than in weekly newspapers.... [and reasoned] As an index of public intelligence and appreciation for the Catholic press this is hardly a favorable showing. There is more vegetation, but the increase is in weeds."

87. Yearbook...1928, p. 16; Yearbook...1930, p. 37. CC. The directory approved in 1930 did not appear until 1932. Meier edited still another directory in 1942 which was published for him by Joseph F. Wagner, Inc. This company issued directories in 1943 and 1945. In 1950 the CPA took over the publication of the directory. See below: Chapter VII.

88. Brother Nicholas [sic-really Lawrence] J. Gonner, SM, "First English-Language Catholic Daily in U. S.," Catholic Press Annual '61, p. 36.

89. Synopsis...1921, p. 5. CC. Gonner had spent seven years studying in Luxemburg according to his son, Brother Lawrence. The 1922 plea was reported in Catholic Review, August 5, 1922.

90. A. J. Beck to F. P. Kenkel, July 16, 1942. CC. Kenkel had asked Beck who had been with the Catholic Publishing Co. for a number of years (1908-1922), to explain why the Catholic daily had failed that summer.

91. Catholic Tribune, July 17, 1920; Bulletin of the Catholic Laymen's Association of Georgia, July, 1920. This editor had high praise for Gonner calling him "One of the leading Catholic laymen of the West and indeed of the country. He is a thinker as well as a doer, a forceful writer and the possessor of a great fund of general and specific information that peculiarly fits him for the great task he has undertaken." The Methodist publication was quoted in "Catholics Launch a Daily Paper," Literary Digest, LXVII (Oct. 23, 1920), p. 36.

92. Beck to Kenkel, July 16 and July 25, 1942. CC.

93. Dr. R. Willman, "Helping the Catholic Press," America, XXXV (June 12, 1926), 215. Willman had been concerned with the apostolate of the Catholic Press for many years.

94. Beck to Preuss, July 19, 1925. CC.

95. Nenning, circular letter of May 13, 1927. Copy received by Kenkel, CC. Notice of the anniversary number appears in a letter from J. P. Clardy of the Tribune business office to Charles Korz, President of the Central Verein, June 17, 1930. CC. For name changes of the daily refer to: Eugene P. Willging and Herta Hatzfeld, Catholic Serials of the Nineteenth Century in the United States; Second Series, Part Six, Iowa (Washington, 1963), p. 23.

96. The Ave Maria, XXV (February 19, 1927), 245.

97. For McGrath's idea see: Frank A. Hall, "Justin McGrath: First Director of NCWC News Service," Catholic Press Annual '62, p. 41. "Note and Comments," America, XXV (October 1, 1921), 554, makes reference to the Cincinnati and Detroit moves. Wey's suggestion appears in Minutes... 1923, p. 3. CPA. Meehan's article is "The First Catholic Daily," America, XXXIX (May 26, 1928), 156.

98. Synopsis... 1921, p. 6. CC.

99. Register (Kansas City), July 5, 1923.

100. Ibid., May 29, 1924; The 1925 convention was reported in

Indiana Catholic and Record, May 22, 1925.

101. Circular issued by "Life Membership Committee of One Hundred" following the 1927 CPA Convention. CC.

102. See: Catholic Review, May 27, 1927; S. A. Baldus, "A Recommendation for the Enrollment of Life Members in the Catholic Press Association and a Proposal to Create a Catholic Literary Awards Foundation." CPA. The plan was summarized in the 1927 circular.

103. J. H. Meier labeled it as such in his Catholic Press Directory (Chicago, 1928), p. 26. As secretary, Meier was anxious to recruit members for the Association. In a letter to Father Daniel Hudson, March 29, 1928, he suggested that The Ave Maria become a life member. Hudson Papers, AUND. Yearbook...1929, lists Hudson as a life member so Meier was successful in this instance. CC.

104. See: Yearbook...1928, p. 21; Yearbook...1929, p. 78; and Yearbook...1930, p. 116. CC.

105. "The Catholic Press Association," America, XXXIX (May 26, 1928), 149.

106. The extra convention day was noted in Catholic Tribune, July 3, 1926; Yearbook...1928, p. 21 referred to the new business methods; Yearbook...1929, p. 18 mentioned the dues increase. CC.

107. See: Yearbook...1929, p. 42; Yearbook...1930, p. 32. CC.

108. Simon Baldus, "Seventeen Years of the 'C. P. A.'," Bulletin, IX (May, 1928), p. 8. For examples commenting on the obstacles see: "Successful Convention of C. P. A." Bulletin, VI (June, 1924), p. 12; Andrue H. Berding, "The Catholics and the Newspapers," America, XXXIV (January 2, 1926), 275-276; and Clarence J. McCabe, "The Press and the Family," Review, XII (January, 1930), p. 18. Discouragement was experienced even by the leaders. In 1923 the dedicated Dr. Hart wrote how hard he was working and remarked: "I am getting very, very tired of the continual grind. I often wonder whether the results justify the sacrifice." Hart to Dietz, July 20, 1923.

Dietz Papers, CC. Likewise, Baldus commented: "It is to be regretted that those who have worked hardest and given their best efforts to the cause of Catholic journalism, derive an income from their labors hardly equal to that of a second rate brick layer, and falling far below that of the professional bootlegger." Baldus to Preuss, March 4, 1925. CC. Those who noted advances include: "The Catholic Press Association Meets," America, XXXV (July 17, 1926), 330; Thomas F. Meehan, "The First Catholic Daily," America, XXXIX (May 26, 1928), 155; and Justin McGrath, "Catholics and the Catholic Press," Bulletin, X (January, 1929), p. 5.

Chapter IV

"Coming-of-Age" to World War II (1931-1941)

In 1931 a very special milestone of progress was commemorated. It was the twenty-first annual convention of the Association, and leaders of the group labeled the gathering the "Coming-of-Age Convention." The site chosen was Baltimore "so that it might be a homecoming, since the city had been the source of so many Catholic leaders."[1] The local committee, chaired by Msgr. Albert E. Smith, editor of the Baltimore Catholic Review, capitalized on the religious aspects of the city. Each delegate was presented with a badge struck from bronze and stamped with a replica of the Baltimore Cathedral, and in his address of welcome Smith dwelt upon the inspiration the delegates would receive from this historic spot. An exhibit of relics of Catholicity in Maryland attracted much attention, and the editors and publishers visited the crypt of the Cathedral to pray at the tombs of Bishop John Carroll, James Cardinal Gibbons and five other bishops of the See.[2] Indeed, the CPA met in Baltimore in "a Catholic atmosphere... [not] duplicated anywhere else in the United States."[3]

In attendance were approximately one hundred fifty delegates made up of almost equal numbers of laity and clergy, and even "two quiet nuns." Missing, however, was Justin McGrath who had died suddenly the week before. As usual, McGrath had been scheduled to address the delegates and present a report of the News Service. His death was a shock, and a committee was named to extend the condolences of the CPA to his family.[4]

The business sessions were varied and numerous. A series of talks considered the place of ethics in subscription promotion, advertising, content, missionary appeal, and reading content. Discussing the last point, Father James M. Gillis of the Catholic World maintained that editors often fail to explore or present various problems to their readers. The reactions of the delegates are not recorded, but the priest-editor of Omaha's True Voice later commented: "As a matter of fact, there has been considerable timidity on the part of Catholic editors when it comes to discussion of Catholic events.... A little open discussion and open confession of our faults and shortcomings can do no harm."[5]

Two business items of note were transacted at the 1931 convention. Acting on the suggestion of Alexander J. Wey, general manager of the Catholic Universe-Bulletin in Cleveland, the convention "directed the executive board to consider arrangements for departmental clinics at the next convention for exhaustive discussion of special problems..." Secondly, following the recommendation of the 1930 meeting, the members adopted a strong nine-point advertising code calling for "accuracy of circulation statements to prospective advertisers, selection of worthy solicitors to represent the Catholic Press, the maintenance of fixed rates for all, rejection of patent medicines and 'cure-all' advertisements, protection of readers by a competent investigation of all advertising copy, and the employment at all times of sound business methods."[6] F. P. LeBuffe, SJ, Chairman of the Circulation Vigilance Committee, reported that the combination of the current economic depression and the lack of funds available to the committee had hindered its work. To remedy this situation a motion was carried providing the member publications increase their yearly contributions to this committee from twenty to one hundred dollars.[7]

Honored at the annual banquet was Bishop-elect Thomas K. Gorman, recently named to the new diocese of Reno, Nevada. Because he was editor of the Los Angeles Tidings at the time of his appointment, the CPA members were especially pleased with Gorman's promotion. The banquet itself contained elements of seriousness as well as much light heartedness. Archbishop Michael J. Curley, the principal speaker, struck out against mixed marriages labeling them "largely unmixed maledictions." Moving to a more congenial subject he lauded the Catholic Press in general and referred to his paper (the Review) as "the apple of my archiepiscopal eye." He also reminded the editors that their convention was but a foreshadowing of other great Catholic events in Baltimore for, in just three years, the Archdiocese would commemorate the centennial of the birth of Cardinal Gibbons as well as the three hundredth anniversary of the arrival in Maryland of the Jesuit Fathers. After the essay contests winners were announced, "Lord Baltimore" himself appeared to present the Catholic history of Maryland to the group. [8]

The final convention session was held aboard ship as the delegates traveled to Annapolis for a sightseeing tour and a reception by Governor Albert E. Ritchie. That evening those who stayed over attended a second banquet at the new St. Mary's Seminary as guests of the students and the Sulpician Fathers. [9] The "Coming-of-Age" theme continued throughout the year. President Benedict Elder in his farewell address to the 1932 convention told the members:

> With this convention, we are completing our twenty-first year. We have grown up. We have taken on the stature of manhood and its consciousness. As a natural person on attaining majority becomes more conscious of his purpose and mission in life, so I trust the Catholic Press Association now that it is rounding out its twenty-first year is more conscious of its purpose and its mission than ever before. [10]

A system of chains or newspaper syndicates, coupled with the trend toward diocesan control also matured during the decade. In earlier periods, private companies had sponsored chains. The 1923 Catholic Press Directory, for example, noted that the Citizen Company of Milwaukee published not only the Catholic Citizen in that city but also three other papers in St. Paul, Minnesota, Memphis, Tennessee, and Washington, D. C. At the same time the Catholic Press Union of Cleveland was issuing three Ohio papers and a fourth in Erie, Pennsylvania. These chains, however, remained static and never attempted a nationwide system. Rather it was two other long-established newspapers which in the 30's set about promoting the chain system.

One, The Denver Register, had been published under the watchful eye of Msgr. Matthew J. W. Smith since 1912 when, as a young layman, he had become editor. [11] In 1924 a second paper, The Register, began to come out on Tuesday while the older Denver Register continued to appear on Thursday. Originally, this move was to ascertain whether Colorado was ready for a daily Catholic paper, but Father Smith's bishop, J. Henry Tihen, president of the Register Company, vetoed the idea of a daily. Instead The Register was reorganized in 1927 as a four page national Catholic newspaper, flashy in appearance and "carrying complete coverage of the national and international Catholic news field."

Two years later Hubert A. Smith, the monsignor's brother and managing editor of the Denver Register, was in Fresno, California, soliciting orders for bundle lots of the national edition. When he approached Father Michael Sullivan, the priest offered an idea that he had been considering for some time. A few years earlier, Sullivan had observed that in East San Diego a weekly newspaper, supported entirely by advertising, had been given free to every local resident. The priest persuaded Smith that a Catholic paper could be circulated in the same way.

Father Sullivan's bishop approved the plan, and he suggested that it be tried on the diocesan level. Although Msgr. Smith was skeptical, in June of 1929 the Central California Register made its appearance. Within a few months the Register Company made similar arrangements in three other dioceses so that by the time the CPA convention opened in 1930, McGrath included a reference to the chains in his annual report:

> Another problem of great concern and of vital interest to the News Service which has become acute during the past year is the establishment by diocesan papers of chain systems... one of our Western Catholic papers has carried the chain system to an extent beyond anything heretofore known in Catholic journalism.

McGrath added that he had called attention to the matter, and the administrative committee of the NCWC had ruled "that an extra subscription [to the News Service] must be paid for each paper published outside the home diocese."[12] Despite this regulation the Register system continued to mushroom. By the middle of the decade twelve dioceses had joined, and by the end of this period almost thirty were numbered among its members. Financing through advertising soon failed, probably due to the severity of the depression, and subscriptions were then sold at a nominal cost.[13]

The second chain was an outgrowth of Our Sunday Visitor, a publication begun in 1912 by the young Father John F. Noll as an antidote to the anti-Catholic propaganda spread by such publications as The Appeal to Reason and The Menace. Intended as a means of continuing education for American Catholics, Our Sunday Visitor's motto was "to serve the Church" and its subtitle, "The Harmonizer."[14] Within two years, Father Noll's Visitor had a circulation of four hundred thousand copies distributed in bundle lots for sale at church doors on Sunday morning.[15] Even in its early days it was referred to as "one of the mysteries of American journalism" because it seldom printed news items, consisted of only four pages, and was mediocre in appearance.[16] Father Noll, who became Bishop of Fort Wayne, Indiana, in 1925, had always contended that his paper was not in competition with other Catholic weeklies. Early in 1926 he began the Fort Wayne edition of Our Sunday Visitor inserting the national edition as part of the paper. Although other bishops asked that he do this for them also, he refused to compete with the diocesan press. After Msgr. Smith developed the Register system, however, Bishop Noll in 1937 accepted the principle. The Visitor Company then perfected two plans: in a number of dioceses the local papers were supplemented by Our Sunday Visitor's national edition as had been done in Bishop Noll's own diocese; for dioceses without their own newspapers, a national news edition was established.[17]

Near the end of the period two other attempts were made to found chains. In 1935 the Witness Publishing Company of Dubuque, Iowa, began publishing the Observer for the diocese of Rockford, Illinois. Four years later Msgr. Peter M. H. Wynhoven of the Catholic Action of the South in New Orleans introduced diocesan editions for Alexandria and Lafayette, Louisiana, and Natchez, Mississippi. Neither attempt prospered. The Observer later became independent, and the Catholic Action papers joined the Register system.[18]

Because the chain papers were less costly, they were welcomed by many, especially in areas where Catholic papers were few or non-existent. But they also had their critics. An editorial in the Oklahoma South West Courier declared: "High speed presses are grinding out editions with no pretence at local news coverage but with an eye to picking up local money. The outside Catholic paper is displacing the diocesan organ in Catholic homes on the strength of a few pennies." And the Quincy paper which quoted this statement added: "... bear well in mind our eight page Western Catholic newspaper is a home product--a diocesan product which has nothing in common with the chain-store type of newspaper."[19] These comments were probably directed at church door sales of the national editions of The Register and Our Sunday Visitor. The chains themselves were built up not by taking over existing papers or by competing with diocesan ones, but by establishing new papers in regions where no

Catholic paper existed and with the initial overtures usually coming from diocesan officials. In addition the depression forced other privately owned papers to sell out so that by the mid-1930's over seventy-five per cent of the Catholic newspapers were under the control of the various dioceses.[20]

Nonetheless, the trend toward diocesan control together with problems arising because of the national editions and the chain systems resulted in a lengthy struggle within the Association which at times threatened to disrupt the CPA, the News Service, or both. Not only the lay editors of the few remaining independent papers but also some of the bishops who sponsored their own diocesan publications resented the competition of The Register and Our Sunday Visitor. Even before Father John J. Burke had succeeded in terminating the controversy of the preceeding decade concerning the News Service, the new conflict had begun.

In May of 1932 a diocesan chancellor wrote at length to CPA President Benedict Elder, referred to the unfair competition of the national weeklies, and urged that the Association investigate the use of the News Service by these papers. Writing immediately to Bishop Noll and to Bishop Urban J. Vehr of Denver, Elder explained that complaints had been voiced and asked that they send representatives to the board meeting to be held in conjunction with the annual convention. Both Noll and Smith (who was delegated by his bishop to handle the matter) declined Elder's invitation insisting that their papers were established to serve the Church, denying that the publication of brief news items was injurious to diocesan publications, and maintaining that they could manage quite well without the benefits of the News Service. Although the executive board discussed the matter at length in three different meetings the directors did not present the problem to the general sessions, deciding instead that letters should again be sent to the parties involved. During the convention, however, Bishop Noll wrote another letter to the president indicating that he would not use the News Service in the future and offering to mediate the differences.[21]

The following year a representative from Our Sunday Visitor met with the board to the satisfaction of all, but the controversy with the Register continued. Father Smith not only declined an invitation to meet with the board, but also charged that the CPA was "taking an inimical stand" toward his publication. He denied that there was "such overwhelming desire" for the Register that other editors need fear it, and he threatened to drop Association membership should the matter be brought up at a general session of the 1933 convention. This reaction prompted Father Burke to request of Bishop Hugh Boyle that "Father Smith be quietly asked not to withdraw his membership" lest the old controversy over non-members receiving the News Service be renewed. A month later when Bishop Vehr visited Washington, Father Burke repeated this appeal to him. Consequently, although the antagonism continued, the Register retained membership.[22]

In February of 1934 the board discussed the Register situation again and considered either changing the release dates of the News Service so that the national editions would not be able to use items ordinarily carried by diocesan papers or stipulating that no other Catholic paper could appear in a diocese in advance of the diocesan publication. It was even suggested that The Register be expelled from the Association. This and every other proposal encountered opposition; no action was taken except for the appointment of a committee to study the situation until the next convention. Through an agreement reached at a Liaison Committee meeting the night before the 1934 meeting opened, the Register problem was once more kept from the general convention sessions.[23] For four years the board continued to discuss the situation often considering retaliatory measures. In the fall of 1937 President Fitzpatrick privately proposed that the CPA break with the NCWC and establish its own news service, but Hall convinced him of the futility of such action.[24] It was President Charles H. Ridder who finally settled the controversy after he took office in 1938 by meeting with Msgr. Smith personally and urging him to cooperate with the Association. Following this meeting, Smith wrote a letter asking the editors of his chain of papers to join the CPA, attend the conventions, and "play ball with the boys." This was done; Hubert Smith read one of the major papers at the 1939 convention, and representatives of the Register papers began attending annual meetings.[25]

Another proposal, related in some respects to the chains and the national weeklies, did find a place in the discussions of the general sessions of the conventions during the last few years of the period, but ultimately it was rejected by the Association. The plan, sponsored by Msgr. Wynhoven and first presented to the 1937 convention, envisioned the establishment of a weekly supplement to be used by every Catholic paper and containing "interesting stories, feature articles by famous writers, specialized pages, sports for the youngsters, and even 'the funnies' for children." The promoter argued that national appeals could be made through this medium, more space could be used in local papers for articles of regional interest, and national "propositions dangerous to Catholic interests and principles, could be better and more uniformly explained and more forcefully brought to the attention of the public." Admitting that this would be an expensive undertaking, Wynhoven contended that the funds initially invested could soon be repaid and that the venture would not only become self-supporting but would even be a profitable enterprise in a short time since it would be relatively easy to obtain national advertising with the projected large circulation. Maintaining that his plan was not an impossibility, Wynhoven pointed to the secular Sunday magazine supplements and asserted: "Our Catholic weeklies can do the same by cooperating and combining."[26]

The priest was not the only one thinking along these lines. When the 1940 convention met in Detroit, a retired automobile advertising executive, Theodore F. MacManus, entertained the delegates at his estate and presented them with a mimeographed prospectus. MacManus had "long wanted to use his publicity talents to benefit the Roman Catholic Church" and had spent the eighteen months of his retirement developing his plan and seeking support for it. Like Wynhoven's, this proposal called for a Sunday newspaper containing all that the regular secular papers provided but Catholic in "editorial inspiration and technique." The MacManus plan differed drastically, though, from that of Msgr. Wynhoven as the publicity executive intended to sell stock "and buy out all the Catholic papers of the nation."[27]

The convention did not act on this second scheme, but in July Msgr. Wynhoven, who had been elected president in Detroit, wrote to Bishop Gannon complaining that one of the CPA directors was "courting Mr. MacManus." He enclosed a copy of a letter that he was sending MacManus in which he reminded that gentleman that the bishops needed to be consulted and the CPA must approve if the project was to be implemented. The monsignor wrote bluntly: "As things stand now, I can definitely inform you, dear Mr. MacManus, that irrespective of what financial backing you may get, the plan will not work for the present, for the Bishops are skeptical about it and the editors in general hostile to it." Inserting a word for his own plan, the president continued,

> I had suggested to Father Benz [a priest connected with the MacManus plan with whom Wynhoven had corresponded] that he propose to you a national Sunday supplement, which would fill a great need, hence very acceptable to all concerned, and would also be imminently feasible at this time with your valuable backing and interest.

When MacManus died suddenly two months later, Bishop Gannon, writing to Msgr. Wynhoven, commented:

> I think this draws the curtain over a scene which had little attraction for me. When I meet you sometime, I will explain the Chicago project with the McCormick Company on which the Cardinal and I worked for some time but which we could never bring to fruition. It was far more attractive than the Detroit plan. Perhaps you can take up where I left off and make a success of it.[28]

At the October board meeting, Wynhoven appointed a Finding Committee to examine the issue of the Sunday supplement. Reporting to the 1941 convention, Father Edward Daily explained that his committee had not only studied the idea of a supplement but also had drawn up a model of such a publication. The delegates, while not showing much enthusiasm for the supplement, raised no objections to it and approved the committee's proposal that the executive board continue to study the matter.[29] Therefore, the following October Msgr. Wynhoven sent Bishop Gannon a "prospectus for a National Magazine... [for his] thoughtful consideration and study," and told the Episcopal Chairman, "We feel that the enclosed plan, if enthusiastically backed, will lend greatly to strengthen the Catholic press and make our endeavors in that field in this country more effective." The "prospectus" was brief. Explaining that such a national supplement would fulfill a purpose and need, would be possible, and could succeed financially, it also contained a provision that editorial policy would be determined by an editorial board "duly approved by the Hierarchy." But Bishop Gannon remained doubtful. He suspected that the larger Catholic weeklies would not cooperate. Again referring to his earlier labors with George Cardinal Mundelein, he reported that they had received many refusals to their suggested "National Editorial Pictorial Supplement."[30]

Msgr. Wynhoven replied that the weeklies were sure

to approve and contended "... it is the Bishops' endorsement which is needed... I sincerely hope Your Excellency can see your way clear to arouse some enthusiasm at the Hierarchical meeting in Washington." Bishop Gannon, however, still hesitated and discussed the supplement plan with Director Hall who found himself "unable to pass judgment on the proposal, for lack of information." He advised the bishop not to recommend the Wynhoven plan but rather to let it fail "for want of facts." In his presidential report the following May, Wynhoven spoke the final words on the matter telling his fellow-editors: "There is only one disappointment that still rankles in my presidential breast namely, the wanton application of a lit cigarette to our National Supplement balloon. But then being an implicit believer in divine Providence, I lose no longer sleep over it."[31]

Although the bishops failed to put their stamp of approval on the supplement plan, they provided the impetus that led to much CPA activity in another phase of the Catholic Press during this decade. At their annual meeting in 1932, the hierarchy took note of immorality present in the secular literature of the day and denounced it. Under the direction of Charles H. Ridder the Catholic Press Month Committee conducted the 1933 campaign as a crusade to substitute good Catholic literature for these immoral publications.[32] That fall the bishops shifted the emphasis from publications to films and named the Episcopal Committee on Motion Pictures to investigate the problem. Bishops Boyle and Noll, both of whom were actively connected with the CPA, were members of this committee which established the Legion of Decency in April of 1934 to promote a campaign "to arouse millions of Americans to a consciousness of the dangers of salacious and immoral pictures and to take action against them."[33] The Catholic Press, Catholics as a group, and even numerous secular and Protestant organizations entered the campaign with great enthusiasm.

By the time that the CPA meetings convened on May 24, 1934, the campaign was well underway. Local groups had been formed, boycotts begun, and pledges signed. In his resumé of the Catholic Press Month activities of 1934, Ridder reported the success of a drive against objectionable magazines carried out in his home state of New York under the direction of Patrick Cardinal Hayes. Likewise, President Richard Reid in his address complimented his fellow-editors on the concerted efforts they had made in publicizing the Legion of Decency campaign and informed them that the result was that "motion picture authorities themselves are demanding a cleanup." The delegates spent the major part of an afternoon discussing the question: "How can the Catholic Press best cooperate with the Episcopal Committee on motion pictures in its crusade against objectionable films?" Later, when the resolutions were drawn up, the group promised full cooperation with the Committee, condemned immoral films, and determined to "unite in every effort designed to eliminate from public sale the indecent books and magazines that have flooded the country with a stream of filth...."[34]

The organization annually reaffirmed its stand on decency. In November of 1937 Bishop Noll, speaking to members of the executive board, urged them to combat immoral entertainment, adding that in his own diocese he had widened the Legion of Decency pledge to include reading matter as well as films. The board, heeding his suggestion, proposed to the Catholic Press that the principles of the Legion of Decency be expanded to "publications generally." Pointing to the "corrupting influence" of some publications, the board called upon the Catholic editors to do all in their power to overcome this great evil.[35]

In October of 1938 the American hierarchy named an Episcopal Committee to organize a nationwide drive against indecent literature. Consequently, the National Organization for Decent Literature (NODL) was formed in December with Bishop Noll as chairman. Response to the drive which formally opened on Sexagesima Sunday was such that "before the end of Lent a concerted campaign was under way under a Diocesan Director in some thirty dioceses." Once again the Catholic Press gave its complete cooperation and support.[36]

After World War II the influence of both the Legion of Decency and the NODL began to decline, but in the mid-30's this reform effort evoked so much support that the decency crusade became known to the entire world. In June of 1936 Pope Pius XI issued an encyclical letter on motion pictures, Vigilanti Cura, in which he praised the campaign underway in the United States and recommended imitation of it to Catholics in other countries.[37]

Not only was 1936 an eventful year for the CPA because of the prestige given to the decency drive through the Holy Father's endorsement, but it was also notable in two other respects. At the 1934 convention, Hall reported that the Catholic Press of the United States had been invited to participate in a World Exhibition of the Catholic Press. The exhibit, planned to commemorate the seventy-fifth anniversary of L'Osservatore Romano, was to be held in Italy in 1936. In August of 1935 the United States National Committee of the World Catholic Press Exhibition was named, but by fall it had made little progress. Response to letters soliciting contributions was slow, Bishop Boyle (the honorary chairman) had not favored the committee's plan to request funds from the bishops, and conditions in Europe were such that the exhibit might have to be postponed. The financial difficulties were worked out eventually, contributions from the bishops supplemented funds given by Catholic publishers, and Ridder (treasurer of the committee) was able to report to the 1936 convention that "all expenses in preparation and shipping of the Exhibit had been paid." Later, however, he requested donations totalling one thousand dollars to reimburse the Vatican Committee for charges entailed in the erection of the display.

Besides these financial matters, the committee undertook the task of collecting data concerning the organization, development, and extent of the Catholic Press within the confines of the United States and of soliciting the Catholic publications for materials to be exhibited. The actual preparation of the physical aspects of the exhibit was entrusted to the Department of Architecture of the Catholic University, and the display was installed in the pavillion under the direction of a graduate student from the University studying in Rome. To house the world exhibition a new building was constructed on a site chosen by the Pope himself. The United States' section occupied the most prominent position in the spectacle, and the exhibit there was one of the best displayed. The CPA portion of the display, arranged beneath a colored plaque, presented graphically the growth of the American Catholic Press as well as an explanation of Association activities; the NCWC section demonstrated the workings of the News Service. In addition to these two major divisions, individual displays submitted by various publications, examples of promotional efforts, special editions, campaign specimens, newspaper systems, and reproductions of earlier Catholic publications were exhibited.[38]

No doubt one reason that CPA members cooperated with the World Press Exhibition and were anxious that the Catholic Press of America make a good showing was that the Association in 1936 was also celebrating its Silver Jubilee.

The convention commemorating this anniversary opened about two weeks after the exhibit and, as at the Vatican Exposition, the general theme was growth and expansion. At the invitation of Bishop James J. Hartley, the anniversary convention was held in the city that gave birth to the CPA, Columbus, Ohio. In addition to Bishop Hartley, Father John J. Burke, James T. Carroll of the Catholic Columbian, Dr. Thomas P. Hart, and other founding members were present. Bishops Boyle and Noll both attended the sessions and addressed the members at the Civic Banquet. Pope Pius XI conveyed to the delegates "his cordial greetings and his fatherly felicitations on the noble work for the propagation and defense of the faith which has been accomplished in the quarter-century of its existence. The Apostolic Delegate also praised the "most creditable record" of the CPA expressing the hope that "still greater success" would be reached in the future.[39]

If the convention itself left some delegates in "a happy frame of mind and a state of anaesthetic enjoyment," it proved exhausting to outgoing President Joseph J. Quinn who had to face several problems of which most of the delegates were unaware. The most serious of these concerned the Civic Banquet which was almost cancelled an hour before the time scheduled for it to begin due to financial difficulties. Nonetheless, arrangements were completed "at the last minute," and the dinner proved to be the occasion of much reminiscing and flowery oratory. Both Bishops Hartley and Noll spoke and President Quinn, reviewing the years past, eloquently declared: "Since that historic session back in 1911, the Catholic Press has broken the fetters of indifference that chained it to mediocrity, has crumpled into pulp the heresy that the Catholic Press is but a weakling and has built its mighty arch across the nation."[40]

Several sessions were devoted to the usual Association affairs with discussion of dishonest solicitors, problems concerning circulation, ways and means of advertising, and the like. There was also a review of the years that had been covered and a forecast of what the future might hold. Commenting on this session, an editorial in America later noted:

> Those who were present at the May convention of this year realized that the future of Catholicism and Americanism would be in greater jeopardy in the years that will follow 1936 than in the years that followed 1911.... The problems before the

> Catholic editors became prodigious during the past twenty-five years. Their problems for the next two and one-half decades would be frightening to any group of lesser courage and lesser Faith.... [41]

In many instances these problems of the editors were intimately connected with the problems of the nation as a whole. Such was the economic depression which continued in greater or lesser degree throughout the decade. In his Press Month appeal of 1932, Bishop Boyle noted that almost no Catholic publication had discontinued because of the financial pressures of the previous year although in some cases the number of pages had been reduced. In spite of their own financial problems CPA members responded to the Pope's plea for assistance for the poor of the world contributing some thirteen hundred dollars to the cause. [42]

The Catholic journalists viewed the depression in various ways. Arthur Preuss held that he had "never seen anything to equal this before in the almost fifty years of my active life. Let's hope that there will be a change for the better before we are all reduced to actual want!" Characterizing the financial difficulties of the Catholic papers as "an arraignment of the Faith of our people" who were falsely economizing by giving up the Catholic publications, Bishop Boyle congratulated the editors for their "courage and resourcefulness" despite the trying conditions. Msgr. Wynhoven looked at the matter differently. At no time did he regard the publication of Catholic papers as a money-making enterprise. Thus, "When hard times come,... we don't feel it as do those of other businesses or of the secular press, because the Catholic journalist... is used to fasting and abstinence in a broader sense, he just pulls tighter the belt about his waist, takes in another notch, and settles down to do better work than before."[43] Apparently numerous editors followed this maxim. A 1937 convention report pointed out that during the worst of the depression period, from 1930-1935, only one Catholic paper had discontinued publication and in the same five years, four new ones had begun. At the end of the decade an article on the Catholic Press maintained that it had "breasted the depression tide in considerably better fashion than its secular contempories."[44]

The CPA was also involved in other social problems of the day. At least three times during the period the question of education was discussed. In 1934, reference was made to Bishop Joseph Schrembs' demand for state aid for Catholic education in Ohio. He had not been successful, but Patrick F. Scanlan declared that nonetheless a great victory had been achieved for "it served the purpose of taking a lot of our people away from their inferiority complex. They realized that their religion not only was a mighty factor and contributing to civic progress, but they realized and recognized that they were victims of injustice." Scanlan argued, "Once our people realize that, once they get off the defensive, then we will be making progress."[45] In his presidential address in 1937, Vincent de Paul Fitzpatrick noted that one of the three most important items that Catholic newspapers had concentrated on throughout the year was the fight against educational discrimination. Two years later Bishop Gorman called upon the government for federal aid. Advocating "a national system of moral education throughout the Republic," the bishop noted that the burden of supporting Catholic schools was a very heavy one indeed.[46]

Some attention was also given to the racial problem. In 1939, President Ridder read a statement prepared by John LaFarge, SJ, in behalf of the Catholic Interracial Council which said in part: "We are encouraged by the innumerable items regarding the Negro that have appeared throughout the year in Catholic publications. We are also grateful for the splendid editorials advocating the full measure of social justice for the forgotten man in American life..." Later, this convention condemned the "spirit of ill will and strife over the matter of racial origins" which was so noticeable in American life of that time.[47]

Labor, too, received some consideration toward the end of this period. In 1940 and 1941 speakers discussed labor problems, and at the later meeting the Association resolved to make known the social principles of Rerum Novarum and Quadragesimo Anno concerning, among other things, "the right of the worker to a family wage and to freedom of organization."[48]

Opinions differed as to just which national and international items should be discussed by the Catholic Press. At one of the first meetings of the decade, a speaker who discussed "The Catholic Editor and Politics" advised the editors to avoid partisan politics because "the business of the Catholic Church is saving souls and not meddling in politics." He did, however, advocate discussion of "moral questions and American principles--growing out of candidacies and legislation..."[49] An editorial round table in 1934 considered "Treatment of public questions in editorial and news columns: to what extent? and in what manner?" Some participants insisted that only Catholic news should be featured, while others held that "all secular news, regardless of its significance, had a place in Catholic papers."[50] In 1940, Bishop Gannon advised the editors to be "cautious" in dealing with the questions of "war, politics, and nationalism."[51] Nevertheless, the CPA consistently included both national and international issues in its deliberations. In 1933 and again the next year, a New Deal measure, the NRA, was considered. The earlier meeting discussed the provisions of the Act concerning trade associations and empowered the board to take measures to ascertain if the CPA was such a group. Ridder, chairman of the CPA Code Committee, reported to the 1934 convention that arrangements had been made with the authorities administrating the Graphic Arts Code allowing the CPA to administer that code for the Catholic Press. During the same convention, a speaker urged the journalists to alert the Catholic laity to the needs of the "thousands of Catholic youths in...[CCC] camps."[52] In 1941 the editors went on record "as wholeheartedly in support of the National Defense Program in so far as it is essential to the preservation of American institutions."[53]

On the international level, the editors advocated Americanism and deplored totalitarianism in all its forms; spoke out against foreign entanglements and pleaded for peace; and condemned the abuse of religious freedom in Mexico and China as well as the strong-arm tactics employed by the dictators in Russia and Germany. However, the issue that was most frequently discussed was the Spanish question. In 1937, President Fitzpatrick commended the Catholic Press on its "struggle to bring out the truth in behalf of religious in strife-torn Spain." The resolutions that year reflected the views of the chairman of the resolutions committee, Charles J. Mullaly, SJ, who had studied and had been ordained in Spain, and who had been interested in conditions in that country for over thirty years. One decried the want of "impartial and truthful information" in secular newspapers concerning the Spanish situation, and another proclaimed the CPA's "sympathy with the present Nationalist party in Spain in its defense of those human rights which all Americans hold fundamental--namely, freedom of assembly, freedom of the press, freedom of the ballot, freedom of education and freedom to worship and serve God according to one's conscience."[54] A resolution in 1938 charged that the Spanish situation had been "generally misrepresented through various agencies which have in many instances succeeded in victimizing parts of the secular press" and urged that the "C. P. A. continue its mission of ascertaining and disseminating the truth and cooperating with that portion of the secular press which desires to present conditions as they are, especially as regards the situation of the Church in that unhappy country."[55] After the 1939 convention heard a letter from the Spanish Ambassador to the United States thanking the CPA "for presenting to its readers the underlying facts in the recent conflict in Spain," the delegates extended "heartfelt congratulations on the victory of Spain over Communism, Socialism, Syndicalism and Anarchism." They also voted to compile a list of secular papers they judged unfair in reporting on the recent Spanish struggle and to communicate their feelings to these papers, with a statement of regret that these had failed to report "adequately and accurately both sides in the Spanish conflict."[56]

This last step was really an outgrowth of earlier action of the Association. A circular distributed before the 1937 meeting projected, among other plans, an organization of Catholic editors to "correct [on the local level] misstatements in secular papers."[57] The Catholic Laymen's Association of Georgia had for many years been involved in this type of Catholic action, and the Bureau of Publicity established within the NCWC under Bishop Gannon's direction in 1938 was designed to counteract misrepresentation of Catholics in secular publications.[58] About this time, too, consolidated Catholic Press committees were operating effectively in such areas as New York and Detroit. In his 1941 report, Hall noted that during the past year the Catholic Press had "applied vigilantly the corrective truth where misstatements were made concerning things Catholic."[59]

These efforts elicited criticism from secular publications. Discussing the New York movement which had concentrated on Spanish Leftist Propaganda, a commentator in the Christian Century described it as a possible prelude to the destruction of both freedom of speech and of the press and suggested:

> Editors are glad to be instructed. They are happy to receive more facts and to listen to the presentation of differing points of view. The consolidated committee will render a real service if it will minister to this desire. But not if it says: This

is the truth; print it because we say so.

A more anti-Catholic critic charged that the American bishops controlled the press and that "... millions of practicing Catholics never question either the news or the news interpretation in the Catholic press."[60]

Catholics, including Catholic editors, disagreed on the last point. A Catholic rebuttal to this critic alleged that the diocesan papers really made very little impression "because so few read them."[61] More than two years earlier Benedict Elder had written, "Should anyone say that the Catholic editors are being bound up by the Catholic hierarchy, we simply answer they don't know Catholic editors, because they can't be bound by anything short of the very fundamental doctrines of the Church and Her Apostolic mission." Continuing, the Louisville editor asserted, "... there is not one of them... that will say he has ever been held down by his Bishop or directed by him contrary to his own fundamental belief."[62] Discussing "official declarations" in an address in 1940, Archbishop Edward Mooney of Detroit said that the "connection between the Catholic Press and the ecclesiastical authority is so close as to impose upon you a heavy and delicate responsibility." Nevertheless, he called for discussion and interpretation according to Catholic principles and advocated that a definite ecclesiastical stand be taken only as a last resort.[63] Addressing the Peoria convention a year later, Archbishop Samuel Stritch went even farther in characterizing diversity of opinion within Catholic publications as good. If some editor spoke unwisely, the remedy was "not to stop legitimate freedom but courageous criticism by other Catholic newspapers."[64]

Other activities during the 1930's were the result of developments within the CPA itself. As noted above, the first convention of the decade decided that in the future departmental clinics should be included. The following year the position of General Counsel was created, and Benedict Elder filled this post throughout the period.[65] In 1933 President Reid suggesting that the organization "rearrange its forces," asked that the magazine and newspaper sections be extended and that special sections be established for publishers, writers, and the Catholic school press.[66]

Other innovations were instigated by Bishop John Mark Gannon who became Episcopal Chairman in 1936. After winning over the CPA officials by requesting a meeting with them so that he might "learn in detail the history, operation and objectives" of the CPA, Gannon, accompanied by Hall, met with President Fitzpatrick to discuss the "affairs, the hopes and the ambitions" of the group. The bishop, expressing the opinion that the CPA should become one of the outstanding Catholic organizations in the country, gave it his hearty endorsement and urged that all Catholic publications join and attend the 1937 convention. He encouraged members of the hierarchy to participate and suggested that the conventions themselves be embellished by making the opening ceremony a Solemn Pontifical Mass.[67] Even "three distinguished members of the Hierarchy and the largest attendance in several years" at the Rochester convention did not satisfy Bishop Gannon. He wanted

> ...the next Catholic Press convention [to] be staged in a metropolitan center under the patronage of a Cardinal Archbishop, with a nation-wide preparation, with a press and literary exhibition along the lines of the Vatican Exhibition, with a mobilization of all Catholic authors, editors, publishers, college leaders and Bishops, --culminating in the great objective of making America Catholic Press-conscious,...[68]

Much of this was realized the following year when Archbishop Joseph Rummel of New Orleans served as host of the convention, five other members of the hierarchy participated, and a Solemn Mass opened the meetings.[69] Likewise, in 1939, Bishop Gannon continued his efforts to bring the Catholic Press into as prominent a public setting as possible. The gathering that year was in New York City under the patronage of Archbishop Francis J. Spellman who presided on the throne at the opening Solemn High Mass.[70] This elaboration of convention externals continued throughout Bishop Gannon's years as Episcopal Chairman. In 1941 twelve members of the hierarchy were in attendance, and the convention itself extended over four days.[71]

Other Association business of the 1930's was concerned with the various bureaus. As a result of the controversy of the 1920's, the News Service Bureau in 1932 was replaced by a Liaison Committee to confer with personnel of the NCWC News Service.[72] Its main concern over the decade were matters relating to the national editions and the chain papers. The Advertising Bureau, having presented its code to the 1931 convention, frequently conducted round table discussions at the annual meetings. In 1934 it recommended a general publicity campaign, but this was not carried out due to lack of funds.[73] In 1933 the Chicago office of the Circulation Vigilance Committee was closed as an economy measure, and its records were transferred to the CPA secretary who conducted this business under the direction of the executive board.[74] By the mid-30's the committee had largely achieved its goals, and it no longer existed by the end of the decade.

The Literature Bureau sponsored no contests in 1931 or 1932, but in 1933 it suggested a motion picture contest with prizes to be given for the best ideas submitted for screen adaptation. This contest was delayed so it could be coordinated with the Bishops' decency campaign.[75] In 1935-1936 the Bureau again awarded prizes for general literary achievements, but in 1937 the Awards Foundation money was allocated to theses on the American Catholic Press presented as graduate requirements in colleges and universities.[76] Other instances of correlation and cooperation between press and education were numerous throughout the period.[77] Of special note was the establishment of the Catholic School Press Association in 1931 by Dean Jeremiah O'Sullivan of the College of Journalism at Marquette University.[78] For several years, Hall advocated affiliation of the CSPA as well as other Catholic groups with the CPA. Finally, in 1939, the CPA created a Catholic School Press Bureau as a tie between O'Sullivan's group and its own organization.[79]

During this decade, Catholic Press Month campaigns continued under the direction of a special CPA committee and with the cooperation of the Press Department. Some Association members thought that even greater publicity was needed. During Advent in 1938, Msgr. Wynhoven, Press Month chairman that year, wrote to all the bishops of the United States asking for "a concise, pungent one paragraph expression on" the Catholic Press to be included in a booklet he was compiling. From Bishop Gannon he requested a statement aimed principally at enlisting the active support of other bishops.[80] Swim--or Sink appeared in the summer of 1939. It contained statements from most of the members of the American hierarchy, numerous brief essays by the author on various aspects of the Catholic Press, an article on the CPA by past-President Quinn, one concerning the News Service by Director Hall, and a third describing the Catholic School Press Association by Dean O'Sullivan.[81] Deemed particularly useful was a section containing "a listing of

Catholic magazines and newspapers according to ecclesiastical provinces and dioceses, together with statistical analyses."[82] Commenting on the publication, Hall stated in his 1939 report to the Association:

> This inexpensive volume,... now becomes the only piece of literature on the Catholic Press generally, which is in available form. It is to be hoped its circulation will be wide. It is hoped also that it will be the beginning of the building up of a considerable literature on our press which can be supplied to the many who desire it.[83]

Although the book was adopted by the CPA board as "the official source of information on the Catholic Press of the country" and designated as the official work for the 1940 Press Month campaign, less than half the first edition of ten thousand copies were sold in the six months following its publication. And despite the fact that the board had endorsed the work, Wynhoven complained in early February that "only an insignificant 250 copies were ordered by three members of the Executive Board of seven."[84]

It appeared that interest in the CPA and the Catholic Press in general was far from enthusiastic, but this was not entirely accurate. Rather, the Association had reached a certain plateau of maturity. True, the fervor of the founders had abated somewhat, and interal bickerings coupled with the feuds over the News Service and the chain papers had dissipated much of the energy of the members. The depression and the prospects of another world war had also taken their toll. Nonetheless, the CPA was actually entering a new phase of its existence, one that would involve fundamental changes in its structures and renewed interest in its activities.

Notes

1. Benedict Elder as toastmaster at the annual banquet noted this. Reported in: "C. P. A. Holds Successful Meeting at Baltimore," CA, XIII (June, 1931), p. 20.

2. Ibid. For other convention reports see: Tablet (Brooklyn), May 30, 1931, and Catholic Register (Kansas City, Missouri), May 14, 1931.

3. *Catholic Review* (Baltimore), June 12, 1931, carried a reprint from the *Bulletin* (Georgia) in which Richard Reid, editor of that paper, made this observation. The same paper reprinted an article from the *Catholic Virginian* (Richmond) reporting on those in attendance.

4. *Catholic Register,* May 28, 1931.

5. *Tablet,* May 30, 1931, reported on the Gillis address. Father Peter C. Gannon's comments are from *The True Voice,* May 29, 1931.

6. *Catholic Review,* May 29, 1931, told of Wey's suggestion. "C. P. A. Holds Successful Meeting in Baltimore," *op. cit.*, reported the code.

7. *Catholic Register,* May 28, 1931.

8. *Tablet,* May 30, 1931, quoted Curley's colorful remarks. Other data is from "C. P. A. Holds Successful Meeting in Baltimore," *op. cit.*

9. *Catholic Review,* May 15 and 29, 1931.

10. *Resume... 1932,* p. 6. CC.

11. For various aspects of the *Register*'s story, see: *The Catholic Tribune* (St. Joseph, Missouri), September 19, 1925; *Time,* December 6, 1954; *The Register,* June 24, 1960; and Charles McCarthy, "The Man Who Proposed the *Register* System," *Catholic Press Annual '63,* pp. 31 and 42, *passim.*

12. *Yearbook... 1930,* p. 80. CC.

13. McCarthy, *op. cit.*, p. 42.

14. *Dedication Booklet* (Huntington, Indiana, 1961), no pagination. Copy procured from *Our Sunday Visitor* office.

15. Reported in *Catholic Review,* June 5, 1936. This was an account of Bishop Noll's explanation of his publication to the Silver Jubilee Convention. Noll had sent his first issue to every bishop and priest in the United States.

16. William C. Murphy, "The Catholic Press," *American Mercury,* IX (December, 1926), 403.

17. Richard Ginder, With Ink and Crozier (n. p., n. d.), p. 129. F. A. Fink in a letter to Rev. Albert Murray, September 4, 1951, says: "It was I who inaugurated the Sunday Visitor plan of publishing special diocesan editions." Copy in CPA.

18. Announcement of the Catholic Action papers appeared in Catholic Action of the South, May 11 and September 14, 1939. They are no longer listed in Catholic Press Directory (1945) but are given in the Directory as Register papers begun in 1954. The Observer was still being published by the Witness Co. in 1942, but in 1945 belonged to OSV chain and was independent by the time that the 1951 Directory was published.

19. The Western Catholic (Quincy, Illinois), March 2, 1934.

20. Reported by Charles H. Ridder, "The United States Catholic Exhibit at Vatican City, 1936," Historical Records and Studies, XXVII (1937), p. 38.

21. Copy of letter from James A. McFadden to Elder, May 6, 1932. NCCB. Letters: Elder to Noll, May 13, 1932; Smith to Elder, May 14; Noll to Elder, May 14 and May 19(?). PDF. See also, Resume... 1932, pp. 40-43. CC.

22. Resumé... 1933, p. 27.(CPA). Copies of letters: Richard Reid to Smith, May 30, and Smith to Reid, June 3, 1933. PDF. Also: Smith to Reid, June 14, 1933, and Burke to Boyle, June 20 and July 21, 1933. NCCB.

23. "Memorandum on Meeting of Executive Board, Catholic Press Association, In Augusta, Georgia, February 9 and 10, 1934," Frank A. Hall. PDF. Also: Frank A. Hall, "Memorandum on C. P. A. Convention, Cleveland, May 24-26, 1934." NCCB.

24. Fitzpatrick to Hall, September 10, 1937, and Hall to Fitzpatrick, October 26, 1937. PDF.

25. "Minutes, Board.. November 25-26, 1938." PDF. Years later, in 1953, both Bishop Noll and Msgr. Smith were honored by the Association. They were given special citations and were guests at a Journalism Awards Banquet at which a testimonial address praised them for their apostolic efforts and the contribution they had made

"to the development of corporate consciousness and cooperation among Catholics of the United States." See: "Convention Honors Bp. Noll, Msgr. Smith as Pioneer Catholic Journalists," CJ, IV (June-July, 1953), p. 4.

26. Catholic Review, May 28, 1937, reported the convention presentation. Discussion of the plan is from Rt. Rev. Peter M. H. Wynhoven, Swim--Or Sink (Marrero, Louisiana, 1939), pp. 127-130. Copies of Wynhoven's original 1937 plan and a six-page explanation of a weekly supplement drawn up by the Advertising Bureau of CPA are in PDF.

27. A copy of the "MacManus Prospectus" and a news story on the plan are in PDF. See also: "Memorandum on the 'MacManus Plan' for Catholic Press," drawn up for the Apostolic Delegate under date of August 26, 1940. NCCB. Newsweek, June 24, 1940, p. 53, ran a story on MacManus and his plan. "Catholic Press Association," Catholic World, CLI (July, 1940), 491 presented the financial aspects. Msgr. Smith also commented on this and other facets of the plan in The Register, June 9, 1940.

28. Wynhoven to Gannon, July 22, 1940; Wynhoven to MacManus, July 22; and Gannon to Wynhoven, September 20, 1940. Gannon Papers, ADE.

29. "Minutes, Board...October 11, 1940." WC. Transcript ...1941, pp. 6-7 and 27-28. CPA.

30. Mimeographed copy of "A National Supplement for Our Catholic Newspapers"; letters: Wynhoven to Gannon, October 29 and Gannon to Wynhoven, November 5, 1941. All in Gannon Papers, ADE.

31. Wynhoven to Gannon, November 7 and Hall to Gannon, November 10, 1941. Gannon Papers, ADE. Proceedings... 1942, p. 18. CPA.

32. Charles H. Ridder, Chairman Catholic Press Month Campaign to "Fellow Member" regarding February, 1933, Catholic Press Month, dated December 16, 1932. CC. Of course, Episcopal Chairman Boyle and Director Hall cooperated in this effort.

33. John T. McNicholas, Archbishop of Cincinnati, "The Episcopal Committee and the Problem of Evil Motion Pictures," The Ecclesiastical Review, XCI (August, 1934), p. 113. There had been a Motion Picture Bureau in the NCWC for years. In the early 1920's those connected with the Bureau had discussed means of protesting "unwholesome motion pictures." See correspondence, December, 1920-January, 1922. NCCB.

34. Résumé... 1934, pp. 56, 24, 7-8, and 62-63 covers the various points. CPA.

35. The Catholic Tribune, December 4, 1937, reported this meeting.

36. Bishops' Committee Sponsoring the National Organization for Decent Literature, The Drive For Decency in Print, 2 vols. (Huntington, Indiana, 1939) I, 5 and 131.

37. P. J. Sullivan, "National Catholic Office for Motion Pictures," New Catholic Encyclopedia (1967), X, 222-224.

38. The most complete report of the exhibit is Ridder, op. cit. Hall's announcement is in Resume... 1934, p. 31. CPA. Difficulties encountered by the committee are recounted in a memo from Hall to Father Burke, December 3, 1935. PDF. For Ridder's request for additional funds see Ridder to Wey, June 30, 1936. WC. For details concerning the physical aspects of the display see: Dr. Frederick V. Murphy, "U. S. Exhibit at the World Catholic Press Exhibition," CA, XVIII (July, 1936), pp. 19-20.

39. Catholic Columbian (Columbus, Ohio), June 5, 1936. For another convention report consult Burke Walsh, "The C. P. A. at Columbus," CA, XVIII (July, 1936), pp. 15-16†.

40. Quinn's speech was quoted in Catholic Review, June 5, 1936. The state of the delegates comes from Catholic Columbian, June 12, 1936. For Quinn's difficulties see: Quinn to Hall, June 10, 1936, and Frank A. Hall "Confidential Notes on the C. P. A. Convention, Columbus, Ohio, May 28-30, 1936." PDF.

41. "Convention of Catholic Editors," America, LV (June 13, 1936), 218. For discussion concerning the sessions see: Walsh, op. cit., and Joseph J. Quinn, "Silver Jubilee of

the C. P. A., " CA, XVIII (May, 1936), pp. 17-18.

42. Most Reverend Hugh C. Boyle, "Catholic Press Month-1932, " CA, XIV (February, 1932), p. 4. Résumé... 1932, pp. 14-16. CC.

43. Preuss made his comment in a letter to Kenkel, July 30, 1932. AUND. Boyle's views are from Catholic Register, February 1, 1934, and Most Reverend Hugh C. Boyle, "A Call to the Laity, " CA, XVII (February, 1935), p. 7. Wynhoven's view is from Swim--Or Sink, op. cit., pp. 105-106.

44. The report in mimeograph form and entitled "The Relation of the Catholic Press Association to the Catholic Press of America, " was drawn up by "Joe" Quinn according to A. J. Wey. WC. The quotation is from "We Catholics and Our Country, " CA, XXXIII (January, 1941), p. 12.

45. Résumé... 1934, p. 29. CPA.

46. Burke Walsh, "C. P. A. Meeting at Rochester, " CA, XIX (June, 1937), p. 12, and Burke Walsh, "The C. P. A. at New York, " CA, XXI (July, 1939), p. 11.

47. LaFarge is quoted in Catholic Review, June 30, 1939. The resolution is noted in Walsh, op. cit., p. 16.

48. E. Francis McDevitt, "The Catholic Press--Auxiliary of the Church," CA, XXIII (June, 1941), p. 9. For the speeches given see: Program... 1940 and Program... 1941. WC.

49. Quoted in the Bulletin of the Catholic Laymen's Association of Georgia, June 11, 1932.

50. Resume... 1934, pp. 39-40. CPA.

51. Burke Walsh, "Detroit Meeting of Catholic Editors, " CA, XXII (June, 1940), p. 7.

52. The New World (Chicago), June 30, 1933, reported the initial NRA action. Results appear in Résumé... 1934, pp. 33-35. The CCC request is in Résumé... 1934, p. 40. CPA.

53. Catholic News (New York), May 31, 1941.

54. Fitzpatrick's remark appeared in: Burke Walsh, "C. P. A. Meeting at Rochester," CA, XIX (June, 1937), p. 12. Father Mullaly's background was explained in the Catholic Review, May 28, 1937. The resolutions were reported in Catholic Tribune, May 29, 1937.

55. Burke Walsh, "The C. P. A. at New Orleans," CA, XX (June, 1938), p. 7.

56. Burke Walsh, "The C. P. A. at New York," CA, XXI (July, 1939), p. 16, noted the congratulatory statement. The Tablet, July 1, 1939, reprinted the entire letter of the ambassador and reported on the listing. For a general study of the attitudes of Americans toward the conflict see: F. Jay Taylor, The United States and the Spanish Civil War (New York, 1956). The author concluded that the Catholic Press, as well as the majority of Catholics, favored the Nationalists.

57. "To the Publishers, Editors, Business Managers, Circulation Managers and Others Associated With the Catholic Press of the United States," n. d. CC.

58. Résumé... 1938, p. 17 records a statement by Bishop Gannon concerning the new Bureau and its similarity to the Georgia group. CPA.

59. Catholic Review, June 30, 1939, commented on the local committees. Hall's comment is from: "Statement by Director, N. C. W. C. News Service, to the Catholic Press Association Convention, Peoria, May 21-24, 1941," p. 6. OSV.

60. "Catholic Pressure on the Press," Christian Century, LV (May 11, 1938), 583, and H. Rutledge Southworth, "The Catholic Press," The Nation, CXLIX (December 16, 1939), 675.

61. Ruth O'Keefe, in a letter to the editor, The Nation, CL (January 20, 1940), 84.

62. Benedict Elder, "Catholic Editors are Independent," reprinted from the Catholic Record (Louisville) in the

Catholic Review, June 4, 1937.

63. Catholic Review, June 7, 1940. See also: Burke Walsh, "Detroit Meeting of Catholic Editors," CA, XXII (June, 1940), p. 7.

64. Catholic News, May 31, 1941.

65. Résumé... 1932, p. 42. CC.

66. Brooklyn Tablet, July 1, 1933.

67. Gannon to Fitzpatrick, November 26, 1936; Fitzpatrick to Gannon, November 30, 1936; circular distributed by Fitzpatrick during February of 1937. Gannon Papers, ADE.

68. Burke Walsh, "The C. P. A. Meeting at Rochester," CA, XIX (June, 1937), p. 10.

69. Burke Walsh, "The C. P. A. at New Orleans," CA, XX (June, 1938), p. 7.

70. Gannon to Spellman, May 15, 1939. Gannon Papers, ADE. A report of the meeting can be found in Catholic Tribune, July 1, 1939.

71. Catholic News, May 31, 1941. However, this four day convention was the only such session until 1950. The next year the usual three day meeting was held, and in 1943 only two days were given over to the convention. It was not until 1957 that a four day convention became the norm. Also, after Bishop Gannon left his post in November, 1943, less effort was made to attract national attention by external elaborations of the meetings.

72. Résumé... 1932, pp. 29 and 42. CC.

73. Résumé... 1934, p. 36. CPA. Wey reported at this session that the circumstances were such that he thought it unwise to make an appeal for publicity purposes at that time.

74. Reported in The New World, June 30, 1933.

75. Record, June 29, 1933; Résumé... 1934, pp. 35-36. CPA.

76. Record, June 4, 1936; Burke Walsh, "The C. P. A. Meeting at Rochester," CA, XIX (June, 1937), p. 12. The report credits Richard Reid with the suggestion. "Notes and Comments," Catholic Historical Review, XXIV (April, 1938), pp. 99-100, lists the requirements and prizes.

77. Résumé... 1934, p. 38 refers to a press exhibit held in connection with the NCEA convention; "Catholic Editors Meet," Commonweal, XX (June 8, 1934), p. 157 tells of a special evening session on Catholic journalism and literature for students from colleges in the area; according to NC Release 11/2/36, following the 1936 convention the executive board at is first meeting suggested that Catholic magazines and newspapers cooperate more closely with the work of Catholic education; and from Michigan Catholic (Detroit), May 30, 1940, we learn that a special youth rally was held as an adjunct of the regular sessions.

78. Margaret L. Whitehead, "Dean O'Sullivan's Dream," The Sign, XX (February, 1941), 403-404. Also, personal interview with J. O'Sullivan on December 28, 1967.

79. Hall to Reid, June 28, 1932; Hall to Quinn, June 18, 1935, refers to such affiliation. PDF. The tie is mentioned in: Burke Walsh, "The C. P. A. at New York," CA, XXI (July, 1939), p. 16. See Chapter VIII.

80. Wynhoven to Gannon, December 15, 1938. Gannon Papers, ADE.

81. Wynhoven, Swim--Or Sink, op. cit., passim.

82. Tablet, June 24, 1939.

83. "Statement by Director, N. C. W. C. News Service, to Catholic Press Association, New York City, June 22-24, 1939," p. 10. OSV. Remember that the last Catholic Press Directory had been issued in 1932.

84. Reverend J. Fred Kriebs, Chairman Circulation Bureau, Catholic Press Association to Associate and Friend of The Catholic Press, January 9, 1940. CC. Wynhoven to Members of the Executive Board of the C. P. A.,

February 10, 1940. Gannon Papers, ADE. The executive board at the May meeting decided to purchase 1,000 copies. The October minutes noted that almost 900 of these were sent to seminaries, universities, and colleges. "Minutes, Board... May 27, 1942," p. 1; "Minutes, Board... October 30, 1942," p. 1. WC.

Chapter V

Internal Developments

Changes in the CPA were evolutionary extending over a period of years and touching on many facets of the organization. Activities of the Association have continued along similar lines from World War II to the present. Hence we can deal with the mature years of the CPA as a unit beginning with a closer examination of certain internal developments.

Already in the mid-1930's lethargy was noted within the CPA membership. In an exchange of correspondence with Frank Hall in June of 1934, President Joseph J. Quinn asked: "Is there something lacking at the conventions or are the delegates hard put to it for railroad fare?" Responding that the convention was the "big activity of the Association," Hall suggested that "the program be prepared well in advance by a hard boiled committee which would absolutely assure itself that every ten minutes turned over to some one would be calculated to bear some fruit."[1] By the fall of 1936 Vincent dePaul Fitzpatrick had ascended to the presidency, and Bishop John Mark Gannon had become Episcopal Chairman of the NCWC Press Department. As noted earlier, both these men were anxious to enhance the prestige of the CPA. When Fitzpatrick consulted Hall about attracting new members and strengthening the organization, Hall advised "that the Association should profitably turn its attention and devote its energies in greater proportion to specific and practical pieces of service to the members..." taking care to publicize these endeavors.[2] The publicity campaigns of Bishop Gannon, previously mentioned, were based on a like strategy.

The biggest burst of activity, though, was that generated by Msgr. Peter M. H. Wynhoven who became vice president in 1938. This priest from New Orleans had a long history of involvement in both civic and religious affairs. He had served as chairman of one of President Franklin D. Roosevelt's U. S. Regional Labor Boards, and had been singularly successful as a mediator. He had also established an employment bureau, a hotel for working girls, and a trades and industrial school for dependent boys.[3] His energetic approach to CPA affairs surely could have been predicted, but probably even he did not realize that the consequence would be an inter-Association struggle resulting in the negation of a long-standing custom.

The matter came to a climax at the 1939 New York convention. In addition to recruiting new members for the Association and managing the Catholic Press Month campaigns of 1938 and 1939, Wynhoven had been vocal in criticizing CPA inertia and was laying plans to revitalize the organization. The nominating committee, composed of two priests and a layman, startled the convention by submitting Wynhoven's name for president and that of Patrick F. Scanlan for vice president.[4] Since the 1911 organizational meeting the presidency had always been allocated to a layman; no president in the history of the group had served fewer than two years, and beginning in 1920 each had held office for a two year term. From the second meeting in 1912 and continuing unbroken with the exception of a few years after World War I, the vice president had been a priest. Finally, at no time had a vice president ever succeeded directly to the presidency. The committee overlooked all this, but the chairman noted that there had been a dissenting vote within the committee. The layman, Claude Becker, obtained the floor to announce that although he admired Msgr. Wynhoven, he respected the tradition that had stood for almost thirty years. Becker, himself a founding father and a very active member, maintained that a layman would be more efficient in dealing with the secular press, and he renominated Charles H. Ridder who had just completed a one year term in the office.

The debate quickly became heated--so much so that a recess was called to allow for the removal of reporters and visitors. When it resumed, many charges and countercharges filled the meeting room. One member contended that a priest would be more acceptable to the hierarchy, whereas another decried the emphasis on tradition and declared that Wynhoven "had done more in six months than the presidents of the CPA had done in years... " Before the suggestion of a priest delegate that the voting be based not on the status of the candidate but rather on merit alone could be carried out, another life-long member, Richard Reid, offered a compromise suggesting that the presidency be alternated between a priest and a layman. Reid noted that he would be happy to nominate Msgr. Wynhoven at the next convention, but he pointed out that refusing to honor Ridder with a second term as had been customary would be most humiliating since the meeting was being held in the president's own territory. At this point, Msgr. Wynhoven withdrew his name, Ridder was re-elected, Scanlan declined the vice presidential nomination, and Wynhoven was elected to that post. As agreed upon, Msgr. Wynhoven was named president in 1940 while a layman, Alexander J. Wey, became vice president. After two years, Wey succeeded to the top office, and the pattern has remained virtually unchanged for another thirty years.[5]

With the order of succession established, the members turned their attention to another problem. For some years there had been talk of a central headquarters and an executive secretary for the Association, but insufficient funds always kept the project in the talking stage. As a result the officers were usually over-burdened and frequently discouraged. Hall reminded Msgr. Wynhoven of the problem in a letter written during the winter of 1941 and suggested the advisability of a paid executive. "That, though, is old stuff," he concluded, "and I am not forgetting at all that you tried very hard to do just such a thing more than a year ago."[6] The priest was not known for giving up easily. In his presidential report to the convention that May he recommended: "For the sake of efficiency, greater strength of the organization and to make things more interesting, I submit that we employ a part-time office executive with some ambition, vision and enthusiasm."[7] His suggestion was ignored for the moment, but when Wey took over the presidency in 1942 he revived the idea and pushed it vigorously. Just before the fall meeting of the executive board he wrote to Msgr. Wynhoven inviting him to attend and brought up the question of the executive secretary and national headquarters:

> I am convinced that until we have the proper kind of a follow-through most of our aspirations will remain just dreams. There are many things that can and should be done, and despite the willingness of officers to sacrifice themselves, there are serious limitations of time and energy. You gave a colossal amount of time and much of your strength, physical and mental, during your terms of office, and I doubt if ever anyone can match the value of

> your service. Until we have a national office, efficiently staffed,... much effort and time will be spent without lasting and growing results.[8]

Shortly thereafter President Wey sent a circular letter to all the board members scheduling the fall meeting, declaring that the "Number One" issue facing the board was that concerning the executive secretary and national headquarters, and stating:

> My brief experience as president has served to crystalize the belief shared by others, that, lacking the modern machinery long since found indispensable to the life and progress of leading national and even local organizations, we shall continue to fall short of the mark set by our founders almost a third of a century ago.[9]

Wey enclosed a proposal for the "Creation of office of Executive Secretary and Establishment of National Headquarters" in which he argued that the lack of a continuous policy and the perennial internal dissatisfaction were due in large measure to this weakness in the structure of the Association. Vice president John J. Considine, MM, agreed with Wey's proposal and suggested that the preparatory work be done by a committee "made up of one man thoroughly prepared to take the responsibility of seeing the thing through, assisted by several others who will act as counselors rather than as legislators,..." For those reasons, he suggested that only three members be named to the proposed committee and that the personnel

> ...be, you [Wey] as chairman, because you will see the thing through at any cost. Your two fellow members should be Dean O'Sullivan and myself. Thus there will be no deadwood but three men with a determination to get the thing going.

This time action was taken; the board passed a resolution calling for an executive secretary and national headquarters, and the committee members named were those listed by Considine.[10]

Within a week the committee met, and a few days later sent out a list of "preliminary conclusions" including the directives that the change be effected "as soon as possible" and that the "headquarters,... be connected with the

Press Relations Department [of NCWC] if possible." Proposals for the duties to be delegated to the secretary and a list of prospective secretaries (three priests and four laymen) completed the report.[11] In a meeting just before the 1943 convention, the executive board examined a plan suggested by NCWC officials providing that a Press Development Bureau be set up in the Washington building with a paid executive spending approximately half his time on this service bureau and the remainder on CPA business. The proposal was adopted by the annual convention, and in a board meeting following the general sessions, a resolution was passed authorizing the president "to negotiate a financial arrangement with Msgr. Ready [of NCWC] to involve expenditure of not more than $3,000.00 for establishment of the office of Executive Secretary...."[12] However, implementing the plan proved to be difficult. When the board convened in October, Wey reported that despite "strenuous efforts" by the committee, a suitable person for the position had not been found because of wartime conditions. Again at the 1944 general session, Dean Jeremiah O'Sullivan reported for the Executive Secretary Committee "that most of the young, aggressive, trained men that we have considered for the job are either in the Army or expecting to go into the Army," but that the search would continue.[13]

As the months passed there were changes among the executive board members and even in the personnel of the Executive Secretary Committee so that by the time the board met in October of 1944 the committee had decided against the earlier proposal of cooperation and coordination with the Press Development Bureau. The members now thought that neither organization would be satisfied under the arrangement and decided instead to engage a man of their own on a part time basis. And the committee had finally found a suitable man for the job, James A. Shanahan, who was introduced to the directors and outlined for them a rather ambitious program. The board voted to hire Shanahan for three months just prior to the 1945 convention and to pay him $2,500.[14] Again the war almost frustrated the plans. In January a government ban on conventions was announced, and the board at a special February meeting cancelled the 1945 gathering. Deciding to adjust the executive secretary plan, the directors hired Shanahan for a year making him directly responsible to the president.[15]

Hence, on March 1, 1945, James A. Shanahan became the first executive secretary of the CPA with headquarters in his own office building in San Francisco. But when the president, Father Patrick O'Connor, reported to the board in October of that year, he noted the dire financial condition of the organization and questioned whether the CPA could continue to employ an executive secretary. He maintained that "the members must soon decide whether the services of such an official mean enough to them to warrant an increase in dues."[16] The outgoing board in a session during the 1946 convention decided in the negative, advising, "in view of the unavailability of finances," that Shanahan's contract not be renewed. But the general membership disagreed, recommending to the new board that the office be continued. In view of this, the board agreed to poll the membership for voluntary contributions to see if $5,000 might be raised to pay Shanahan's salary.[17] Within a few days the new president, Humphrey E. Desmond, had a circular in the mail asking that the average contribution be "about one and one-half times the former annual dues," but suggesting that larger donations would also be needed to make up for those unable or unwilling to contribute.

> Here is your opportunity to say whether the Catholic Press Association is to go forward or backward. If it is to serve a greater purpose than that of bringing the membership together once a year, the Executive Secretary program is the way. It is the plan followed by all successful, progressive associations.

In less than a month President Desmond reported that the program would indeed continue and Shanahan had been rehired for another year.[18]

The executive secretary was again engaged on a part-time basis with a new office address in Chicago, but progress was not so rapid as had been anticipated. By the next spring some members, including the president, were doubtful about retaining Shanahan. Before Shanahan was hired, Desmond had suggested that perhaps a priest would be best for the position, and now he revived that plan. In company with Father Paul Bussard he visited Msgr. Howard J. Carroll, General Secretary of the NCWC, and presented a proposal whereby a priest would act as executive secretary of the CPA and work from NCWC headquarters. Even though this project had the approval of the Episcopal Chairman, Archbishop John G. Murray of St. Paul, others including Murray's assistant, Bishop Thomas K. Gorman, Msgr. Carroll, and Director Hall had reservations. These three felt that it would look as though the bishops were taking over the Association, and this in turn would lead to a renewal of difficulties between the two groups. The plan came to naught, and President Desmond himself recommended to the board that Shanahan's contract be renewed.[19]

Within a year, however, Shanahan indicated his intention to resign, and the board accepted a temporary solution suggested by Father Bussard who had been named president by the 1948 convention: the work of the executive secretary would be done through the Catholic Digest office and under the direction of Father Bussard. This arrangement lasted only a few months for by October another plan, also advocated by Bussard, had matured. Shortly after becoming president, the priest had written to Alfred Barrett, SJ, chairman of the new journalism division at Fordham University, asking that CPA headquarters be located on the campus with Barrett directing the affairs of the Association. Father Barrett and Father Robert I. Gannon, President of Fordham, agreed, and the board implemented the plan. On Barrett's recommendation, Mrs. Helen Walker Homan of Fordham was hired as executive secretary and the priest assumed the title of executive director. To help finance the new arrangement, Father Bussard offered $1, 800 toward the salary while another board member, George A. Pflaum, gave $1, 000 with the promise that $500 more would be given annually for the next four years to help keep the project going.[20] The transfer which took place in November was never satisfactory. Both Mrs. Homan and Father Barrett were employed by Fordham as well as by the CPA, the division of their duties was not specified clearly, and difficulties arose almost immediately. As a result, Father Bussard asked for and received Mrs. Homan's resignation before the 1949 convention. Barrett then took over all the duties working without a salary and using the $5, 000 for operating expenses of the headquarters. Because Father Bussard who had hired him was completing his term as president in 1950, Barrett submitted his own resignation at that time "to leave the new president free."[21]

Much to his surprise, the board accepted Barrett's resignation and made plans to engage a full-time executive secretary.[22] When the matter was brought to the floor of the convention, the delegates voted to set up a national office, to employ a full-time secretary, and to increase membership dues in order to finance the plan. Since this increase would not be legal without a constitutional revision, they accepted a voluntary increase for the 1950-1951 interim. As a full-time executive was not available immediately, the board re-hired Father Barrett for three months while the search for a suitable man was underway.

When a committee named to hire a secretary reported its lack of success to a July meeting of the directors, the board drafted one of its own members for this job. Chosen was James F. Kane, general manager of the Paulist Fathers' publication, Information. A newcomer to the CPA, having been a member for only four years, Kane had been elected to the board at the May convention. The Paulists readily released Kane from his contract, and he was hired by the CPA for a three-year period to begin in September.[23] Nevertheless, Jim Kane began working unofficially for the Association in July with his first task being the location of a suitable, yet inexpensive office site. Economy was the controlling factor, but in the opinion of Msgr. John S. Randall who aided Kane in the search, the location obtained was good.[24]

Therefore, on September 20, 1950, the national headquarters of the CPA officially opened in two large rooms located on the sixth floor of The Carroll Club building in midtown Manhattan staffed by Kane and his associate, Miss Norah Geddis. There had been little continuity in the workings of the Association, very few records had been preserved, Kane and Miss Geddis were over-worked, and finances remained a problem. Nevertheless, when the secretary made his report to the members at the annual convention in May, he concluded on a positive note: "It is my solid conviction after nine months in office that your National Office will be able to contribute heavily to the continued expansion and greater effectiveness of the Catholic press."[25] Apparently the board members were not quite so idealistic as their secretary. At the fall meeting, they drew up a list of "The duties of the executive secretary for the year 1951-1952." These were listed in "their order of importance," and "the first and most important duty" was not the "expansion and greater effectiveness of the Catholic press." Rather, the secretary was commissioned to procure $5,000 in additional revenue for the CPA; his "other chief duties" were enumerated as those connected with the annual convention, the Association's house organ, Catholic Press Month activities, and publication of the Catholic Press Directory. Kane accepted the challenge. He not only exceeded the financial goal by almost $3,000 and carried out the secondary projects listed by the board, but he also obtained many new CPA members, worked with Association committees concerned with postal increases and newsprint difficulties, and succeeded in bringing about closer relations with other trade associations within the publishing field.[26]

Besides involvement with all these same activities during 1952-1953, Kane also continued to give special help to the smaller publications among the membership and in general strove "to raise the professional tone and publishing competence of member publications."[27] Therefore, the board "most reluctantly" accepted Kane's resignation submitted in the fall of 1952 to be effective on the expiration date specified in the 1950 contract. In his final report to the organization, Kane had three recommendations to offer regarding the national office. Pointing out that its role ought to be coordination and preliminary planning, he warned against continuing the practice of expecting it to function as a money-raising body. He maintained that in reality it should be a service bureau and advocated that Association committees, and not the central headquarters, should be responsible for most of the CPA's work. In conclusion he told the members: "...there is literally nothing this Association cannot do once you make up your minds to act together on a vigorous and clear cut program with definite purposes clearly in mind."[28]

A national headquarters with a full-time secretary had functioned successfully for a period of three years,[29] but the summer of 1953 was a real test of its durability. A new secretary took charge on June 15, new quarters were occupied in mid-summer, and on July 10 Miss Geddis completed her last day as office manager. Despite this almost complete change of personnel, the headquarters continued to operate efficiently and to the satisfaction of the board.[30] For the next five years the Association's affairs were directed by G. Roger Cahaney. During this time progress continued, the location of the national office changed as demands for additional space were met, and the staff grew in number as the work of the office increased. It was with genuine regret, then, that the board received Cahaney's resignation in the spring of 1958 to become effective on June 1. Msgr. Randall, President, paid tribute in his convention report to the "devotion and loyalty" of the retiring secretary noting that Cahaney had but one concern--the CPA.[31]

As soon as Cahaney's resignation was received, the officers constituted themselves as an employment committee and began interviewing likely prospects. By the end of April, James A. Doyle had been hired as the third full-time executive of the CPA. According to the president, "... his varied background in editorial, promotion and advertising work, his managerial experience and his experience with Association work made him the unanimous choice of the officers."[32] From the beginning, Doyle concentrated on the service aspects of the central office. In September, he submitted a report to the board announcing that he "had begun a program of regular Service Bulletin newsletters... to insure some Association contact on a helpful plane with active members..." That winter Doyle started a series of membership solicitations, and he set up a member-publisher display center in the national office. When President John J. Daly reported to the convention in May, he praised the new secretary and labeled him "a top-flight executive."[33]

Changes occurred over the years as office personnel came and went. In the fall of 1959 Mrs. Eileen Nugent, who had begun working on a part-time basis during the first year of the operation of the CPA headquarters and had later taken a full-time position with the Association, was named Office Manager. Another office re-organization was announced in 1964 at which time Mrs. Nugent and Mrs. Margaret Casey were designated as staff associates and assumed responsibility for specific areas of office administration. Meanwhile the office had moved once more--to 432 Park Avenue South. Francis Cardinal Spellman officiated at the blessing, an open house was scheduled for the occasion, and Doyle reported that this affair "was an example of the best in public relations for the CPA."[34]

By this time Jim Doyle had served as executive secretary for a longer time than any of his predecessors and had proven to be a competent and trustworthy administrator of the business of the Association. Therefore, certain members began efforts to enhance his stature within the organization. In April of 1963 a resolution had been presented to the board calling for a "clearly-defined and more fully responsible role for the man in the CPA who is the mainstay of the organization."[35] This was finally written into the bylaws following action taken by the 1965 convention with the title of the executive changed from "secretary" to "director." Despite various suggestions that he also be given additional powers and responsibilities, no action was taken until two years later when a motion was passed calling for a change in the by-laws clearly indicating that the director's position had indeed been strengthened. In the 1968 session this was done by approving a constitutional change designating the director as "the day-to-day operating executive of the Association, responsible for the initiation, implementation and execution of policies and programs adopted by the Board of Directors." He was also made an ex-officio member of all CPA committees and of the board.[36]

Previous to this the board had undergone several other changes. The original constitution provided for a board of directors composed of the officers and three other members chosen annually at the national convention. Though the 1916 revision referred to the governing body as the executive board, the composition of the group remained the same, and there was no other change until 1939 when the Episcopal Chairman became an ex-officio member.[37] That same year President Ridder appointed a Catholic Press Planning Committee with Msgr. Wynhoven as chairman. Among the proposals presented by this committee to the 1940 convention was one suggesting that the reorganization of the executive board as discussed at the 1939 meeting be implemented. This provided that the number of directors remain unchanged, but that one of the directors be chairman of the newspaper division, another of the magazines, and the third of the Catholic School Press. The published constitution of 1942 contained a revision to this effect, but by October of that year the executive board had already recommended another change which provided for continuity in the governing body.[38] The proposed changes were discussed at the 1943 convention and finally adopted the following year with the revised by-laws providing for nine elected members with a three year term of office. One member was to be a representative of the Catholic School Press while four each were to be chosen from the newspaper and magazine divisions. To provide for stability in the group, the 1944 convention elected three board members for a one year term, another three for a period of two years, and the remaining three for three years. The cancellation of the 1945 convention disrupted this procedure, but the pattern was stabilized in 1946. The provision for a three year term had continued to the present as has the stipulation that the president, vice president, and treasurer be elected by the convention delegates from among the board members, but that the secretary be chosen by the board from its own members.[39]

Changes have occurred in regard to the number and selection of the board members. At the closing business session of the 1952 convention a motion asked that the ninth elected member be chosen at large rather than from the Catholic School Press. Since a by-law revision was necessary before this could be implemented, the proposal was not considered at the time.[40] In his report to the 1953 meeting, Secretary Kane recommended that the CPA continue its ties with the Catholic School Press Association, suggested that there be a better representation of all members on the board, and advocated that the number of elected directors be increased to twelve. To expedite the transaction of current business, Kane further advised that the officers be authorized to act as an executive committee. The 1954 revised constitution incorporated these proposals stating that the twelve directors should include two members at large plus five magazine and five newspaper members and that the officers might act as an executive committee between board meetings provided the board empowered them to do so.[41]

Two years later a question arose concerning an honorarium for the officers. Actually, since 1944 the constitution had carried a provision that all board members could be reimbursed for necessary expenses incurred, but in practice this had not been done as the officers and other directors alike had either paid their own expenses or had been financed by their publications. The board discussed this financial matter twice in 1956, and in May of the following year unanimously approved a motion providing one thousand dollars annually for the expenses of the president. Recent constitutions state that the amount of reimbursement for the president be determined by the board of directors. The provision that other board members may submit legitimate expenses still remains, probably because it has occasionally been used to assist a needy director, but it is seldom evoked.[42]

The officers functioning as an executive committee also caused some discussion. In May of 1959 one of the directors remarked that there was a tendency for the officers to be overly secretive about Association business, and this was brought up again at the fall board meeting.[43] A few years later the general membership challenged the aura of secrecy surrounding board meetings, and the 1964 convention approved a motion asking that important action taken by the board be made known to the members either through the Catholic Journalist or by means of special bulletins.[44] This was done, but in recent years as the executive director has taken on additional duties and the national office has handled more of the CPA business, the board and even the officers have had less to do with the ordinary day-by-day functioning of the Association.

A development paralleling that of the establishment of the national headquarters with a full-time executive secretary was regionalization. Not only did the proposition concerning regions survive a lengthy preliminary stage before it became an actuality, but the regional plan also reached culmination in the early 1940's. President Benedict Elder in his farewell address in 1932 suggested regional meetings, and the following year President Richard Reid again brought the matter to the attention of the convention. "Is there any reason why we may not have groups organized, also, along geographical lines, to meet from time to time during the year with programs headed up toward the general program of the Catholic Press Association of the entire United States?" he inquired. Again in 1934 Reid urged the members to consider the feasibility of "subsidiary groups in geographical sections meeting from time to time..." His recommendation was approved "in principle," and the board was "authorize[d]...to work out the details of this organization."[45]

Six more years elapsed, however, before the plans for regional meetings were finally outlined to the 1940 convention by Msgr. Wynhoven's Press Planning Committee. Wynhoven explained that the regional meetings would help the "struggling, financially-handicapped editors" who found it impossible to attend the annual conventions. He seemed to fear, though, that unless the regions were securely under the control of the parent CPA, they might act in such a way as to jeopardize the Association or even develop into independent organizations. It was finally decided that there would be no danger if the regions were allowed to choose their own chairmen with the approval of the president and the directors.[46] The board, acting on the report of the committee and the wishes of the delegates, approved the formation of five regions based on geographical location. The president was instructed to appoint a temporary chairman for each region and to make arrangements for the organizational meetings.[47]

By mid-August the Pacific Region had met, thus

achieving the distinction of being the first area to put the plan into action. A month later the Eastern Region convened and by unanimous vote chose former President Reid as chairman. In early October the Mid-West organizational meeting was held in Chicago, and in mid-November the Southern Region met in St. Louis. Only the Western Region failed to take action in the fall, but before the 1941 convention met in May it had organized, and the Southern Region not only had sponsored a second meeting in New Orleans in March, but also had met just previously to the general convention.[48]

In the interim the directors had decided that the national association should pay the organizational expenses of the regions and that thereafter each should be self-sustaining. Msgr. Wynhoven prepared a "Guide for Regional Conference Groups of the Catholic Press Association" which by early November had undergone minor revisions as suggested by Vice president Wey and had been approved by Bishop Gannon and the executive board. The December issue of the Association's house organ carried the "Guide" which included the rules for the regions as well as the duties of the chairmen.[49]

Two matters dominated the discussion concerning regions at the 1941 convention. The first centered on a resolution from the Eastern Region regarding the degree of autonomy that each section might exercise without disrupting the central association. The members voted that the board should clarify the rules governing the conferences and prepare an amendment to the section of the constitution referring to regional divisions. The delegates also had suggestions about the geographical boundaries of the regions. Since these were chosen arbitrarily by the board, the changes proposed were readily approved, and the matter was turned over to the board for execution.[50]

Regional sessions were held again in 1941. A year later the board considered the possibility of alternating general and regional meetings every other year, but this was not carried through. Even though the 1942 convention heard Father Thomas A. Meehan speak on the "Benefits of Regional Conferences," Father Patrick O'Connor reported in October of 1944 that he was reappointing temporary chairmen for the regions despite the fact that no region had met "within the past three years."[51] The Mid-Western Region did convene in November of that year, and members were informed that meetings of the Pacific and Eastern conferences would be held early in 1945. In 1953 a new region--the Pacific Northwest--was activated, and five years later the Southern Region was dissolved and replaced by the South Central and Southeastern Regions. With the exception of the Western Region, the groups continued to meet annually. [52]

Canadian members in the mid-1950's began advocating a region of their own, but the board ruled that Canadian members should affiliate with the Pacific Northwest. Two years later a Canadian member reported to Doyle that a Catholic Press Convention for Canada was being planned, repeated the suggestion for a Canadian region within the CPA, and proposed that the matter be discussed at the 1959 convention. A Canadian Conference of Editors was held before the 1960 convention met, and a Canadian Affairs Committee operated within the CPA during the early 1960's. For a few years, too, Canadian members held special sessions just before the beginning of the annual conventions. Although there was a move toward establishing an independent Canadian CPA in 1963, enthusiasm for a separate organization was short-lived. [53]

Just how successful regional meetings have been is debatable. President Daly praised them in his 1960 report, and Doyle told the board the next year "... there is no question in my mind that they serve a useful purpose."[54] Too often, however, the meetings have been poorly attended and the programs mediocre. After Doyle suggested that the central office take a more active role in planning and promoting these sessions, the officers and past presidents in a special meeting in 1964 endorsed the suggestion. Two years later the director reported that the national office was taking "a major part" in the organization of the regional conferences. [55]

Regional divisions were in reality a reflection of the growing membership of the CPA which was not accidental but the result of concerted and sustained efforts. In November of 1938 the board asked Bishop Gannon to contact the bishops of the country and suggest that all diocesan papers under their control join the CPA. The directors also recommended that dues be decreased as an incentive to wider membership, and named Msgr. Wynhoven as Press Month Chairman. [56] The priest combined membership recruiting with the press month activities so well that he added thirty-four new members bringing the total number to one hundred forty-two. The following year Wynhoven became chairman of the Membership Committee, continued his solicitations, and told the 1940 convention that the active membership had reached one hundred seventy. He sustained this effort during his two years as president writing numerous letters and even visiting a number of the bishops personally.[57] In 1942 when Wey became president and Father J. Fred Kriebs took over the duties of secretary, they carried on the work of actively seeking new members. For the first time in the history of the Association, copies of the Convention Proceedings were sent to members of the hierarchy, and Father Kriebs corresponded with all non-member publications suggesting affiliation with the CPA.[58]

Membership dropped in the late 40's, but increased again when the national office began under the direction of a full-time executive. In 1955 Association Secretary Floyd Anderson reported two hundred eighty-six active members noting that this was almost double the 1950 membership.[59] Nonetheless, it has been necessary for the executive secretary and the officers to work continuously at keeping members once they join the organization. At present there are over three hundred active members from a possible total of about five hundred. As has been true throughout most of the history of the CPA, the majority of non-members are the less known publications with small circulation figures.[60]

No doubt the major reason for the lack of stability in the membership has been the matter of dues. The 1938 convention had endeavored to attract members by reducing dues drastically. A sliding scale whereby members were assessed twenty to one hundred dollars per year was replaced by a new structure having but two rates: publications with less than ten thousand circulation paid ten dollars annually and those above ten thousand were charged twenty-five dollars.[61] As services increased the amount brought in through dues was entirely inadequate to cover the expenses entailed. In the fall of 1945, Secretary Shanahan began working towards a dues increase. Former president Wey complimented him on this maintaining that it was imperative that members start paying a "reasonable amount instead of a mere pittance."[62] The board appointed a committee to study constitutional revisions and directed that it give "especial attention" to the question of an increase in dues; subsequently they were doubled with rates set at twenty and fifty dollars.[63]

This meagre increase proved to be insufficient when the Association considered a permanent secretariate. In 1949 the president, Father Bussard, appointed a committee to study the rate structure and to report to the board in the fall. The committee drew up a new schedule of dues ranging from twenty-five to three hundred dollars per member and calculated to produce an income of over fifteen thousand dollars, twice that obtained under the previous system. After surveying the field of non-members, it concluded that another seven thousand would be possible if these publications could be persuaded to join. The report, then, not only recommended the dues increase but also called for a "concerted drive" for new members.[64] The board approved, and the 1950 convention accepted the revised schedule agreeing to follow it voluntarily until the constitutional change was effected. Nonetheless, finances continued to be insufficient, and in 1952 the board voted for a twenty per cent increase in dues. The proposal, submitted to the regional meetings where it was studied and discussed, was adopted by the 1953 convention.[65]

In 1956 a Special Finance Committee, appointed to work on a revision that would eliminate "certain inequalities" that had become evident in the existing arrangement, at first recommended an increase in dues, but later decreed that it should be delayed for the time being.[66] Msgr. Randall argued that raising dues at that time would be "inopportune" as it might force smaller publications to drop CPA membership.[67] When the board convened in September, however, all the special committees recommended programs requiring additional funds. Because the report of the treasurer "showed a steadily receding cash position and an abnormal imbalance between the Association's costs and income," the directors advised an increase which in February they set at thirty-five per cent.[68] In the interim the Special Finance Committee had received from one of its members the suggestion that dues levied be based not only on circulation but also on frequency of issue and subscription price. The use of such an index system would "charge a member with his exact share of the total circulation and of the total dues."[69] Although this proportionate dues structure was approved by a general session of the 1958 convention, complications arose in its application because the larger newspaper members complained that their share under the new plan was unfair. When the officers met in January, Doyle reported some of the difficulties including the fact that five resignations had already occurred because of the increase.[70] As the large newspaper members continued to demand a ceiling on their dues, a special committee was named in 1959 to study the dues structure again. The 1960 convention approved the committee's recommendation that the request of these members be respected.[71]

This settled the matter momentarily. But in February of 1963 William Holub, CPA treasurer, reported to the officers that even though additional income was not imperative to meet current operating expenses, it was necessary to raise dues if projects under contemplation were to be carried out. Repeating his proposal later to the entire board, Holub recommended especially that smaller members pay more since they benefited most from membership. Again in November, as chairman of a Dues Study Committee, he urged that the increase be accepted charging that the CPA was "at a stalemate." Holub also presented a revised schedule whereby dues, still calculated by means of the index system, would fall between seventy-five and six hundred dollars.[72] By the spring of 1964 members had taken sides on this issue. Two of the past presidents, Msgr. Randall and Father Albert J. Nevins, mailed a circular to the members explaining their opposition to the move and asserting that the increase would "be an intolerable burden" to many thereby resulting in loss of membership. Holub followed their circular with one of his own refuting the arguments of the priests and maintaining that if the measure was defeated, services would have to be curtailed at a time when members were demanding that they be increased. He insisted that the proposed increases were "reasonable and in keeping with the potential of the organization..." When the opening business session of the annual convention considered the matter, feeling was strong and discussion prolonged, but in a vote taken by secret ballot, the increase was approved.[73]

Concomitant with the efforts to increase income by raising active membership dues were campaigns to bolster Association funds by enrolling Associate Members, "Catholic writers of good repute," in the CPA. This class of membership had been included in the organization since 1920, and dues were only two dollars. Little was done to encourage Associate Members until the over-all revitalization of the CPA in the early 1940's. During 1942-1943 the vice president, Father Considine, who led the campaign for individual memberships succeeded in admitting nineteen, and the following year the secretary reported an increase of twenty-five Associate Members.[74] In October of 1945 the board laid plans to enroll "several thousand" Associate Members. Secretary Shanahan, who had pushed the drive through circulars and advertisements sent to publications holding active membership, wrote in February: "Every mail brings new applications for Associate Membership." By May the number had skyrocketed to four hundred twenty-eight compared to eighty-seven just one year before. In his presidential report, Father O'Connor labeled this increase "gratifying," but declared that the CPA should also provide services that would make "membership gratifying to the associates."[75]

The phrase was overlooked for the present. Rather, the 1947 convention adopted a resolution raising Associate dues to five dollars. The increase, lack of attention to the needs of Associate Members, and a decline in promotional efforts combined to discourage individual memberships. When in the early 1950's the number had dropped to fewer than one hundred fifty, a 1952 constitutional amendment expanded Associate Membership to include any Catholic "interested in the furtherance of the cause of the Catholic press..." In July of 1954 President Charles J. McNeill named a committee to study the possibilities of enrolling as Associate Members Catholics who were free-lance writers or working in the general field of publishing and to draw up a program that would be of interest to such members. Some months later the committee members, reporting that the chief desire of these potential members was information that would enable them to "do a better job of writing for and selling to the Catholic Press," recommended that a page in the Catholic Journalist be set aside to supply this information.[76]

A year later the board empowered this committee to draw up a letter to be mailed through the national office to prospective members. Although this effort resulted in fifty new members, the committee was not allowed to repeat a similar mailing because it had already exceeded its budget for the current year.[77] By 1958 Associate Members had again fallen in number, but efforts to provide services for them have continued.[78]

In addition to the Active and Associate Members, Life Members were also sought by the CPA. Undertaken in 1927, this project was expected to finance awards for Catholic literature, but was discontinued when the depression struck. In 1944 Simon A. Baldus, reporting for the Literary Awards Committee, urged that it be revived and completed; two years later President Humphrey E. Desmond suggested reactivation of this plan to realize $50,000. Twenty-seven new Life Members enrolled before the 1947 convention met, and solicitations continued into the next year, but it was not until 1956 that definite action was taken to recruit Life Members. At a meeting of the board following the annual convention that year, Richard Reid spoke to the directors encouraging such a campaign and in July he was named chairman of a committee composed of the officers.[79]

When it began its work, the committee envisioned a much more ambitious program than simply completing the Literary Awards Foundation. The members contacted the Community Counseling Service, Inc. (CCS), of New York City to obtain professional advice concerning a possible nationwide drive to establish a fund of five hundred thousand dollars that would earn enough income to finance a number of projects sponsored by the Association. Preliminary work was completed during the fall and early winter, and representatives of CCS spoke at the January board meeting. Although several members were skeptical and others completely opposed a fund-raising campaign, the board authorized a preliminary survey to cost seven hundred fifty dollars. Episcopal Chairman Thomas K. Gorman, upon his return to Texas, wrote to the president suggesting that the entire plan be dropped. He characterized it as "a nice dream," but insisted that there would never be sufficient interest and cooperation to make it a success.[80] When CCS representatives presented the results of their survey to the officers several weeks later, their findings seemed to substantiate the opinion of the bishop. Reporting a lack of "warm feeling" for the program and mentioning that many of the Association members contacted seemed unsure of what benefits were theirs as members of the CPA, they acknowledged a "negative reaction" as far as the editors' hopes for support from the hierarchy was concerned.[81]

In mid-March of 1957 CCS representatives again discussed the survey at a meeting of the entire board. Asked outright if they were confident that the money could be raised, one of them admitted that until the campaign was "sold" to the membership, the answer was no. Acting on this statement, the board planned a program of education naming committees to examine various activities of the Association.[82] Notifying the members of these committees during the annual convention, Msgr. Randall mentioned that it was the hope of the directors that the program would be ready for presentation at the regional meetings. It was February of 1958, however, before the Special Committee on CPA Life Memberships presented its report. After listing specific purposes for which the funds were to be used, the report advocated that the money collected should not be added to the Literary Awards Foundation, but remain a distinct fund. It vetoed the idea of employing a professional fund-raising company for the drive, suggesting instead that a prominent Catholic layman head up a committee to conduct the campaign.[83]

The board discussed possible chairmen for the drive, set a minimum goal of sixty-five thousand dollars, and designated the fund as the Catholic Press Association Foundation. By May, Francis A. Fink had accepted the chairmanship of the fund-raising campaign which was later renamed the "Catholic Press Development Program." The project never materialized; Fink was unable to recruit members to serve on regional committees, and he delayed sending out letters to the bishops inviting them to become Life Members.[84] During the next few months efforts were made to secure money from the Eli Lilly Foundation for some of the CPA projects, but this did not succeed either. In the end, the fund-raising effort was abandoned, and the Association resorted as usual to dues as the chief source of income.[85]

The unsuccessful Catholic Press Development Program was but one of several abortive attempts made during this period to re-evaluate the structure and objectives of the CPA. For, despite the progress made during the 1940's and early 1950's, some members remained dissatisfied. These advocated ambitious programs for the Association, visualized a prestigious organization, and urged that the CPA engage in self-studies to determine ways and means of achieving these goals. In his final report as executive secretary, Kane suggested that a committee be appointed to draw up a five year program for the Association since "lack of plan or purpose" was undoubtedly the "major weakness" of the individual members and of the group as a whole.[86] Cahaney, Kane's successor, did distribute a publicity blurb outlining "The Purpose and Program of The Catholic Press Association," but this laid greater stress on the current activities of the organization than on any plans for future developments.[87] Although the Life Membership Committee of 1956-1957 conceived a very broad prospectus involving financial security and a greatly expanded service program, the membership as a whole evidenced but meagre interest. In January of 1961 the board spent a session discussing two topics: "Impact of the Catholic Press on Non-Catholic America" and "How We Can Get Greater Professional

Acceptance of the Catholic Press Association." Although the directors had many suggestions, they failed to take action that would implement their ideas.[88]

The next year, John Reedy, CSC, Chairman of a Special Projects Committee, submitted a "Self-Promotion Plan for the Catholic Press," basing his study on a presupposition which regarded the Catholic Press of the United States as a unified institution. Reedy admitted that his proposal was not intended as "a detailed plan of action," but as "an indication of a direction which deserves consideration; ... a type of cooperation which we are not presently using;... a fresh approach to responsible membership...." Copies of the plan were presented to the directors, but again no action was taken.[89] Speaking to the regional meetings in the fall of 1965 and calling for a self-study of the organization, President William Holub told the members that a committee was working on an evaluation.[90]

This report, presented to the board in January of 1966 by a Basic Services Committee, was the work of Father Reedy, the committee's chairman. Entitled "The Purposes and Policies of the Catholic Press Association," it traced the growth of the CPA, but also pointed out a "widespread restlessness" within the membership. Reedy concluded that the most important reason for this dissatisfaction was the "deep frustration" brought about by "the unrealized potential of the Association." Emphasizing once more the necessity of viewing the Catholic Press as an institution having a "distinct service to render to the Church," he questioned the wisdom of confining CPA activities to services to members and called for "wider vision" and "more forceful leadership." To achieve these goals, he asked for a "radical reorientation" in the thinking of the members and in the structure of the organization. Finally, the priest advocated discussion by the members concerning "the general problem of Association policy," asked that the position of the executive director be strengthened to provide continuous and forceful leadership, and requested "more responsible activity" from the individual members.[91] The paper was published in the Catholic Journalist so that members could study it in advance, the committee reported to the convention, and the delegates took part in the discussion which was labeled a "little Council" by President Holub who appointed a commission under the leadership of Father Reedy to continue working on this self-study.[92] In August the commission sponsored a two-day conference in Des Plaines, Illinois.

This meeting examined the relevancy of a Catholic editor in today's world and how a more professional Catholic Press might be developed, and spent much time discussing the role of the CPA and especially the element of leadership within it.[93] The regional meetings that fall heard reports on this conference, but then interest in the movement waned. Of the goals projected by Father Reedy only one was implemented: the strengthening of the position of the executive director.[94]

To effect this change and others discussed in this chapter, it was necessary to amend and revise the constitution and by-laws several times. Various changes were discussed and approved in the 30's, and finally in 1942 an up-to-date version was published in booklet form.[95] Revised constitutions issued from 1944 to 1966 were printed as four page inserts in the Catholic Journalist. At last in the summer of 1968, the members received the latest version which, for the first time in more than a quarter of a century, appeared as a published pamphlet.[96]

In examining these various constitutional revisions it is interesting to trace the name changes that have occurred. The organization was incorporated in the state of New York in 1912 as the Catholic Press Association, Inc. When the 1916 constitution was published, it declared: "This Association shall be known as the Catholic Press Association of the United States and Canada," and this same title was repeated in the published constitution of 1921. A 1937 mimeographed version reverted to the 1911 name, but the 1942 published rendition became The Catholic Press Association of the United States.[97] The executive board in the fall of 1942 and again a year later discussed discrepancies in the legal name. At this time the organization was re-incorporated, and the Association was registered as The Catholic Press Association of the United States, Inc.[98] Through an oversight the CPA was dissolved in 1952. After an investigation brought this to light the next year, it was re-incorporated retaining the name adopted in 1943.[99] When the Canadian editors had their meetings in the mid-1950's, it was suggested that the name be changed to the Catholic Press Association of America or the Catholic Press Association of the United States and Canada. In October of 1956 the board officially approved the first of these titles, but nothing was done, and in September of 1958 the board rescinded the motion.[100] The matter then lay dormant until the fall of 1964 when the board approved a change in the Certificate of Incorporation that would have included Canada in the title.[101] Again, no action followed, and today the legal name of the organization remains the Catholic Press Association of the United States, Inc.

Notes

1. Quinn to Hall, June 13, 1934; Hall to Quinn, June 28, 1934. PDF.

2. Hall to Fitzpatrick, December 4, 1936. PDF.

3. An article appearing in the Catholic Register (Kansas City, Missouri), November 2, 1933, mentioned all these activities.

4. It is possible that there had been some pre-convention politicking in behalf of the priest. Hall indicated as much in a letter written almost twenty years later to John J. Daly who was then vice president. Hall to Daly, January 24, 1958. DC. On the other hand, it may be that some members were quite oblivious of the custom. The previous year Bishop Gannon had written to Msgr. Wynhoven congratulating him on being elected vice president. He continued: "This most probably places you in line for the presidency next year." Gannon to Wynhoven, n. d. Gannon Papers, ADE.

5. Details of the session are in a memorandum dated June 26, 1939. PDF. A few exceptions to the succession must be noted: in the summer of 1943 John J. Considine, MM, serving a second term as vice president resigned, and the board named Msgr. Wynhoven to complete the year in that office. Therefore, at the 1944 convention Father Patrick O'Connor became president without having been vice president, and Humphry E. Desmond was elected vice president. When Father O'Connor accepted a special assignment in the Orient in December of 1945, Desmond took over his work but was designated "Acting President" until his own election in 1946. Desmond was re-elected in 1947, and the transition remained untroubled for another ten years. Then, in 1958, a pre-convention scheme to keep Vice president John J. Daly from

the presidential office failed despite a few deft maneuvers. (See Hall's letter to Daly, January 24, 1958. PDF. Also, Mrs. Helen Daly, in a personal interview on July 18, 1968, brought up this matter.) A few years later, Floyd Anderson who had been elected president in 1962 and re-elected in 1963, resigned in July, 1963, to become Director of the NC News Service. Msgr. Robert G. Peters who was then vice president assumed the title and office of president, and the board named William Holub to the office of vice president even though he was then serving as treasurer. Holub was elected vice president at the following convention and then moved on to the regular two years as president. In 1967 John O'Connor was chosen vice president but in the fall of that year, following a dispute with his bishop, he left the Catholic Press. Thereupon, Joseph Gelin was named by the board and duly elected by the delegates at the 1968 convention. See Appendix C for all CPA officers.

6. Hall to Wynhoven, January 16, 1941. PDF.

7. Resumé... 1941, p. 8. PDF.

8. Wey to Wynhoven, October 2, 1942. WC.

9. Wey to The Members of the CPA Executive Board, October 16, 1942. WC. There is a copy of the proposal in the same collection.

10. Considine to Wey, October 26, 1942; "Minutes, Board... October 30, 1942," p. 4. WC.

11. A copy of this report is in WC.

12. WC also contains a copy of this plan. Actually, the CPA Executive Secretary Committee had authored the plan and had brought Hall and Msgr. Ready to their way of thinking on the matter. See: memo from Hall to Ready, February 11, 1943; Considine to Ready, April 14, 1943; and Ready to Wey, May 17, 1943, for materials giving the evolution of the plan. NCCB. CPA Secretary Father J. Fred Kriebs quoted the resolution in a letter to Wey dated June 17, 1943. WC.

13. Memo from Hall to Ready, October 28, 1943. NCCB. Proceedings. . . 1944, pp. 25 and 26. CPA.

14. Memo from Hall to Ready, October 26, 1944. PDF. "Minutes, Board. . October 20, 1944," p. 47. Father O'Connor had known Shanahan for some time, and it was through the president that Shanahan was secured according to C. P. A. Bulletin, IV (December, 1944), p. 1.

15. "Minutes, Board. . . February 17, 1945," pp. 57-58. It was later disclosed that certain funds made available through the convention cancellation helped finance this longer period. See: Desmond's circular of June 4, 1946. WC.

16. "Report of the President of the CPA to the Executive Board," October 25, 1945. CPA.

17. Abbreviated Report. . . 1946, pp. 15, 17, and 19. WC.

18. Desmond to Fellow Members, June 4 and July 2, 1946. WC. Actually, the contract was made out for thirteen months to provide for "continuity of secretarial services during the period when arrangements for the Executive Secretary's contract" would again have to be made. This from the secretary's report to the board, "Minutes, Board . . . October 17, 1946." CPA.

19. Desmond to O'Connor, August 24, 1944. CPA. Memos and correspondence, April-October, 1947. NCCB. Abbreviated Report. . . 1947, p. 13. WC.

20. "Minutes, Board. . May 21, 1948," p. 3; "Minutes, Board. . October 1, 1948," passim. Both in CPA.

21. Naturally, Mrs. Homan and Father Barrett each blamed the other for the resulting situation. See: Mrs. Homan's Report to the Executive Board, June 15, 1949, and a letter from Barrett to Bussard dated June 11, 1949. In his final report Father Barrett traced the developments at Fordham, explained what he had tried to accomplish, and suggested a permanent headquarters. All in CPA.

22. A letter from F. A. Fink to Kane dated August 8, 1950,

indicated that Father Barrett was quite upset that the move was made. CPA.

23. The above material is based on a personal interview with Mr. Kane on January 25, 1968, and on President Fink's report to the 1951 convention, a copy of which is in CPA.

24. Msgr. Randall to Father Albert J. Nevins, August 18, 1950. CPA. Father Nevins also aided in the search.

25. CJ, II (October, 1950), p. 1 reported the opening. Kane's "Report on the Operation of Your CPA National Office," to the 41st Annual Convention is in CPA.

26. For Kane's duties see: "Minutes, Board...October 18, 1951." PDF. His successes are recorded in: F. A. Fink, "Report of the President to the 42nd Annual Convention," June 19, 1952 (CPA) and CJ, IV (October, 1952), p. 1.

27. Kane to author in a memo dated January 26, 1968.

28. The resignation was announced in NC Release 10/27/52. Kane's recommendations are in: "Report of the Executive Secretary," 43rd Annual Meeting, May 7, 1953. CPA.

29. Kane in the January 26, 1968, memo to this writer contended: "The project could never have succeeded without the wholehearted and self-sacrificing cooperation of many, many CPA members who collectively spent more in time and money on Association affairs than the total CPA budget." He paid special tribute to Fink, Msgr. Randall, and Father Nevins.

30. CJ, IV (April, 1953), p. 1 noted that the changeover would be moved up to that date; Ibid. (June-July, 1953), p. 1 gave the new location; Ibid. (August, 1953), p. 3 told of Miss Geddis' departure for a Dominican convent; "Minutes, Board... May 14, 1954," recorded the board's satisfaction. CPA.

31. Msgr. Randall, "Report of the President," May 14,

1957, commented on the expansion; an example of the board's reaction to Cahaney's resignation is Floyd Anderson's comment on the secretary in a letter to the officers dated April 5, 1958; Randall's remark is from "President's Report" to the General Business Session, May 21, 1958, p. 5. All are in CPA.

32. Randall's 1958 report, pp. 5-6, and a memo from him to All Members, Board of Directors, April 28, 1958, give the board's action and Doyle's qualifications. Doyle had been with the Howes Publishing Company in NYC for over ten years and had worked as a newsmagazine editor, promotion manager, circulation director, and advertising salesman. CPA.

33. James A. Doyle, "Executive Secretary's Report," to Board of Directors, September 22, 1958; Ibid., May 12, 1959. CPA. Daly's remark is from "President's Report," 1959 Convention. DC.

34. Doyle, "Executive Secretary's Report," to Board of Directors, September 23, 1959. CPA. Ibid., October 7, 1964, PC. Ibid., May 26, 1964. PC.

35. "Minutes, Board... April 30, 1963." PC. However, several years before others had called for upgrading of the executive secretary. See: John Reedy, CSC, to Holub, June 19, 1959. AMF.

36. "Annual Business Meeting," May 17, 1967. HC. For the constitutional change see: "Constitution and By-Laws Catholic Press Association of the United States, Inc." Revised to May 15, 1968, Art. VI, Section 7; Art. V, Section 1.

37. For these changes see: "Constitution of the Catholic Press Association," 1911, Art. IV, Section 1; "The Constitution of the Catholic Press Association of the United States and Canada," 1916, Section IV, 1 (CC); and Resumé... 1939, p. 9 (CPA).

38. Transcript... 1940, pp. 83-85. CPA. "Minutes, Board ... October 31, 1942," p. 5. WC.

39. Proceedings... 1944, pp. 7 and 44-45. CPA. Abbreviated Report... 1946, p. 9. WC. "The Catholic

Press Association of the United States, Inc. Revised By-laws adopted by Members of CPA in Milwaukee, Wisconsin, May 11, 1944," Art. V, Sections 1-4 and Art. VI. PC.

40. "Minutes Closing General Business Meeting," June 20, 1952, p. 1. CPA.

41. Kane's suggestions are in "Report of the Executive Secretary" to Annual Meeting Catholic Press Association, May 7, 1953, pp. 3-4. CPA. The revisions appear in "The CPA by-laws... adopted at the convention in Chicago, Ill., on May 14, 1954," Art. V. WC. Except for the addition of the executive director as an _ex-officio_ member of the board, the present governing body of the CPA remains as it was designated in this constitution.

42. The provision is in "The Catholic Press Association of the United States, Inc. Revised By-laws adopted by Members of CPA in Milwaukee, Wisconsin, May 11, 1944," Art. V. Section 7. Discussions concerning these finances appear in "Minutes, Officers... July 12, 1956," p. 4; "Minutes, Board ...October 10-11, 1956," p. 6. Approval is in "Minutes, Board... May 17, 1957," p. 3. Discussion concerning other board members is found in "Minutes, Board... February 13-14, 1958," p. 23; _Ibid._, March 2, 1967, p. 6. All in CPA.

43. See: "Minutes, Board... May 15, 1959," p. 7, and September 25, 1959, p. 2. CPA.

44. "Minutes, Board... May 26, 1964," p. 5 and "Minutes Business Meeting," May 29, 1964, pp. 3-4. CPA. The _Catholic Journalist_ is the CPA's house organ.

45. Elder's suggestion is in _Resumé... 1932_, p. 7. CC. Reid's recommendations are in _Resumé... 1933_, p. 34 and _Resumé... 1934_, p. 25. The resolution is also in _Resumé... 1934_, p. 64. CPA.

46. _Transcript... 1940_, pp. 85-91. CPA.

47. _Resumé... 1940_, p. 6. CPA.

48. Notices concerning the meetings are found in NC Re-

lease 9/24/40; In Vain, I (September 14, 1940), p. 1 (December 30, 1940), pp. 1, 3-4 (May 10, 1941), p. 4; Transcript... 1941, pp. 4-5. CPA.

49. The directors' decision is in "Minutes, Board.. October 11, 1940." This plus a copy of the "Guide" with a letter from Msgr. Wynhoven to Wey under date of October 18, 1940, and a copy of the revised "Guide" and letters from Wynhoven to Gannon, October 29, 1940, and Gannon to Wynhoven, November 1, 1940, are all in WC. The regional rules are from In Vain, I (December 30, 1940), pp. 3-4.

50. See: Transcript... 1941, pp. 16-26 for discussion concerning autonomy and pp. 14-15 for suggestions on geographical boundaries. CPA.

51. The discussion on alternating meetings is in "Minutes, Board.. October 31, 1942," p. 5. WC. Meehan's speech is in Proceedings... 1942, pp. 116-118. O'Connor's remark is in "Minutes, Board.. October 20, 1944," p. 42. Both in CPA.

52. At present there are again five regions. The Mountain (Western) Region did not disband, and the South Central and Southeastern Regions met as a unit (Southern Region) in 1968. Personal interview with Jim Doyle, October 24, 1968.

53. The Canadian action can be traced through "Minutes, Board.. October 10-11, 1956," p. 10; Rev. G. Laviolette to J. A. Doyle, September 24, 1958; "Report of the President," May 10, 1960, p. 6 (CPA) and "Report of Canadian Affairs Committee," May 26 and October 7, 1964 (PC). In a personal interview on October 23, 1968, Msgr. J. G. Hanley of Kingston, Ontario, stated that in his opinion the Catholic Press in Canada is too weak to support an independent organization.

54. "Report of the President" to Board of Directors, May 10, 1960, p. 6. CPA. "Executive Secretary's Report," October 26, 1961, p. 3. CPA.

55. Doyle's suggestion is in "Executive Secretary's Report," November 21, 1963, p. 5. PC. Minutes of

"Special Meeting of Officers and Past Presidents of CPA," April 23, 1964, p. 3. Also PC. "Minutes, Board... August 4, 1966," p. 3, refers to the major role taken by the national office. CPA. This had been suggested years before by the first full-time secretary. In a letter from F. A. Fink to James Kane dated August 8, 1950, Fink wrote in part: "I like your ideas about tying in the regional meetings of the C. P. A. more closely with the Executive Board." CPA.

56. "Minutes, Board... November 25 and 26, 1938," p. 2. PDF.

57. Membership reports are found in Resumé... 1939, p. 12; Resumé... 1940, p. 10 (CPA); and Resumé... 1941, pp. 6-7 (PDF).

58. A. J. Wey to author under date of December 11, 1967, mentioned the mailings to the bishops. Kriebs' activity is found in Proceedings... 1943, p. 17. CPA.

59. "Minutes, Board... May 25, 1955," p. 1. CPA.

60. Personal interview with Doyle, October 24, 1968. For membership statistics, see Appendix A.

61. Resumé... 1939, p. 7. CPA.

62. Wey to Shanahan, September 11, 1945. WC.

63. Circular: Shanahan to All Members, November 9, 1945, and Abbreviated Report... 1946, pp. 10 and 14. WC.

64. "Minutes, Board... June 17, 1949," p. 1, and "A Survey Report Relating to an Increment of Annual Funds of the Catholic Press Association through the Readjustment of Annual Dues," July 25, 1949. The quotation is in part 4. CPA.

65. "Minutes, Board... October 24, 1952," p. 4. CPA. CJ, IV (October, 1952), pp. 1-2 and (June-July, 1953), p. 4.

66. CJ, VII (October, 1956), p. 6 referred to the inequal-

ities. The committee action is in "Minutes, Board ... May 14, 1957," p. 4. CPA.

67. "Report of the President," May 14, 1957, p. 4. CPA.

68. CJ, VIII (October, 1957), pp. 1-2 records the recommended increase. The percentage was arrived at in "Minutes, Board.. . February 13-14, 1958," p. 6. CPA.

69. "Report of Special Finance Committee to President Randall," and "Frederick C. Dyer's Opinion," February 12, 1958. DC.

70. Rev. Edward C. Foster to Rev. Frank Gartland, September 8, 1958, mentioned the difficulty of application. V. Rev. Msgr. John M. Kelly of the New World (Chicago) to President Daly, January 17, 1959, noted the disproportionate rates. DC. The resignations were reported in "Minutes, Officers... January 15, 1959," p. 1. CPA.

71. Convention action is in "Closing Business Meeting," May 15, 1959, p. 3 and ibid., May 13, 1960, p. 1. CPA. Ceiling demands are found in letters of Rev. Joseph R. Crowley to President Daly, January 29 and May 5, 1960. DC.

72. "Minutes, Officers... February 20, 1963," p. 4; "Minutes, Board... April 30, 1963," p. 1; and "Report of Dues Study Committee," November 21-22, 1963. PC.

73. Circular: Msgr. Randall and Father Nevins to CPA Members, n. d., but April or early May, 1964; Circular: William Holub to CPA Members, May 15, 1964; "Business Meeting," May 27, 1964, p. 2. The vote was recorded as 88-79. PC.

74. The provision for this class of membership is in "Amendments to the Constitution of the Catholic Press Association of the United States and Canada," adopted at Washington, D. C., January 24, 1920. CC. Considine's success is recorded in Proceedings... 1943, p. 17. CPA. Father Kriebs, the secretary, noted that most of the new associate members had been obtained by two active members,

the editors of The Victorian and St. Anthony Messenger; therefore, they must have been Robert K. Doran and Father Hyacinth Blocker. See: Proceedings... 1944, p. 44. CPA.

75. For data on the drive see Circular: James A. Shanahan to All Members, November 9, 1945, and Shanahan to All Active and Associate Members, February 16, 1946. WC. Results were reported in CJ, II (May-June, 1946), p. 7. O'Connor's report which was by letter from Japan is in Abbreviated Report... 1946, p. 7. WC. Shanahan had himself been an Associate Member for years. His name appears in Minutes... 1923, p. 2. CPA.

76. "The CPA by-laws... [revised to] May 8, 1953," Art. I, Sec. 3. PC. The committee report, dated November 3, 1954, and in the form of a memo from the Associate Membership Committee to the Board of Directors and others, was discussed at a board meeting on November 11, 1954. CPA.

77. "Minutes, Board.. November 3, 1955," pp. 9-10; "Report to the CPA Board from Associate Member Committee," and "Minutes, Board.. October 10-11, 1956," p. 10. CPA.

78. "Minutes, Board.. May 20, 1958," p. 11. CPA. Cahaney reported that "about 35" associate members had been lost in the past year. "Minutes, Officers ... January 15, 1959," p. 1. CPA. Doyle reported at this meeting that a market guide for writers was in preparation for Associate Members. This type of service has continued to the present.

79. Proceedings... 1944, p. 53. CPA. The reader is reminded that Baldus had suggested the drive in the first instance. Desmond's suggestion is found in "Minutes, Board.. October 10, 1947," p. 1. The 1947-1948 successes are noted in "Minutes, Board ... May 19, 1948," p. 125; Reid's suggestion in ibid., May 18, 1956, p. 1; and his appointment as chairman in "Minutes, Officers... July 12, 1956," p. 4. All in CPA.

80. The early work of the committee can be traced through Memo: Chairman Richard Reid to All Members,

Life Membership Committee, September 5, 1956; "Minutes, Board.. October 10-11, 1956," pp. 7-9; Ibid., January 21, 1957, pp. 1-7. Gorman's letter to Randall is dated January 24, 1957. All in CPA.

81. "Minutes, Officers... March 1, 1957," pp. 1-4. CPA.

82. "Minutes, Board.. March 15, 1957," pp. 1-5. CPA.

83. "Report of the President," May 14, 1957, pp. 5-7; "Report on [sic] Special Committee on CPA Life Memberships," to Board of Directors, February 13, 1958. Both in CPA.

84. "Minutes, Board.. February 13-14, 1958," pp. 3-5. The committee report had suggested chairmen and recommended the name. Fink's acceptance is noted in "Minutes, Officers... July 17, 1958," p. 1, and his troubles in ibid., January 15, 1959, p. 3. All in CPA.

85. "Minutes, Board.. May 15, 1959," p. 7; Ibid., September 25, 1959, p. 4; Ibid., January 5-6, 1961, p. 4. All mention contacts with Lilly. DC. In "Dues Study Committee" to Board of Directors Meeting, November 21-22, 1963, Holub laments the abandonment of the fund-raising endeavor. PC.

86. "Report of the Executive Secretary" to the Board of Directors, May 7, 1953, p. 4. CPA.

87. There is a copy of this with "Minutes, Board.. November 11, 1954. CPA.

88. "Minutes, Board.. January 5-6, 1961," pp. 6-11. CPA.

89. Rev. John Reedy (CSC), "Self-Promotion Plan for the Catholic Press," May 15, 1962. PC. In 1964 Reedy who had been asked to serve on another CPA committee declined in a letter to Doyle dated July 9. One reason he gave was lack of action taken on committee reports. He mentioned this particular plan which he recalled he had "submitted to the Board in the Spring of 1962--without ever hearing anything of its fate." CPA.

90. William Holub, "Address to Regional Convention of CPA," Fall, 1965, p. 1. CC.

91. Rev. John Reedy (CSC), "The Purposes and Policies of the Catholic Press Association - A Position Paper," n. d. CC.

92. CJ, XVII (July, 1966), pp. 9-10 reported the convention action.

93. Ibid. (October, 1966), pp. 3, 9, and 11 reported the Des Plaines meeting.

94. Other recommendations made by participants were implemented. These included a thorough study of the News Service, advisory committees for consultant services, survey of salary scales and the like in the Catholic Press, and publication of a standard style book. "Executive Director's Report," Spring, 1967. AMF.

95. "Constitution and By laws [sic] of the Catholic Press Association of the United States," 1942. CPA.

96. "Constitution and By-Laws Catholic Press Association of the United States, Inc."-Revised to May 15, 1968. CPA.

97. "The Constitution of the Catholic Press Association of the United States and Canada," 1916, p. 5. CC. "Constitution and By-laws [sic] of the Catholic Press Association of the United States," 1942. CPA.

98. "Minutes, Board...October 30 and 31, 1942," p. 4; "Minutes, Board...October 18, 1943," p. 4. WC. The proposal was made at the earlier meeting and the fact that it had been accomplished was reported in 1943. "Certificate of Change of Name," June 19, 1943. CPA. The document was signed for the CPA by President Wey and Secretary Kriebs.

99. Kane to Secretary of State, Albany, N. Y., January 12, 1953; Victor Wirth of Department of State to Kane, January 14, 1953; "Certificate of Annulment of Dissolution, Reinstatement and Report of Corporate Existence of The Catholic Press Association of the

United States, Inc.," January 20, 1953; Kane to Andrew McGivney (CPA General Counsel), January 26, 1953. All in CPA. The dissolution was merely a legal technicality.

100. Requests for the change were many. Memos and letters dating from July of 1955 to June of 1956 are in the DC. The official request is noted in "Minutes, Board... November 3, 1955," p. 10. Approval is found in ibid., October 10-11, 1956, pp. 4-5. "Minutes, Board... September 22, 1958," p. 10 records that the motion was rescinded. All minutes in CPA.

101. "Minutes, Board... October 7, 1964," p. 2. PC.

Chapter VI

Business Affairs

Fortunately, the question of its proper legal title did not interfere with the activities of the CPA during this period. Among these concerns the more important involved business matters relating to publication costs, advertising, and circulation, as well as the almost perennial involvement in efforts to procure newsprint and to stymie Congressional action intended to increase second class postal rates.

The problem of publishing costs had always plagued Catholic publications, but World War II gave an added boost to all costs and made the position of the publishers even more precarious. Simon A. Baldus, addressing a 1942 convention session of magazine editors, claimed that the periodical publishing business had suffered particularly from the economic conditions brought on by the war. He pointed out that not only had costs gone up but that income had also diminished through losses in advertising revenue and an overall decrease in the purchasing ability of the American consumer. Baldus, suggesting that raising rates would result in a large number of cancellations, advised that it might be better for Catholic publications to streamline departments and make a concerted effort to increase circulation by offering readers a better and more attractive product.[1] An indication that the editors agreed is found by examining subscription prices of the period. The 1943 Catholic Press Directory shows that most Catholic weeklies of that year were listed at one or two dollars, and the most popular monthlies ranged from two to five dollars. In the Directory published two years later, these rates remained virtually unchanged.[2]

By early 1947, however, Secretary James A. Shanahan reported to the membership: "Catholic newspapers all over the country have been forced to increase the subscription price of their publication due to increased running costs, ..." The trend continued with the coming of the Korean conflict. In 1950 James F. Kane reported: "The pinch of pyramiding costs is beginning to hurt Catholic publishers too. Upward revisions in circulation price of Catholic newspapers have already been announced,... " Kane, however, advocated rate increases as an alternative to lowering editorial quality or taking other steps that might result in an inferior product.[3] Again the editors seemed to agree. Thirty-one newspapers had raised subscription prices by 1952, and the median rate had reached three dollars. Kane restated his view recommending "prompt price increases" and arguing that "Our readers, and the Church... cannot get continued editorial improvement today without paying more."[4] By 1954 fifty-nine of the Catholic weeklies were charging three dollars per year, "an increase of more than 135 per cent over the 25 papers shown in the first subscription survey made in 1951." In the survey the following year three dollars remained the prevalent rate, but twenty-five weeklies cost more than that. Four years earlier the number of weeklies costing more than three dollars had been six.[5]

G. Roger Cahaney, Kane's successor, believed that the CPA's annual surveys accounted in part for the increase in rates; he also admitted that the central office had emphasized the surveys to encourage papers to "bring their rates into closer alignment with" their publication costs.[6] Cahaney's studies continued, and so did the rate increases. By 1956 only nine papers were still charging under three dollars per year, and a short twelve months later, although the three dollar category remained the largest, there was a decided increase in the number raising rates to three and one-half or even four dollars. By the end of the next decade, most Catholic weeklies listed their annual subscription price as either four or five dollars.[7]

One reason that the subscription rates continued their upward climb was that efforts to attract national advertising were unsuccessful. Advertising Round Tables occupied much of the attention of convention delegates in 1939 and 1940, and sessions on advertising were included in numerous conventions from then until the present. In 1947 Secretary Shanahan, planning a national advertising service beginning with the newspapers and then moving into the magazine field, mailed a questionnaire to the members. Returns showed such a disparity of rates that he was unable to carry out this project.[8]

Catholic publications sometimes complicated the advertising issue by accepting questionable copy. Kane late in

1951 urged editors to "blue pencil doubtful ad copy" as readily as they struck out unacceptable editorial material. Discussing the same subject in 1954, Donald Thorman argued that "significant numbers of Catholic publications" were selective in the type of advertisements used. He emphasized that the dilemma demanded united rather than independent action and called for a positive approach suggesting a national Catholic advertising council that would issue a stamp of approval on proposed advertisements. A speaker at a 1957 convention session maintained that questionable advertisements would undoubtedly "diminish the effect" of the editorial matter and asked that copy accepted be such that it not "conflict with" the basic purposes of the publication. Two years later Robert G. Hoyt, while admitting that some Catholic publications were still harboring distasteful ads, noted that financial conditions were the root cause. His solution was to improve the product editorially to the point where it would attract numerous readers thereby making it a marketable medium for worthwhile advertising.[9]

In the 1960's a CPA Advertising Sales Study Committee chaired by Msgr. John S. Randall recommended a research program of the American Catholic market. The directors appropriated a thousand dollars in the fall of 1964 to be used in furthering the study. Although the committee continued its investigations, it received little support from the board, and advertising personnel who were interested primarily in the present situation complained that they were being over-looked in the convention programs.[10] Emphasis thus moved from the theoretical to the practical, and the board arranged for advertising sessions to be held in conjunction with the 1966 regional meetings. The Toronto Convention of the following year also included a full-scale advertising seminar on its agenda.[11]

Despite avid interest in ways and means of securing advertising, a number of Catholic publishers were for many years reluctant to disclose the circulation figures of their publications. In 1914 the Audit Bureau of Circulation had been organized by publishers, advertisers, and advertising agencies, and it issued periodical statements regarding the circulation of its members providing verified figures to potential advertisers. By 1940 many advertisers refused to consider buying space in publications not giving ABC circulation figures. The obvious advantages of submitting to an ABC audit notwithstanding, Catholic publishers held aloof. The Evangelist of Albany, New York, had joined as early as 1927, but by 1940 a mere half-dozen held membership.[12] Leaders in the CPA tried to convince their fellow members that identification with ABC would be to the best interests of individual papers as well as to the Catholic Press as a whole. Writing in one of the early issues of the CPA house organ, Vice president Alexander J. Wey asked: "In the presence of this fundamental circulation yardstick,... isn't it a bit unreasonable to expect the national advertiser to take our word for it,... that we have so many paid subscribers?" Wey was speaking from experience since the Cleveland paper with which he was affiliated was an ABC member. He explained the advantages of the audit reports and concluded: "A. B. C. membership should help immeasurably to gain for the Catholic press the respect and the business it deserves from local as well as national advertisers."[13]

Delegates to the 1941 and 1943 conventions heard a representative of ABC explain that association and benefits of membership in it. In questioning the speaker, the editors, concerned because of their limited budgets, concentrated on cost. The speaker assured them that this item was not prohibitive. Attention was drawn also to the advisability of group action. At the earlier convention, Wey stressed this aspect of ABC membership, and at the second meeting the ABC agent urged his listeners to "adopt a united front" as the best means of winning both national and local advertising.[14]

One of the obstacles to membership on the part of Catholic publications was the ABC's definition of "paid circulation." The Bureau insisted that the purchaser (that is, the reader or subscriber,) must himself pay at least half the listed subscription price.[15] Many Catholic newspapers were not sold directly to individual subscribers but in bulk lots for sale at church doors or in a "full coverage" circulation plan, and ABC officials were reluctant to modify their regulations to include these categories. The "full coverage" arrangement, an effort to get the Catholic weekly into all Catholic homes, was of most concern to CPA members since it had become very prevalent by the late 1940's. Sometimes the pastor entered a subscription for each of his parishioners using either general funds or money obtained through a special collection. Accordingly, the publication was not meeting the ABC specification. In the early 1950's CPA officials initiated action hoping to remove this barrier. In the fall of 1951 a committee from the Association, appointed to meet with an ABC committee, reported that the Bureau had agreed to establish a new category for the religious press. President Francis A. Fink told the 1952 convention that three meetings had been held on the matter and that the religious classification, along with provision for the one hundred per cent parish subscription plan, would be instituted within the year.[16]

Changes were slow in coming. Secretary Kane, at the October board meeting, deplored the fact "that CPA has failed generally to follow up its earlier vigorous efforts on this point," and in May the outgoing board "resolved that the succeeding Board of Directors should continue to press for a favorable decision" regarding this matter.[17] The new board re-activated a committee to negotiate with ABC and to act with other religious publications seeking the same goal. A cooperative Committee of the Religious Press was formed with Msgr. Randall as chairman, and in December H. H. Kynett, chairman of the ABC committee, wrote the priest that his committee had decided to recognize the religious press as a separate classification. Acknowledging that the solution reached in 1952 was the most acceptable one, he advised Randall that the Bureau would make a decision in March regarding both the bulk and the "congregation-wide" sales.[18] This time the vote was favorable, but CPA members failed to show appreciation for the new listing. Eight months after the break-through was an accomplished fact, an ABC official commented: "... no applications have been received from any of the Catholic publications since the new rule... was adopted, neither have we received a single inquiry." The situation remained unchanged even through the convention of the following year.[19] For the next few years a CPA committee attempted to recruit members for ABC. A brochure describing the service of the Bureau was distributed to the 1956 convention members. During the following year letters were sent to non-members by both ABC and CPA committees, but in general results were disappointing.[20]

One reason that interest in ABC abated was that a new advertising problem had won the attention of CPA members. The Standard Rate and Data Service (SRDS) had been listing Catholic newspapers in its magazine consumer book causing confusion among advertising media groups and had limited listings to such Catholic newspapers as held membership in ABC. A special ABC-SRDS committee named by President Charles J. McNeill in 1954 recommended that SRDS insert a special section in its daily newspaper book for

Catholic weekly newspapers and remove the restriction regarding ABC membership.[21] The president of SRDS agreed that the listing was misleading and promised to study the CPA proposal. As negotiations continued for several months, Catholic weeklies were listed temporarily in SRDS's weekly newspaper book. At last the committee announced that an agreement had been reached whereby CPA-ABC members would be listed free of charge in the SRDS weekly newspaper book published twice a year while subscribing members would also be included in the daily newspaper book issued each month.[22]

Thirty-five papers, approximately one-third of the diocesan weeklies, participated in the new project and sponsored a two-color insert divider for their section.[23] This number remained static despite sporadic promotional efforts by the ABC-SRDS Committee, in part because all CPA committees "automatically disbanded at convention time each year." Some members felt that greater continuity in effort would be achieved if the national office, rather than a committee, would handle SRDS listings, billings, and other details.[24] In the spring of 1959 the ABC-SRDS Committee recommended that SRDS committee work be transferred permanently to the central office.[25] But the SRDS Committee remained active, and in the fall of 1962 the board decided that one of the papers using the service should handle the listings or that the member publications should themselves find other means of carrying out the necessary work. Still, it was later agreed that billing and collecting could be channelled through the CPA office.[26] This was done until the convention of 1968 at which time the financial statement showed that CPA was servicing SRDS members at a loss, and the board decreed that since so few papers were involved, SRDS accounts would be turned over to a new advertising sales organization then being formed independently of CPA.[27]

Throughout this period Catholic newspaper publishers were often involved in organized endeavors to attract national advertisers. Usually these attempts, though not CPA sponsored, were discussed at board meetings and conventions, and leaders were invariably members of the Association. One of the first of these ventures began in the Eastern Regional Meeting of 1952 when members considered banding together to obtain advertising. As one condition was that all papers in the area must join, and not all the delegates had come with the authority to commit their publications to such a plan, the projected advertising service did not materialize.[28]

About the same time Wey had been urging Kane, who had announced his resignation as executive secretary, to establish himself as a national advertising representative for Catholic newspapers. Executives of the New England advertising agency, Newspaper Representatives, contacted Kane and invited him to join their firm and work through their office. Evaluating this offer as "the best chance Catholic papers have ever had to get national advertising,"[29] Kane drew up a proposal for the project, suggested that it be called the Catholic Advertising Service, and included not only the publications in the Eastern Region but also those in the Middle Atlantic area and the District of Columbia. Four interested publishers meeting informally with Kane in December ruled that the advertising agency should be called Catholic Newspaper Representatives but in other respects accepted Kane's proposal. Constituting themselves into a Publishers' Sponsoring Committee, the men scheduled a meeting for all Catholic newspapers in February and decided that since the bishops owned most of the newspaper press, Episcopal Chairman Thomas K. Gorman should be invited.[30]

At the February meeting newspaper members of CPA "voted overwhelmingly" to support the CNR plan, and Bishop Gorman promised his active assistance. Humphrey E. Desmond, however, warned the publishers not to expect "any great return" in the early stages of the project. Although the CNR members all belonged to the CPA, the venture was not under the auspices of the Association so the sponsoring group was retained under a new title, Publishers' Advisory Committee.[31] The advertising agency published a brochure giving statistics on the Catholic market, circulation figures, and advertising rates. But interest soon waned among the members who seemed to forget Desmond's admonition. Only twenty-four newspapers sent representatives to a CNR meeting held at the close of the 1954 convention, and the group disbanded when the contract between the members and the CNR terminated a year later.[32]

Still hoping to keep the newspapers united in the advertising effort, Kane drew up another proposal reminding the publishers that some success had been achieved despite the many difficulties encountered: "The alternative to action is defeatist inaction; a refusal to tackle problems because they're hard must result eventually in decay and defeat."

Wey also pleaded that the project not be abandoned: "We are at the stage where smooth and uninterrupted continuity of our effort must be sought, or our equity in the initial cooperative effort will be lost."[33] CNR members met in April, 1955, and heard a message from Bishop Gorman urging them "to continue their cooperative advertising efforts." Although thirty-two of the forty-three affiliated papers voted to accept Kane's new proposal, the plan was abandoned since some of the larger papers from major cities refused to cooperate.[34] President McNeill told the convention that year that he "bitterly" regretted this action and labeled it "a sad thing for the Catholic press." At a session held in conjunction with the same convention, the newspapermen did vote to continue the Publishers' Advisory Committee and commissioned it to "explore the possibilities" of establishing a successor to the defunct CNR.[35]

By October the committee had set up the Catholic Newspaper Advertising Bureau (CNAB) with thirty-one members under contract for two years. CNAB consisted primarily of a centrally located information service rather than a direct sales agency and was intended "to save the good will built by CNR and to maintain among potential advertisers an awareness of the Catholic newspaper market."[36] The director of the service, Thomas F. Murphy, addressed a session of the 1956 convention on "What is the C. N. A. B. ?" By October, 1957, the question was irrelevant, for the organization had passed from the scene, to be succeeded by still another plan, Catholic Family Newspapers (CFN). Forty-one members comprised this group which was represented by the New York firm of Bogner and Martin.[37] By January of 1959 CFN membership had reached fifty, but within five years this group had gone the way of its predecessors, and Msgr. Randall's request that the national office establish an answering service to handle newspaper advertising was rejected.[38]

In October of 1967 the persevering Msgr. Randall presented another proposal. Twenty-five papers wanted to organize and seek national advertising; Randall asked that they be allowed to operate through the national office. Though approved, his plan was later modified, and the Catholic Major Markets Newspaper Association came into being. It occupied office space on the same floor as the CPA headquarters and relied on the Association staff for telephone coverage for a brief period each day.[39]

Advertisers who wanted their sales material to reach as many potential buyers as possible naturally looked for publications with large and widespread readership. CPA members had been struggling since the Association's founding to build up circulation, but were caught in a vicious circle--to increase circulation one had to have money; to get money advertising was needed; but advertisers in turn demanded a big circulation. Everything seemed to conspire against small papers. Their problems in maintaining standards of professional competence had an adverse effect on circulation. Geographic and ecclesiastical limitations also affected the distribution of Catholic publications. Though this was particularly true of the diocesan weeklies, specialized magazines (such as those devoted to missions, devotions, children, etc.), encountered a similar restriction. Only the general magazines, journals of opinion, and the national weeklies had a large potential market; but even the national Catholic market was limited by the educational background of the Catholic population.[40]

Surveys conducted in the late 1950's concluded that there was still a great circulation potential to be cultivated. A study of the diocesan weeklies showed that their average coverage was but thirty-nine per cent of the Catholic population, and although Catholics numbered about one-fifth of the population of the United States in 1959, the total circulation of all Catholic magazines being published that year did not equal that of the "combined top three in the secular field."[41] Nonetheless, circulation figures have increased steadily over the years. Whereas less than six million copies were circulated in 1920, the figure had moved closer to seven million in 1930 and to almost nine million ten years later. The following decades witnessed a large increase with fifteen million approximated in 1950, twenty-six million by 1960, and close to twenty-eight million at present.[42]

Some of the increases could be attributed to population growth, but much was due to the determination and efforts of the Catholic journalists. In the early years of the Association, direct mail promotion was supplemented by solicitors and subscription agencies. These led to so many abuses that it became necessary to name a Circulation Vigilance Committee and establish a bureau to investigate questionable agents. Field selling continued to be used especially by the magazine publishers, and in June 1951, the United States Supreme Court heard a test case involving door-to-door solicitation. When the decision in Breard vs. Alexandria,

Louisiana, upheld a local ordinance outlawing such selling methods, a number of towns and cities at once began formulating legislation of this type referred to under the general name of Green River Ordinances.[43]

The CPA joined other national groups in fighting this legislation. Secretary Kane, while admitting that abuses sometimes occurred in direct selling, maintained that these were not serious enough to "justify vicious and ill-conceived legislation that threatens basic American liberties."[44] At its fall meeting, the board agreed that such ordinances would cause "extreme hardship" for some of the CPA member publications. In a resolution calling an ordinance pending in the Chicago area "odious" and a danger to freedom of the press, the board condemned "in principle" any such ordinances and called on its members to unite with other agencies in using "all lawful means to oppose them..."[45] The national office distributed to the publishers involved a packet of literature on the issue supplied by the National Association of Magazine Publishers. Msgr. Joseph B. Lux of Extension Magazine led the fight against the Green River Ordinance in Chicago, and Peter B. Wiethe, OFM, of St. Anthony Messenger took the issue to the Midwest Regional Meeting for consideration and discussion. In general, the effort proved very effective.[46]

By this time, however, other ways of obtaining subscriptions were far more popular than the use of agents in the field. As early as 1939 and 1940 Circulation Round Tables held as part of the annual conventions featured papers on several of these methods and discussed the techniques involved. Some still advocated direct mail contacts as well as agents, but most of the attention was given to bulk sales at church doors, campaigns involving school children, and the full coverage or one hundred per cent plans. Bulk sales which required the cooperation of the pastors and promotional talks from the pulpits could result in substantial financial savings by the publishers, but the Catholic editors noticed that the first element was sometimes difficult to secure since pastors hesitated to sponsor a plan that could inflict a financial loss if parishioners became careless about taking copies without paying for them.[47] To carry out the second plan, the publishers had to obtain the authorization of the bishop and of the superintendent of schools as well as the interest and cooperation of the staffs of the schools involved. Once this was achieved, it was usually "very advantageous... easy of operation... economical... successful... [and of] educational value." Individual prizes were given to children selling a designated number of subscriptions, and additional awards were usually allocated to the schools as incentives for participation.[48] The full parish plan flourished only where the pastors were actively interested in the Catholic Press. As first used, parishioners were contacted for individual subscriptions, and then provisions were made for those who were either unwilling or unable to pay.[49]

The full parish coverage gradually developed into the one hundred per cent plan or complete diocesan circulation which some dioceses introduced in the 1930's.[50] After Bishop John Mark Gannon presented such a plan during his term as Episcopal Chairman of the Press Department of NCWC, complete diocesan coverage became more common. Parish collections financed the subscriptions and papers were mailed directly to Catholic homes by the diocesan paper using lists submitted by the pastors. Although the editors favored this method, some pastors objected, and the parish collections presented the biggest obstacle. Ultimately, the one hundred per cent plan prospered, but more often than not individual subscriptions were first solicited as had been customary earlier in the full parish coverage method.[51]

Because they could not rely on parish or diocesan support and no one hundred per cent plan was possible, magazines had a much more difficult time than newspapers in devising circulation schemes. Specialized magazines appealed only to certain groups, and the general magazines were too numerous for any one of them to have a large circulation. Necessarily, they had to continue direct sales methods or employ field agents. Too often content was inferior, and magazines were sold not on any inherent qualities but as a means of supporting apostolic works or promoting certain religious devotions. Some publications perpetuated the image by bribing subscribers with cheap premiums which suggested that the publication itself was not worth the subscription price.[52] Perhaps due to this proliferation of magazines or because of a keener competitive spirit arising from an open sales territory, Catholic magazine publishers made fewer attempts at organized sales endeavors than did the newspaper publishers. Nonetheless, their circulation problems were more serious, the discontinuation of magazines was common, and the situation has become even more acute in the recent past.

Cooperative efforts attempted were basically unsuccessful and therefore short-lived. Following the 1953 convention a resolution drawn up by magazine circulation managers interested in attempting to secure wider circulation by means of church door sales was presented to the board. Although the directors expressed appreciation of and encouragement for the proposal, they insisted that the promotional literature of the organization should not contain references to the CPA.[53] A year later the group had organized the Catholic Periodicals Cooperative with the goal of promoting sales through the use of racks in parish churches. Eight magazine members and two general Catholic publishers comprising the cooperative scheduled a private meeting during the convention that year.[54] This project proved ineffective as did similar attempts, but another plan flourished for a few years in the 1940's and 50's, creating in the process one of the major controversies in the history of the CPA.

During the 1940's secular publishers instituted school circulation plans operating much like the student campaigns of the Catholic newspapers. Soon some of the Catholic publishers added their magazines to the listings of the two leading plans, Curtis and Crowell, even though others noted that such campaigns sold "relatively few Catholic magazines" and were actually detrimental to Catholic circulation plans.[55] At the same time a number joined the Catholic Digest's National Catholic Decency in Reading Program promoted through Catholic schools.[56] When the CPA met in 1950, the Catholic Digest held a special magazine session and urged that those connected with the secular school plans sever these ties and support its plan. Some of the Catholic publishers, interpreting this action as an attempt to gain a monopoly in the Catholic field, refused to heed the request.[57] Nevertheless, the Digest plan prospered, paralleling the success of the Catholic Digest itself for a number of years. Whereas slightly over ten thousand subscriptions to Catholic magazines were obtained in 1945, by 1957 that number had climbed to almost three hundred thousand.[58] Toward the end of that period, the influential Catholic publishers who had remained with Curtis sponsored with that company a plan called the St. Thomas Aquinas Reader Service for sales in the Catholic field.[59]

In the early fall of 1957, a circular entitled "The Magazine School Plans--An Evaluation" was distributed to a number of CPA members independently of the Association. The unsigned statement examined financial aspects of these plans, noted that there had been "a complete lack of group scrutiny" of them, and repeated the earlier argument that school plans which included secular magazines were "detrimental to the Catholic press as a whole." It also charged that Catholic magazines were being used as a "door opener" for a much larger volume of secular publications, and called for "a sincere, open and honest study of the magazine school plans."[60] Although the document referred to all such plans operating in Catholic schools at the time, only the National Catholic Decency in Reading Program reacted to it openly. Father Bussard, publisher of the Catholic Digest, in the December issue of that magazine made a statement about the Digest plan explaining to his readers that sixty-one Catholic and seventy-one so-called "secular" magazines participated and that, in effect, the secular publications were under-writing the cost of the Catholic magazines distributed in this way.[61]

Later in the month Bussard sent a letter to Catholic publications along with his appraisal of the original evaluation. Though it was then generally known that the author was John Reedy, CSC, Bussard stated that "several others" were involved, and he named James F. Kane as the priest's "consultant." That same month the officers of CPA discussed two aspects of the controversy: first, that the school plans violated a section of the Code of Fair Publishing Practices adopted by the membership in 1955; second, a suggestion that the board "consider a motion of censure against the known authors both for the content of the Evaluation and for the method of its distribution."[62] The Association's legal counsel, Thomas A. Brennan, reporting that the CPA had the right to take action in such a situation, recommended that a "special committee of people with high standing and prestige in the Catholic press" be named as a fact-finding group to examine benefits and liabilities deriving to Catholic publications using the plans. The board at the February meeting took this action naming Brennan as committee chairman. Reporting this decision to the membership, Msgr. Randall stressed that it was done in answer to the many letters received requesting action and with the approval of the two parties involved.[63]

Shortly thereafter Kane issued his statement on the plans. Denying co-sponsorship of the original evaluation, he gave the historical background of the subject and asked a number of pointed questions concerning the operation, rebate percentages, and apathy of most of the publishers involved in the plans. He asserted that secular magazines comprised eighty per cent of the sales volume and that fifty per cent of the Catholic sales were for the Catholic Digest. Kane echoed Father Reedy's call for an open discussion on "the basic issues" and urged "responsible and diligent over-seeing of the school plan operations" by those participating in them.[64] In May the fact-finding committee made its report to the board. The conclusions were meager, the committee hoping by restraint "to restore amity and confidence and harmony to the Association and to eliminate any ill feelings that may have resulted." Questioning whether the committee had actually tried "to conduct an impartial investigation," a director suggested that it had rather worked "to arbitrate a feud." But several others agreed that the controversy was harmful to the well-being of the CPA and should be quieted as quickly and as unobtrusively as possible. The board decided to give little attention to the report at the general meeting and to take no other action beyond presenting the report of the committee to the two parties concerned with the reminder that they had agreed to accept its conclusions.[65]

After President Randall gave a brief history of the school plan controversy to the opening general session of the convention, Brennan repeated his report to the members. The discussion that followed was very general and calm, but the matter was brought up again at the closing general session. A member who stated that he represented others dissatisfied with the report of the fact-finding committee charged that the report contained "no facts" but merely "two generalized conclusions." He moved that the matter be re-investigated and a new report containing actual facts on the situation be drawn up. A voice vote proved inconclusive as did a show of hands. Finally, a roll call vote was requested, and the motion lost by four votes.[66] Supposedly the issue was closed. Nonetheless, the strife continued with Catholic newspapers carrying stories on the school plans in the fall, and Father Bussard and other supporters of this method attempting to refute the arguments presented.[67]

In the spring of 1959 at meetings hosted by the Digest in Chicago and New York, Father Bussard told the participants that the contention over the school plans had resulted in a combined total decrease of one million in circulation plus about one hundred ten thousand dollars financial loss to his magazine. He intimated that criticism of the plan had been supported chiefly by small publishers hopeful of obtaining control of the CPA by securing a majority of directors on the board. Thus, the main topic of these gatherings was not the school plan itself but the larger issue of Association leadership. The Digest faction asserted that too many of the board members were "young" and "inexperienced" and that the directors had been overly involved in "areas of censorship and punitive powers." They determined to present a united front and to support a slate of candidates for the annual elections at the coming convention.[68] This they did. Moreover, the Digest secured the election figures and published them, contrary to the usual policy of secrecy. This greatly disturbed a number of the members, and another series of editorials on the school plans appeared in the general Catholic Press.[69]

In November of 1959 Archbishop William O. Brady of St. Paul, Minnesota, home of the Catholic Digest, wrote Father Bussard that the bishops regretted the controversy and particularly "its too long continued acrimony." He informed the priest that Bishop Albert R. Zuroweste as Episcopal Chairman "would see to it" that the matter was closed within the CPA. Assuring the publisher that the bishops found "nothing contrary to good morals" in the Decency in Reading Program, he asked only that the permission of the local ordinary and of pastors be obtained before introducing the program into any locality.[70] As the school plans continued to suffer serious losses, the Catholic Digest presented its resignation to the CPA central office in December of 1961. But in the spring of 1962, the annual CPA convention established a Board of the National Decency in Reading Program with Bishop Zuroweste as honorary president. A year later this board, representing seventy publications, sponsored a Circulation Seminar just before the annual convention.[71] The directors of the Association took belated action regarding the school plans when in January of 1964 Secretary Doyle circulated a statement by the board which referred to the 1958 study of them and noted that the special committee had at that time reported favorably concerning the plans. The statement concluded with a recommendation that "...pastors in Dioceses where the Ordinary and school officials permit school plans to operate... use this method to encourage their people to subscribe to Catholic periodicals in addition to the Diocesan paper,..." When Bishop Clarence Issenmann became Episcopal Chairman he, too, endorsed the school plans.[72] The reason for this change in policy was not that the Catholic Digest's position had at last been vindicated, but rather that the Catholic magazines had encountered serious circulation problems and every effort possible was being made to prevent further losses.

By the time that the CPA members assembled for their 1962 meeting, the general downward trend of most magazines was already cause for grave concern. Outgoing president, Father Albert J. Nevins, deplored the situation and recommended that a letter be sent to all members of the hierarchy asking for their support and assistance. The board heeded his advice, and magazine publishers united behind the proposed board for the National Catholic Decency in Reading Program referred to above.[73] Father Nevins, addressing a magazine session a year later, presented magazine circulation figures beginning in 1958 and labeled the trend "unexpected and alarming." While "intellectual" magazines were on the increase, and the mission organs in fair condition, general Catholic magazines and those in the juvenile field were definitely down. He also found that during the five year period sixty Catholic magazines had discontinued publication. Calling for "immediate action," Nevins asked that the hierarchy be alerted to the situation and recommended that the CPA establish a Catholic Magazine Promotion Committee.[74] A special meeting of the officers and past presidents held in the spring of 1964 discussed the situation as did the board at its fall meeting that year. The directors allocated two thousand dollars to the Standing Magazine Committee named to draw up a survey on magazine circulation in answer to Father Nevin's proposal. The situation continued to deteriorate so that by the winter of 1966 a report to the board characterized the Catholic magazine field as being in "a state of crisis" and in need of "professional help."[75]

Part of the problem, of course, was that times had changed so much that the secular press in certain instances was competing with Catholic publications in treating religious news. Also, some editors who had tried to change the nature of their magazines to bring them into closer accord with Vatican II had alienated their traditional readers, while those who postponed change were deserted by the up-dated Catholics. Members of the CPA magazine committee discussed all these aspects at a special winter meeting in January of 1968 and approved a letter to be sent to members of the hierarchy. Accompanying the letter was material supplied by the CPA national office explaining that ten Catholic magazines had ceased publication during the past year alone. Declaring that Catholic magazines were actually improved "in format, content, [and] impact," it urged that bishops actively promote the religious magazines and even discuss the problem in the priests' senates in the various dioceses.[76]

Although securing advertising was mainly a concern of newspapers,[77] and circulation harassed magazines more than newspapers, both groups were affected by difficulties regarding print paper. Major newsprint problems continued over a period of approximately fifteen years extending roughly from 1942 to 1957 and were of two types: the difficulty of procuring an adequate supply of paper for publishing purposes and consistent price increases. Both aspects of this problem had caused intermittent disturbances since the founding of the CPA, but they assumed added significance with the outbreak of World War II. Since the demand for paper soon outdistanced the supply, the newly formed War Production Board named a Newspaper Industry Advisory Committee in October of 1942. Following the advice of this group, conservation measures were enacted, including in January of 1943, the WPB orders (L-240 and L-244) restricting newspapers to the amount of paper they had used in 1941 and reducing magazine paper consumption by ten per cent.[78]

Because the CPA was not represented on the NIAC, President Wey appealed the case of the Catholic publishers and was informed that L-240 was intended to curtail the amount of paper used by "the multi-page metropolitan daily newspapers." A Print Paper Committee named by Wey met with WPB officials and was promised that the Catholic Press would receive "fair and generous treatment." By December the WPB was forecasting that paper shortages would become even more acute and would surely continue after the war ended.[79] Catholic publishers joined their secular counterparts in salvage campaigns and in additional conservation measures. Several of the newspapers adopted a tabloid format, and magazines not only changed print type and paper weight, but also reduced the number of pages per issue in efforts to make better use of the amount of available paper.[80] Shortages did indeed remain even after the war ceased. Secretary Shanahan reported to the members in September of 1945 that revocation of L-240 before the end of the year "would produce a chaotic condition." When rationing ended, Catholic newspapers generally were not able to get extra tonnage.[81]

The Senate Committee on Small Business conducted a hearing in March of 1947 regarding the newsprint situation.

Representing CPA was Father Randall who urged an "equitable distribution" of available stock among all concerned. President Desmond informed the annual convention that such a movement was underway, but a month later Randall, appearing at a hearing of the House of Representatives Select Committee on Newsprint, maintained that conditions had not improved. He again recommended "voluntary cooperation," and he pointed out that paper manufacturers were reluctant to deal with the small publisher at all. The committee chairman assured the priest that his group would foster cooperation among publishers and would work "to establish a larger permanent [paper] supply."[82] Several months later Father Randall reported that the outlook was bleak since Canadian manufacturers were reluctant to invest added capital in equipment because of the "uncertainty of world conditions." In June of 1950 Father Nevins predicted that the situation would "get worse before it improves," explaining that American sources bought eighty per cent of their paper supply from Canada where labor shortages existed in the forests and where a movement was under way toward a greater development of overseas markets.[83]

The situation was intensified by the outbreak of the Korean conflict which was accompanied by "panic buying" by some publishers. Shortly thereafter a Canadian railroad strike caused added difficulties,[84] but the major problem continued to be greatly increased consumption of paper by the United States. While the central office and Randall's Newsprint Committee continued their vigilance, Father Bussard was actively engaged for several months working with Protestant and Jewish press groups so that the religious press might present a united front should government action become necessary. The Newsprint Committee also handled "hardship cases" among the newspaper members, and by early 1952 the outlook was brighter.[85] The relief was only temporary, and when the squeeze tightened again, some CPA members turned to centralized buying as a solution.

The creation of an agency for this purpose was proposed to the board in February of 1954. D. F. McGrann, author of the plan, expected that the organizing company would control a sufficiently large volume of business to enable it to obtain special concessions from producers. The board tabled the proposal at that time, but the Newsprint Committee conducted a survey of paper consumption by the Catholic Press. Although the report was presented to the

1955 convention, no action followed. In November Msgr. Randall told the board that the newsprint situation was critical, and he urged that the directors re-consider McGrann's proposal. After stipulating that any such venture must be independent of the CPA, the board empowered the Newsprint Committee to continue negotiations with McGrann. Shortages continued into 1956, but by May of the following year conditions had eased to the point where a surplus was expected by 1958. Partly because of this trend, the McGrann proposal was never implemented.[86]

Even when Catholic publishers were able to obtain a sufficient supply of newsprint, they had to contend with ever-increasing prices in that commodity. In 1938 the cost per ton had been fifty dollars, the figure at which the Office of Price Administration froze paper in 1942. Before price controls were removed in 1946, however, the ceiling had risen to eighty-four dollars, and by August of 1948 newsprint manufacturers had advanced it to one hundred dollars.[87] Although paper prices had already doubled in the decade, the increases continued. Canadian manufacturers surprised American publishers by raising the price to one hundred sixteen dollars in mid-1951, and a year later increased it another ten dollars per ton. Msgr. Randall called the 1952 increase "wholly unjustified" and explained that the new price would amount to approximately two hundred fifty thousand dollars a year, constituting "a grave threat to the Catholic press."[88]

Again in 1955 increases evoked strong protests from CPA members. Charging that the augmentation would "wreak havoc" on the religious press, the board issued a strong statement. "From our viewpoint," it concluded, "such an increase is a constriction of trade to the extent that it threatens freedom of the press."[89] Nonetheless, by 1957 paper had reached one hundred thirty-four dollars and remained at that price until 1964 when it was reduced ten dollars per ton, "the first widespread decline in 30 years." The respite was brief; two years later paper manufacturers were contemplating restoring the cut.[90]

Hard hit by the rising cost of newsprint, CPA members were also confronted by the prospect of higher postal rates. This area, too, had been one in which there often had been threats to the financial well-being of the Catholic publishers. These proved relatively minor until March of 1947 when Postmaster General Jesse M. Donaldson proposed that second class rates be increased from the traditional cent and a half to two and one-half cents per pound.[91] CPA President Desmond, appearing before the House of Representatives Committee on Post Office and Civil Service, charged that the proposed rates would "triple the postage bill of the average Catholic publication" and pointed out that less than a half-dozen Catholic publishers could absorb the higher charge "without going into red ink." Estimating that the new rates would cost the Catholic Press a million dollars a year, Desmond told the committee that such a move would curtail religious publications, and therefore be detrimental to the American way of life. Desmond's arguments were "sympathetically received," and approximately three hundred telegrams from his fellow Catholic journalists gave much support to his position. The measure reaching the House floor contained a provision exempting "religious, scientific and educational publications owned and operated by non-profit corporations."[92]

But instead of taking action on this bill, the House decided that the entire postal system should be investigated. Therefore, the issue subsided until 1949 when the Post Office Department, backed by President Harry S. Truman, again attempted to obtain increases including new rates for second class mail.[93] At once the CPA protested. Father Bussard, then president of the Association, appeared before the House committee as had his predecessor. Repeating the arguments used by Desmond, the priest explained that the increases could result in less rather than more revenue from Catholic publications since so many of them would be forced out of business. Asserting that the result would be deprivation in the areas of knowledge and culture, Bussard told the committee: "It would be much wiser to get that additional revenue by renting out a wing of the Library of Congress." Comparing the small Catholic editors to the pioneers and capitalizing on the "Red Scare" of the period, he noted that religious editors were "pushing back the frontiers of light against the evils of darkness and Communistic intolerance." Father Bussard went before the Senate committee the following month, informed it that the Post Office Department had nurtured religious publications by keeping second class rates at a minimum for over a century, and asserted that if the special concessions were now withdrawn, "several hundred publications" which had emerged and continued because of the favorable legislation, would disappear. Other religious publishers agreed with Bussard. The *Register* noted: "Many Protestant editors have declared that the bill would increase postage rates 300 per cent in the first year and an additional 50 per cent in the second year. 'There would be no third year,' one editor commented."[94]

Action on the bill was postponed, but early in 1950 a new measure was reported out of committee which retained the provision for the exemption of religious, educational, and other non-profit organizations. The Senate did not act on this bill, and in 1951 still another effort was made. Because this new measure was not favorable to religious publications and proposed that both second and third class rates be doubled, the CPA joined representatives of Protestant and Jewish publications in testifying before the House committee. This joint action "impressed the Congressmen a great deal," and every member of the committee present at the hearing assured the press group that he would oppose increases affecting religious publications.[95] In addition, CPA members renewed their campaign to alert Congressmen of their wishes, and some urged their readers to do the same.[96] When the convention met, the issue was still undecided, but Secretary Kane told the members: "The unity displayed ... in this instance is the most striking example of the value... and the possibilities inherent in a professional and cooperative approach to your common problems." In November, President Fink notified the members that the bill that had just been signed into law represented "a major victory" for the CPA and estimated that it would save the Catholic Press "three million dollars <u>every year</u>." He also praised the cooperative efforts of the members asserting: "It proves beyond question what results we can achieve when we act together, promptly and decisively, as an Association."[97]

Neither President Truman nor Postmaster General Donaldson was satisfied with the bill, however, and third class exemptions proved to be such a burden to postal officials that they urged that such concessions be dropped. Although a new bill was written in 1953, no action resulted so that it was spring of 1955 before any major change occurred. At that time postal officials requested salary increases, and it was thought that higher rates should cover this new cost. Because of the national elections to be held the following year, the CPA Postal Committee reported in November that there was no immediate danger. Postal bills re-introduced in May of 1956 included the preferred status for religious publications.[98]

Watchful waiting resumed until early in 1958 when another major crisis threatened. The convention that year heard an address by Francis R. Cawley, Vice President of Magazine Publishers Association, Inc., who decried the fact that the federal government seemed unaware of the difficulties of small businesses. Charging that the Administration was attempting to transform the Post Office Department into a business concern when it had been established as a service agency, Cawley advocated that losses incurred through the preferential treatment of non-profit newspapers and magazines be financed by the United States Treasury rather than by increasing rates in other postal categories.[99] William Holub, chairman of the Postal Rates Committee, reported to the fall meeting of the board that the new law had incorporated the preferential rates, asked that the members express appreciation to the Congressmen who had supported the bill, and then requested that they be very careful to "cooperate with their local post offices," particularly in the matter of zoning, so as to retain the good will of postal officials. The following spring Holub suggested that the Association publish a CPA postal manual to assist the members in interpreting postal regulations. Published in April of 1960, the handbook was sent to all members of the Senate and House committees and to Protestant publishing groups as well as to CPA members.[100]

About this time, too, the inter-faith group was reactiviated; it was instrumental in securing favorable postal legislation the following year, and continued to operate as a unit. At Senate hearings in August of 1962, Ford Stewart, publisher of The Christian Herald, and Edward E. Grusd, editor of National Jewish Monthly, joined CPA President Floyd Anderson in protesting against the current postal bill. Anderson, after telling the committee that operating margins of religious publications were so narrow that "What might appear to be even a small increase could be disastrous for many of the publications which our Association represents," appealed to the committee "to keep the religious non-profit press the strong and vital organs of public opinion they are, and ensure their growth by continuing the existing postal rate structure, which has traditionally made this possible."[101] Nonetheless, the draft reported by the Senate committee contained objectional provisions. A prompt and concerted movement by Catholic publishers resulted in a last minute amendment striking out the proposed increases for non-profit religious publications.[102]

The CPA Postal Committee once more assumed its position of watchfulness until the fall of 1964 when Postmaster General John Gronouski considered the possibilities of increases on non-profit publications. Representatives of the inter-faith group visited Gronouski in February to explain the problems of the religious press. They not only found him receptive, but they were also invited to suggest a member of their group to serve on a special advisory committee then being activated. CPA Postal Rates Committee Chairman William Holub was chosen.[103] Nonetheless, Doyle informed the members in August that this new committee had recommended abolishing the preferential rates. Asking members to write their Congressmen in protest, Doyle suggested that they remind them that implementing zip code regulations was already adding to publishers' expenses. This protest action continued into 1967 as did the activities of the inter-faith group. Testifying in June of 1967, members of this group agreed that any increases would have adverse effects on their publications and urged the committee to reconsider.[104]

They were successful to the extent that only minimum increases were approved by the House for third class mail of non-profit publications. But provisions regarding second class matter included a new schedule for the advertising portion of a non-profit publication to begin in 1968 and gradually increase until 1973. In October Holub called the measure then before the Senate "the most drastic yet," and the board mailed letters of protest to all Senators. These were unsuccessful insofar as the graduated schedule was retained, but increases for non-profit publications were placed at a lower level than other categories. The Postal Rate Committee promised to work for an amendment and made plans with the Associated Church Press to produce a new postal manual explaining the latest regulations.[105]

Thus, despite consistent attention to the business problems peculiar to their field and unified action in attacking them, CPA members were not really much better off in these areas in 1968 than they had been thirty years earlier. Obviously, most of these matters would continue to trouble them in the future.

Notes

1. <u>Proceedings... 1942</u>, pp. 51-59 records Baldus' address.

CPA.

2. Joseph F. Wagner, Inc., Catholic Press Directory (New York, 1943 and 1945), passim.

3. CJ, XII (January, 1947), p. 1; Ibid., II (October, 1950), p. 6; and (August, 1951), p. 6.

4. See: Ibid., IV (September, 1952), p. 8 for increases and (December, 1952), p. 6 for Kane's statement.

5. The quotation is from CJ, V (September, 1954), p. 2; the 1955 survey was reported in ibid., VI (September, 1955), p. 2.

6. CJ, VI (September, 1955), p. 6.

7. Ibid., VII (October, 1956), p. 2; Ibid., VIII (September, 1957), p. 1. Catholic Press Directory (New York, 1968-69), passim.

8. Shanahan reported on the survey in CJ, XII (January, 1947), p. 1 and (March, 1947), p. 1. His explanation of the difficulties is in "Minutes, Board.. October 10, 1947," pp. 120-121. CPA.

9. Kane's remark is in CJ, III (November, 1951), p. 6; Donald Thorman, "The Catholic Advertising Dilemma," Catholic World, CLXXVIII (February, 1954), 357-363; the '57 speech was reported in CJ, VIII (July-August, 1957), p. 5; Robert G. Hoyt, "Ads in the Catholic Press," Commonweal, LXIX (February 20, 1959), 538-540.

10. The committee began its work in the fall of 1962 and made various progress reports. A recapitulation of its work can be found in "Advertising Sales Study Committee" report to Board of Directors Meeting, October 7, 1964 (PC). The board's role is from "Minutes, Board..October 7, 1964," pp. 1-2 (PC) and ibid., August 17, 1965, p. 3 (CPA). A representative of the advertising personnel reported to the board following the 1966 convention. See" "Minutes, Board.. May 13, 1966," p. 2 (CPA).

11. "Minutes, Board.. August 4, 1966," p. 4 and Program ...1967 which listed a total of eleven advertising

sessions. Both in CPA.

12. Proceedings... 1940, pp. 21-23, contains an address, "The A. B. C. What It Is And How It Works," which noted the position of advertisers. The same source on pp. 15-20 has a second address by Father Gerald H. Kerwin who identified the other members and gave the dates they had joined as follows: Sunday Visitor, 1934; Catholic Universe Bulletin and Chronicle, 1939; Brooklyn Tablet and Catholic Review, 1940. CPA.

13. Wey's comments on A. B. C. are from In Vain, I (May 10, 1941), p. 3.

14. Cost was discussed in Transcript... 1941, pp. 98-101; group action is from ibid., p. 102 and Proceedings ... 1943, pp. 55-56. CPA.

15. This was explained to the 1941 convention by Carl Gazley of A. B. C. See: Transcript... 1941, pp. 95-96. CPA.

16. Fink announced the new committee in a circular letter to CPA members in late summer of 1951 (CPA); its successes were reported in "Minutes, Board... October 18, 1951," p. 3 (PDF) and Fink, "Report of the President," 42nd Annual Convention, June 19, 1952, pp. 4-5 (CPA).

17. "Minutes, Board... October 24-25, 1952," p. 3 and ibid., May 6, 1953, p. 1. PDF.

18. The new committee was reported in CJ, V (October-November, 1953), p. 5. The ABC decision is from a letter from Kynett to Randall, December 7, 1953. CPA.

19. William F. Hoffmann to Randall, November 23, 1954. Randall reported this to a general session of the convention: "Minutes Opening Business Meeting," May 25, 1955, p. 2. Both in CPA. However, CJ, VI (January, 1955), p. 5 had reported that forty-seven Catholic weeklies and nine magazines held A. B. C. membership--quite an increase over the 1940 figure.

20. "Minutes Opening Business Meeting," May 16, 1956, p. 1 and "ABC-SRDS Committee Report" to convention, May 15, 1957. Both in CPA.

21. "Report of the ABC-SRDS Committee" to Board of Directors, November 11, 1954. CPA.

22. Randall reported the SRDS president's decision in a letter to McNeill, February 15, 1955; "Minutes, Board... May 16, 1956," p. 3 reported the temporary listing (CPA). CJ, VII (September, 1956), p. 4 announced that the new conditions would become effective in October.

23. "ABC-SRDS Committee Report" to Opening Business Meeting, 1957 Convention, May 15, 1957. CPA.

24. The quotation is from a letter to President Daly from Gerald M. McCue under date of February 6, 1959. Other letters containing similar comments are Wey to Daly, March 10, 1959, and Bob Labonge to SRDS Committee, March 18, 1959. All in DC.

25. "ABC-SRDS Committee Report" to Board of Directors, May 12, 1959. CPA.

26. "Minutes, Board... September 20, 1962," p. 1 (PC) and "Minutes, Officers... February 20, 1963," p. 4 (CPA).

27. "Minutes, Board... May 14, 1968," p. 2. CPA. But publications not belonging to the new organization are still taken care of by CPA central office according to Director Doyle in an interview, October 24, 1968.

28. NC Release 11/17/52.

29. James F. Kane, Memo to Catholic Newspaper Publishers on National Advertising Program, November 26, 1952. CPA.

30. James F. Kane, "Supplement to the National Advertising Program for Catholic Newspaper Publishers," December 21, 1952. CPA.

31. The report of the February meeting is from CJ, IV

(March, 1953), pp. 1-2.

32. CC contains a copy of the brochure: "Detailed Analysis of the Catholic Newspaper Markets represented by CNR." The meeting was reported in *CJ*, V (June-July, 1954), p. 7 and the disbanding in *ibid.*, VI (April-May, 1955), p. 7.

33. Kane, Memo to Catholic Newspapers regarding General Advertising Proposal, March 9, 1955; Wey Co-Chairman CNR Publishers Advisory Committee to CNR Member, March 16, 1955. Both in CPA. Humphrey E. Desmond was the Co-chairman.

34. *CJ*, VI (April-May, 1955), p. 7 reported the New York meeting.

35. Charles J. McNeill, "Report of President to Catholic Press Association," 45th Annual Convention, May 25, 1955, p. 4. HC. The special session was reported in NC Release 5/30/55.

36. *CJ*, VI (October-November, 1955), p. 1 announced CNAB. Its purpose was set down in a letter from Thomas F. Murphy to N. J. Morgan, September 28, 1955. CPA.

37. Murphy's address is listed in *Convention Journal and Buyers' Guide*, May 1956, p. 18. CC. Information on CFN is from a reprint of an advertisement from *Advertising Age*, December 9, 1957. DC.

38. *CJ*, X (January, 1959), p. 5; "Minutes, Board.. May 10, 1966," p. 2. CPA. The death of Joseph Bogner, Sr. was in part responsible for the disappearance of CFN according to Director Doyle. Interview, October 24, 1968.

39. "Minutes, Board..October 27, 1967," p. 4 and *ibid.*, January 19, 1968, p. 2. CPA. There are now 22 papers with Catholic Major Markets. Doyle interview, October 24, 1968.

40. An editorial in *America*, XCII (February 5, 1950), 470 maintained: "Inevitably a hundred Catholics will be interested in controversies over parish bingo to every one who wants to know how Catholic social

principles apply to the problem of disposal of U. S. farm surpluses."

41. The diocesan weekly study appeared in CJ, VIII (November, 1957), p. 1. However, an earlier survey reported in C. P. A. Bulletin, II (March, 1943), p. 1 had found only thirty per cent coverage by Catholic weeklies, so the average was gradually rising. Brother Lawrence Gonner, "Facts and Hopes of Our Catholic Press," Social Justice Review, LI (February, 1959), 331 discussed the circulation of Catholic magazines.

42. Early figures are from a circulation table compiled for I am The Catholic Press (San Francisco, 1946), p. 6. WC. Later figures are from the following sources: NC Release 7/28/52; CJ, X (July, 1959), p. 1; and CPA, Catholic Press Directory (New York City, 1968-1969), Inside Back Cover.

43. Reported in CJ, III (October, 1951), p. 2. Green River Ordinances provided "that solicitation may not be made on residential premises without a prior invitation to call." This from CJ, VI (February, 1955), p. 7.

44. Kane's reaction was reported in CJ, III (October, 1951), p. 6.

45. Appended to "Minutes, Board...October 18, 1951." PDF.

46. CJ, III (November, 1951), pp. 1 and 6. Also, ibid., IV (January, 1953), p. 8.

47. Proceedings... 1939, pp. 31-37. CPA.

48. Ibid., pp. 37-42. CPA.

49. Ibid., pp. 42-45. CPA.

50. Proceedings... 1940, pp. 50-54. CPA. Rev. H. H. Ross explained how the Diocese of Peoria, Illinois, had succeeded in this project after a precarious beginning in 1934.

51. Ibid., pp. 44-50. Joseph J. Quinn who discussed the

plan sided with the pastors arguing: "In fact, few pastors can whip their parishioners into a state of enthusiasm over the coal bill, much less the Diocesan paper which furnishes more light but less heat." (p. 45). Polls taken among the editors showed that they consistently favored a complete coverage plan above all others. See: CJ, XII (February, 1947), p. 1; Ibid., V (September, 1954), p. 1; and NC Release 12/14/66.

52. Father Paul Bussard referred to this abuse in his presidential address. See: CJ, II (June, 1950), pp. 2-3.

53. "Minutes, Board... May 9, 1953," p. 3. PDF.

54. CJ, V (March, 1954), p. 5 and (April, 1954), p. 6.

55. CJ, II (August, 1950), p. 4. The comments against the school plans were attributed to Frank Gartland, CSC, of Catholic Boy. Other earlier discussions of the school plans can be found in Our Sunday Visitor, January 1, 1950 and November 12, 1950.

56. The Decency in Reading Program started in 1945 with Catholic magazines only and "...the results were meager. Then in 1951 we began to sell all the decent secular magazines along with the Catholic ones,..." Father Paul Bussard to writer, January 28, 1969.

57. "A Statement by James F. Kane on School Plans," March 17, 1958, p. 3. DC.

58. An interesting article on the beginnings and phenomenal growth of the Catholic Digest can be found in James W. Whalen, "The Catholic Digest: Experiment in Courage," Journalism Quarterly, XLI (Summer, 1964), 343-352. Subscription figures are taken from "Catholic Digest Report," Appendix III, late 1958. DC.

59. "A Statement by James F. Kane on School Plans," March 17, 1958, p. 3. DC.

60. "The Magazine School Plans--An Evaluation." The reason for not giving the names of those behind the

proposal was that the supporters wanted the weight of the arguments rather than the prestige of the backers to influence those who read it. John Reedy, CSC, to Roger Cahaney, October 17, 1957. AMF.

61. Catholic Digest, XXII (December, 1957), inside cover and pp. 126-127.

62. A copy of Bussard's cover letter dated December 27, 1957, is in DC. Bussard later privately retracted his statement concerning Kane. See: Bussard to Kane, January 13, 1958. AMF. For the board action see: "Minutes, Officers... December 12, 1957," pp. 3-4. CPA. Also, Randall, Memo to Officers Re. School Circulation Plans, December 31, 1957. DC. The section of the Code in question was: "We will not promote or sell our publications in combinations of any sort with non-Catholic publications whose content or policies are inconsistent with Catholic doctrine, values or attitudes." Father Bussard had circulated the members of the Decency in Reading Program charging that since the good names of those involved had been unjustly damaged, the censure should be made.

63. Brennan's decision is recorded in a Memo to Officers from G. Roger Cahaney, n. d., but obviously between the December 1957 and February 1958 board meetings. Randall's report to the members is dated March 7, 1958. Both in CPA. Most of the letters had been written at Father Reedy's request made because the board refused to take action unless members showed concern in the issue.

64. "A Statement by James F. Kane on School Plans," March 17, 1958, passim. DC.

65. "Minutes, Board... May 20, 1958," pp. 4-9. CPA. The parties involved had simply agreed not to pursue the matter further according to Father Reedy. Interview, February 14, 1969.

66. "Minutes General Business Meeting," May 21, 1958, pp. 1-3 and "Minutes Closing General Business Meeting," May 23, 1958, pp. 2-3. CPA. The vote was 48-44. The general conclusions in the

report were that "there is nothing inherently wrong or detrimental in the operation of the Magazine School Plans" and "securing such subscriptions is not un-economical." This from "Report of the Fact-Finding Committee of the Catholic Press Association of the United States" to the Board of Directors, May 20, 1958. CPA.

67. The Catholic Universe Bulletin (Cleveland) initiated the discussion with a series of articles, comments, and letters in September.

68. A report on the New York meeting is found in a Memo to President Daly from Father Albert J. Nevins, March 13, 1959. CPA. Other data is from "The Digest's Summary," March 12, 1959. CPA.

69. Election figures are reported in Memo, Father Paul Bussard to the Publishers Participating in the Decency in Reading Program, n.d. DC. In the same collection are a number of letters to the president expressing regret and concern that this had happened.

70. William O. Brady to Father Bussard, November 23, 1959. CPA. Brady did not permit the plans to be used in his Archdiocese according to a survey done by the Universe Bulletin before it ran the articles on the school plans. AMF.

71. A circulation graph sent to Doyle by Bussard in April of 1964 showed that the Catholic magazine circulation had consistently increased from 1952 to 1958 when it reached a high of over thirteen million. Conversely, from 1959 to 1964 the number had steadily decreased with the estimate for the current year placed at about nine million. CPA. (In retrospect, it seems likely to this writer, who was teaching in Catholic schools during the period, that the school plans would have declined even had they not been attacked. The triumph of the Russians in their October, 1957, launch of "Sputnik" and the subsequent manned flight in 1961 led to severe criticism of the American educational system and a re-examination of school activities by both public and Catholic educators. Anything interferring with "educational excellence" became anathema.) The

resignation gesture is from a letter dated December 21, 1961, signed by Andrew P. Stack, Controller. CPA. Notices concerning the new board appeared in CJ, XIV (February, 1963), p. 16 and (March, 1963), p. 1.

72. Circular: James A. Doyle, January 27, 1964. CPA. Issenmann's action is mentioned in "Minutes Closing Business Meeting," May 13, 1966, p. 2. HC.

73. "Minutes Opening Business Session," May 16, 1962, p. 1 (PC); Father Albert J. Nevins, "President's Opening Statement," May 16, 1962, p. 3 (CPA); NC Release 5/17/62.

74. Father Albert J. Nevins, "The Circulation Challenge to the Catholic Magazine," CPA Magazine Address, April 30, 1963. CPA. Nevins also noted in this speech that even though the board had agreed the previous year to send a letter to the hierarchy, it had not been done.

75. "Minutes Special Meeting of Officers and Past Presidents of CPA," April 23, 1964, p. 5. CPA. The funds were allocated by the board in October: "Minutes, Board... October 7, 1964," p. 3. PC. The survey proved to be of little use: "Minutes, Board... March 2, 1967," p. 1. CPA. The crisis state was pointed out in "Minutes, Board... January 20, 1966," p. 5. CPA.

76. "Minutes Winter Meeting of the Magazine Committee, Catholic Press Association," January 18, 1968. CPA. A report of the meeting and the CPA materials appeared in NC Release 2/16/68.

77. Less than fifty per cent of the Catholic magazines carried advertising according to a 1947 survey. See: CJ, XII (March, 1947), p. 1.

78. Edwin Emery, History of the American Newspaper Publishers Association (Minneapolis, 1950), p. 164-65.

79. Wey's action and the results were reported in the C. P. A. Bulletin, II (January, 1943), pp. 1 and 4; (March, 1943), pp. 1 and 4, and ibid., III (December, 1943), p. 1.

80. C. P. A. Bulletin, II (March, 1943), p. 4 and ibid., III (December, 1943), p. 3 refer to the tabloids. Salvage campaigns and number of pages are reported in ibid., III (February, 1944), pp. 1 and 3.

81. Circular: James A. Shanahan to All Members, September 26, 1945. WC. CJ, XII (February, 1947), p. 1.

82. CJ, XII (April, 1947), p. 1; Abbreviated Report... 1947, p. 4 (WC); NC Release 6/17/47.

83. CJ [no volume given] (November, 1948), p. 2 printed Randall's view. The priest had been named a Very Reverend Monsignor by this time. For Nevins' ideas see: CJ, II (June, 1950), p. 5.

84. CJ, II (October, 1950), p. 8.

85. For examples of the treatment of hardship cases see: CJ, II (August, 1951), p. 5 and ibid., III (December, 1951), p. 8. The brighter outlook is noted in CJ, III (January, 1952), p. 2. For a report of the work of the various committees see: James F. Kane to Directors, February 12, 1951. CPA.

86. The McGrann negotiations can be traced through the following: "Outline of Proposal to Organize Purchasing Power of Members of The Catholic Press Association;" "Minutes, Board... February 12, 1954;" "Report on C. P. A. Paper and Printing Survey," to Closing Business Session, May 27, 1955; "Minutes, Board... November 3, 1955," p. 3; CJ, VII (February, 1956), p. 2; and "Minutes, Board... May 14, 1957," p. 3. All minutes and reports in CPA.

87. Emery, op. cit., pp. 164-5. The secular publishers were, of course, struggling with similar problems.

88. CJ, II (August, 1951), p. 5 and ibid., III (June, 1952), pp. 1-2.

89. NC Release 11/7/55. The statement was sent to selected trade journals and all the wire services according to CJ, VI (December, 1955), p. 7.

90. Editor and Publisher, XCIX (March 5, 1966), p. 16.

91. Emery, op. cit., p. 175. The ANPA, like the CPA, fought proposed postal increases at this time; however, they concentrated on other provisions of the bills.

92. Desmond's arguments before the House Committee were reported in NC Release 3/24/47; support from other editors in CJ, XII (April, 1947), pp. 1 and 3; and the House measure in Abbreviated Report... 1947, p. 5. WC.

93. Emery, op. cit., p. 176.

94. NC Release 3/14/49 and "Statement of Rev. Paul Bussard, President Catholic Press Association of the U. S. before U. S. Senate Post Office Committee Hearing on S. 1103," April 6, 1949 (CPA) cover the priest's statements. The Protestant reaction was reported in the Register (Denver), April 17, 1949.

95. CJ, I (October, 1949), p. 11; Ibid., II (October, 1950), p. 8; and (March, 1951), pp. 1-2 kept the members informed concerning postal legislation. Fink in a letter to Secretary Kane, March 19, 1951, reported the reaction of the House committee. CPA.

96. "Minutes, Board... May 16, 1951," p. 3 recommended contacting Congressmen. An example of alerting readers is "The Post Office and the Catholic Press," Extension Magazine, XLV (May, 1951), p. 22.

97. Kane, "Report on the Operation of Your CPA National Office," to the 41st Annual Convention, May 16, 1951. CPA. Fink to CPA Member, November 9, 1951. PDF.

98. This action may be traced through: Fink, "Report of the President," to the Annual Convention, June 19, 1952, p. 4 (CPA); CJ, IV (October, 1952), p. 7; (August, 1953), p. 4; Ibid., VI (March, 1955), p. 7; "Minutes, Board... November 3, 1955," p. 5 (CPA); and Charles J. McNeill, President, "Report to CPA Convention," May 16, 1956, p. 3 (CPA).

99. "CPA Postal Rates Committee Report," to General Business Meeting," May 21, 1958. CPA. Francis R. Cawley, "Postal Policy and the Press," Address

to CPA Convention, May 22, 1958. PDF. Such a postal service, suggested later, failed to win the approval of the House Appropriations Committee. See: CJ, X (April, 1959), p. 11.

100. "CPA Postal Rates Committee Report," to Board of Directors, September 22, 1958 and May 12, 1959. CPA. The handbook was announced by Doyle in "Executive Secretary's Report," to Board of Directors, May 10, 1960, p. 4. CPA. A revised edition was published in 1966. CC.

101. "Minutes, Board... May 10, 1960," p. 2 CPA. NC Release 7/17/61; Floyd Anderson, President of the Catholic Press Association of the U. S., Inc., "Statement to the Senate Post Office and Civil Service Committee," August 16, 1962. PC.

102. "Special Report on Postal Rates," James A. Doyle to CPA Member Publications, October 22, 1962. PC. Doyle reported that the rates would become effective on January 7, 1963.

103. "Postal Rates Committee Report," to Board of Directors, October 7, 1964. PC. CJ, XVI (March, 1965), p. 4.

104. Doyle to CPA Members, August 17, 1965 (CPA); "Minutes, Board... March 2, 1967," p. 1 (CPA); NC Release 6/28/67.

105. Doyle reported the graduated rates in "Executive Director's Report," August 15, 1967. CPA. Holub labeled the bill drastic in reporting to the board: "Minutes, Board...October 27, 1967," p. 2. CPA. A report on the letters of protest appeared in NC Release 11/8/67. CJ, XX (April, 1968), p. 8 reported the proposed manual. Mr. Holub in an interview on October 24, 1968, emphasized that this graduated schedule will prove to be a real burden as it moves toward the upper limits in the next few years.

Chapter VII

Other Association Activities

Even though the CPA has devoted much time and attention to business affairs in the last three decades, it has continued a number of the activities of the earlier periods such as Catholic Press Month campaigns, the presentation of Literary Awards of one kind or another, and interest in current happenings. In addition, the Association has fostered a system of Journalism Awards for both newspapers and magazines and has instituted its own CPA Award given annually to individuals within the Catholic Press. It has also established and maintained a house organ, taken over the publication of the Catholic Press Directory, and issued various other publications for shorter periods of time.

Press Month campaigns, which had begun early in the history of the CPA and continued with varying degrees of enthusiasm into its mature years, were re-invigorated by Msgr. Peter M. H. Wynhoven, Press Month Chairman in 1938 and 1939. Acting on a suggestion from one of the newly formed regions, the members in 1941 discussed the possibility of producing a special Press Month poster as a promotional item. So many questions arose concerning the practicability of adapting a single poster to the diverse Catholic publications that the matter was referred to the executive board. A committee named to study the proposal encountered the same difficulty; they later found so little interest in posters that the project was abandoned.[1] Nevertheless, when Secretary James A. Shanahan received authorization to spend two hundred dollars to promote the 1948 Press Month, one of the items included in his promotional package was a poster.[2] Shanahan did not repeat the project, but three years later James F. Kane again introduced a Catholic Press Month Package to aid members in their promotional efforts, and a poster proved to be its most popular item. In his farewell address President Francis A. Fink pointed to the promotional packages as one of the most important achievements of his administration.[3] Whereas Kane's "packages" were designed for the use of member publications, G. Roger

Cahaney developed another Press Month Kit for use by outside organizations. This was well accepted for a few years but gradually became less popular and was discontinued after the 1963 drive.[4]

For several years Press Month promotion was handled almost entirely by the executive secretary. After Cahaney's report showed that the 1956 campaign was a "qualified success," the board reactivated a special Catholic Press Month Committee for this work.[5] However, enthusiasm for Press Month never again reached the level that it had attained in earlier years, and some members questioned keeping it in February. Father Paul Bussard, in his 1950 presidential address, recommended that Press Month be transferred to November since he believed that the "reading time of the year" began in the fall and had found that subscriptions to magazines were popular Christmas gifts. A special committee reported to the board a year later that the reasons advanced were insufficient "to overcome the disadvantages and inconveniences of a change in Catholic Press Month."[6] In 1957 a Chicago member petitioned that Press Month be moved to the fall, preferably October, and the board in May of 1964 discussed whether February was really the best month for such promotion. As recently as the 1968 convention the journalists discussed the request of a newspaper member recommending that such promotional activities be transferred to October. Since the meeting lacked a quorum, the question was taken up by the directors who also deferred action[7] in part because some of the members had been questioning the feasibility of conducting a Press Month campaign at all. The 1962 Press Month Committee had called for year-round promotion, and the decline in magazine circulation led the board to a similar conclusion two years later.[8] In May of 1965 James A. Doyle informed the board that Press Month was in need of "serious examination" as most present day publications were capable of producing their own promotional pieces and "almost as many editors poke fun at Catholic Press Month as give it serious thought." He repeated his arguments in August basing them on the premise "that the circumstances which existed when Catholic Press Month was begun and developed in the 20s and 30s no longer are the same."[9]

Actually, the board had much earlier taken steps to insure continuous promotional activities at least as an adjunct to the Press Month campaigns. In 1957 in connection with the proposed drive for Life Memberships, a CPA Press

Promotion Committee was established. This group instituted a course of study in the Catholic Press at Mt. Angel Abbey, a seminary in Oregon conducted by Benedictines, where candidates from nine dioceses studied. Later this committee began an extensive campaign to foster cooperation with other Catholic organizations and to make these groups aware of the importance of the Catholic Press. As activities of this committee increased and those of the Press Month Committee declined, the value of continuous promotion became more evident. Finally in 1964 the Press Promotion Committee absorbed the Catholic Press Month Committee.[10]

In addition to the perennial Press Month drives and the later activities of the Press Promotion Committee, other attempts were made to make the general public more aware of the Catholic Press. Sometimes exhibits of member publications were displayed at CPA conventions and at meetings of other Catholic groups.[11] In 1950 the Association lauded a proposal of the College of Journalism at Marquette for the development of a Catholic Press Archives at that University and promised complete cooperation in the project. The Archives never became an actuality,[12] and shortly thereafter efforts were begun "to make the National Office [of the CPA] more of a center for information about the Catholic press." In the spring of 1959 a continuing display of member publications was introduced, and the following year the secretary suggested building a reference library on the Catholic Press in the central office. Six years later Doyle, reporting that the project had finally made "significant progress," added "that the amount of written and/or published material on the history, theory, techniques and practices of the Catholic press is pitifully small."[13]

The CPA has made its own modest contribution in some of these areas through its various publications over the years. A house organ appearing under three different titles has carried articles relating to publishing techniques and practices as well as items of interest to the members. Perhaps the earliest advocate of such a medium was NC Director Frank Hall who suggested a bulletin to the board in 1935 and was strongly supported by Wilfrid Parsons, SJ.[14] Four years later, still trying to persuade others of the worth of such an organ, he wrote to President Charles H. Ridder that Msgr. Matthew Smith had initiated a circular letter for the Register group. Hall believed that the priest had "got the jump on the Association," and he inferred that at least Register members might well question why an association of nationwide stature was unable to compete in this respect with a small band of "some twenty." Ridder agreed that a bulletin would be a good idea, but thought it would be difficult to find an editor. Hall replied immediately with a suggestion: "...I wonder if you have thought of that bustling gentleman, Monsignor Wynhoven of New Orleans." Mentioning that Wynhoven had been working to recruit new members, Hall added "... he seems to be so vigorous in his activities that he might be willing to take it up."[15]

After the stormy 1939 session, Hall wrote CPA Secretary, Humphrey E. Desmond that a regular house organ would remind the members that "the Association is alive and doing things." He even drew up a format for the publication and repeated an earlier offer to mimeograph the bulletin in the Press Department office.[16] The board at the close of the 1940 convention finally approved a publication to be "issued by the Executive Board under the direction of the president" and to be sent to all the bishops as well as to CPA members, "at least four times during the year." Volume I, #1, of In Vain, dated September 14, 1940, carried Msgr. Wynhoven's name as editor and declared the purposes of this "official organ" to be "a means of information; ... a medium of expression; ... [and] a stimulant to better and more fruitful efforts...." The title of the publication was taken from a statement of Pope Pius X that had long been a favorite of the American Catholic editors: "In vain will you build churches, preach missions, found schools: all your good works, all your efforts will be destroyed, if you cannot at the same time wield the defensive and offensive weapons of a press that is Catholic, loyal and sincere."[17] In a 1941 convention discussion of In Vain, Msgr. Wynhoven told the members that there had not been a great deal of interest shown in the bulletin and asked, "... is it worth-while to continue this?" It was agreed that the organ should continue since it was one way to make the hierarchy more aware of the aims of the Catholic Press. It was also decided that Wynhoven should remain editor-in-chief and that the board of five editors should be responsible for defining a policy for the publication.[18]

By 1942 the house organ was so well established that the directors were unanimous in their opinion that it be continued. As Wynhoven was no longer on the board, John J. Considine, MM, vice president, became the editor. When Volume II appeared it was entitled C. P. A. Bulletin with no explanation given for the change. Father Considine advocated using the publication as an educational device in spreading the Apostolate of the Press.[19] He resigned his office in 1943, however, and Hyacinth Blocker, OFM, was named editor. Father Blocker, envisioning the time when the publication would have a national reputation, suggested that the Bulletin might well accept advertising and become "not only self-supporting" but even "a source of revenue" for the Association.[20] He was replaced as editor before he could carry out his plans as it remained customary for the editor to be a member of the board, and his term had expired. Therefore, Desmond took over after the 1944 convention. His first (and only) issue did not appear until December, but it contained several suggestions regarding future Bulletins including monthly issues, an eight instead of the usual four page format, and articles on technical matters.[21]

Desmond relinquished his duties as editor when Shanahan became temporary secretary in March of 1945. The first publication under Shanahan's editorship was dated June 1945, contained eight pages, devoted the back cover to advertising, and was called The Catholic Journalist. Shanahan distributed copies to non-CPA publications in an attempt to recruit new members. Because he expected to convert The Catholic Journalist into "a practical trade journal," he issued a special mimeographed bulletin containing supplementary materials touching on everyday matters such as paper shortages, postal rates, and the like.[22] Although the board was anxious that the Journalist be a monthly, publication was irregular until Father Alfred Barrett's first number in August of 1949.[23] During the first ten months of his editorship, it was mimeographed, but in June of 1950 a printed bulletin reappeared. Father Bussard told the convention that year: "Our trade association paper is not yet something to boast about, but it is headed in the right direction."[24] Kane and Cahaney continued the house organ making only minor changes in content and format, and the publication appeared about ten times a year.

During his first several months as executive secretary, Doyle made no innovations, but as early as the fall of 1959 he began advocating changes. A special report on Catholic Journalist expansion which he presented in May of 1960 aimed at making the publication a strong trade journal, producing an impressive format, and procuring sizeable advertising revenue.[25] Examining the first revised issue at its January meeting in 1961, the board found it most praiseworthy. Doyle reported later in the year that although the

Catholic Journalist had been well received in the new magazine format, printing and distribution costs were excessive and a source of disturbance.[26] The deficit continued, and Doyle devised a new plan whereby he would publish the Catholic Journalist in the magazine form on a bi-monthly schedule with a Catholic Journalist Newsletter to be published at a reduced cost in the alternate months. The Newsletter was given a good reception when it appeared in August of 1963. Doyle expressed hope that in time both publications might be issued monthly, but advertising sources failed to materialize, and the secretary presented a pessimistic report on the house organ in the spring of 1965. Acknowledging that the magazine was "not impressive," he listed lack of editorial assistance and insufficient financial backing as the main reasons. He asked that the board "give serious consideration... to revamping the Catholic Journalist to give it new strength and new stature." But revenue continued to decline, and beginning in January of 1966 it was necessary to place the Catholic Journalist magazine on a quarterly basis with the Newsletter published the other eight months of the year.[27]

Miscellaneous publications have supplemented the house organ from time to time. To commemorate the CPA's thirty-fifth anniversary, Shanahan prepared a special brochure entitled I am The Catholic Press. Originally Shanahan had planned to publish the booklet in time for the 1946 Press Month campaign, but as orders were slow in coming in, publication had to be delayed. Although the secretary estimated that "at least 100,000" copies could be distributed to pastors, employees, and advertisers, advance orders numbered slightly over 13,000 thereby reducing the initial run to only 15,000 copies.[28] The twenty page booklet purported to be an "interesting factual study of the entire Catholic Press in America." It included a survey of circulation figures, quotations of the Popes concerning the Catholic Press, lists of past presidents and convention sites, and a page of important dates in American Catholic Press history. It also contained very brief histories of the NCWC Press Department and the CPA as well as a page devoted to St. Francis de Sales, and one to a discussion of the training of Catholic journalists.[29] Hall praised the booklet, noting that he had "been plugging for something of this sort for a good many years." He particularly commended its value as a means of recruiting CPA members, but he also thought it would be useful in several other areas including advertising and education. By the fall of the year, the first edition was exhausted and Shanahan asked for permission to reprint the booklet. However, requests for re-orders did not warrant a second printing.[30]

Beginning in 1951 and continuing throughout that decade the central office published a special convention booklet each year. During Kane's period this was magazine size, approximately twenty pages in content, and contained the convention program, pictures of convention "personalities," and advertising. It was entitled CPA Buyers' Guide and Convention Annual. Cahaney produced a convention guide following that format in 1954, but after that he issued a booklet size convention number containing similar material. During some years no Catholic Journalist was published in the month of the convention as the Buyers' Guide replaced it. As his first effort, Doyle issued a CPA Convention Journal using the same format as that followed by Cahaney though it was several pages longer and sub-titled "The Catholic Journalist for May, 1959."[31]

The Association's Golden Jubilee was celebrated in 1960, and the secretary decided that the "anniversary Journal should be an historical document, which would be of lasting value and importance." Work had scarcely begun when Doyle indicated that he favored a Catholic Press Annual not just for the jubilee celebration but for "the next several" years.[32] The first Annual received some criticism especially concerning type styling and art layout. Advertising revenue was significant, however, and Doyle began immediately to plan a better Annual for 1961. Although a new art editor was secured for the second edition, advertising revenue reached less than half that anticipated. The secretary attributed this to the fact that the Catholic Journalist was being revised at the same time, and promotional efforts had been concentrated on that rather than on the Annual. This was remedied with the 1962 number which Doyle characterized as "a definite contribution to the work of recording and defining the history of the Catholic Press and promoting this press here and abroad, within and without our field."[33] The Annuals continued through 1966 when at Doyle's recommendation they were discontinued.[34]

During the years that the Association was publishing the convention guides and the annuals, the organization was also producing the Catholic Press Directory which had been published from 1923 to 1945 at irregular intervals by Joseph H. Meier and Joseph Wagner, Inc. The CPA had given its endorsement to the Directory as early as 1928, and in 1940 had contemplated publishing it.[35] In 1946 the board discussed a proposal presented to Shanahan by the Wagner company whereby the CPA would assume the publication of the Directory, and the former publisher would receive ten per cent of the gross sales for ten years. The board rejected this offer, but the directors instructed Shanahan to continue negotiations. A year later no progress had been made, and the board told Shanahan that if Wagner continued to demand ten per cent, the secretary was "to inform him that we will publish our own directory without his help."[36] In August of 1949 Father Barrett announced via the pages of his first issue of The Catholic Journalist that "Through the generosity of Clement Wagner, president of Joseph F. Wagner, Inc., complete rights of publication and ownership of the Catholic Press Directory have been given to the Catholic Press Association,..." Two provisions were attached to the "donation": first, a new edition was to come out "prior to 1950," and second, the company requested "a two page spread in each and every edition of the 'Catholic Press Directory'."[37] By October the executive secretary had received answers to his request for suggestions regarding the new directory, had succeeded in getting a press directory board named, and had secured a printer and an advertising manager. But the Directory Committee had difficulty obtaining the necessary information from Catholic publishers,[38] Kane replaced Barrett as secretary, and complications arose over the transfer of the Directory. Even though the Wagner company had made its offer on June 15, 1949, and it had been publicly acknowledged by the Association in the Journalist as well as at a regional fall meeting, no official transfer had been effected. When a new CPA board took office in 1950, these directors contested the qualification that Wagner, Inc. receive two pages of free advertising indefinitely. The company in return threatened that "Any attempt to ignore the terms of our agreement or to circumvent these conditions... will not go unchallenged." A compromise finally settled the matter in September with an understanding that free advertising would terminate after five issues, and that in the last two "free" issues Wagner, Inc. would be given the option of buying the front cover at the regular advertising rate.[39]

The Directory was delayed until January of 1951 due to continued lack of cooperation of publishers in returning needed information. Of the initial print run of ten thousand copies half were sent free of charge to advertising agencies and the remainder offered for sale at one dollar each to members or five dollars to others. As advertisers had patronized this first issue very well, the book not only filled a need but also showed a financial profit. Moreover, Kane reported to the 1951 convention that the Directory was "exceptionally well received in advertising circles" and that it had added much prestige to the Association.[40] The Catholic Press Directory was, therefore, a success from the beginning and has remained an annual publication of the Association. Beginning with the second edition the general price was reduced to three dollars and remained at that rate until 1964 when it was again raised to five dollars.[41]

Even as some members fostered and improved the Directory with notable success, others devoted their time and efforts to work connected with the Literary Awards which eventually were abandoned by the Association. In 1937 the Literary Awards committee had announced a contest offering prizes for the best theses on the Catholic Press, but when the 1941 convention met, entries in this contest had not as yet been judged. After a member in a general discussion session pointed out that the CPA had "lost the faith of a lot of young people through the tactics that have been used in this contest," it was agreed that it must be terminated and awards given. Winners were at last announced in the March 1942 issue of In Vain.[42] From 1942 to 1946 the Literary Awards Committee sponsored short story contests divided into two categories, magazines and newspapers, and conducted through CPA member publications. Winners in the local contests were submitted to a board of judges, and final winners were announced at the annual convention. Stories remained mediocre because prizes were small and contestants too often amateurs. For these reasons a nationwide contest was sponsored from 1947 through 1951.

The Literary Awards Foundation was revived briefly in 1947-48, and the fund was enlarged slightly by the enrollment of some Life Members, but prizes also were increased each year and by the time the contests were suspended the Awards were costing not only one thousand dollars earned from the restricted Literary Awards Fund but still another thousand from general Association funds.[43] One of the CPA by-laws stated that life membership fees must remain in a separate fund and that income from this account be used "to give encouragement to Catholic authors and writers..." In 1951 the board approved a proposal to amend the by-laws to remove this restriction, and the following year Father

Philip Kennedy, CPA treasurer, was named as a committee of one to investigate the Foundation. After reporting "that there was no binding power upon the organization and these funds could be used for the general good of the Association," Father Kennedy stated that only a change in by-laws would be necessary.[44] This decision was contested by Charles H. Ridder, one of the oldest members, who wrote that life members had been solicited with the understanding that money received from them was to constitute an endowment fund or foundation. Arguing that this meant a permanent fund, Ridder advocated completing the original foundation rather than diverting money from it. Since others failed to join him in the cause, the 1954 convention approved a revision of the by-laws deleting any reference to the use that was to be made of income from the Literary Awards Foundation and merely stipulating that "only income from such fund shall be expended and the principal thereof kept intact." Expenditures remained under the jurisdiction of the board.[45]

The 1954 Literary Awards Committee, chaired by William Holub, submitted for consideration of the board at its fall meeting a proposal that it maintained could be financed with the income from the Foundation and still be working toward the goal envisioned by the contributors. The plan called for the publication of an anthology every two years beginning in 1956 with collections alternating between fiction and non-fiction writings culled from Catholic publications and edited and published in a professional and competent manner. The board unanimously approved this project, and Riley Hughes, free-lance writer and English professor at Georgetown University, agreed to edit the first collection containing works of fiction.[46] Publication of the book was announced for February to coincide with Catholic Press Month, and the title chosen was <u>All Manner of Men</u>. In general the collection received favorable reviews. A literary critic "hailed it as a 'triumph'," and the Thomas More Book Club selected it as its April book. Among the less enthusiastic was Flannery O'Connor who commented that "Riley Hughes, having little to choose from, has chosen wisely."[47] The book went into a second printing; the board discussed arrangements for French and Dutch editions, and a Dublin company published the same book under a new title, <u>All Kinds of People</u>, in 1958.[48]

Despite objections by some members of the board, work on the non-fiction book began even before the first anthology appeared. By the fall of 1956, the committee had presented preliminary suggestions and had requested that Riley Hughes be authorized to begin planning for a 1960 fiction collection. By May, Dan Herr and Clem Lane had been named as co-editors, and members had submitted extensive material for use in the non-fiction book tentatively entitled "The Positive Approach" because the editors hoped to stress positive attitudes.[49] Publication was again scheduled for February; the title for the published version was Realities from a quotation from Christopher Dawson: "What is vital is... to bring home to the average man that religion is not a pious fiction which has nothing to do with the facts of life, but that it is concerned with the realities, ..." Once more the anthology was well received, and by the end of April almost five thousand copies had been sold.[50]

There had been controversy over the contents of the non-fiction book as some directors feared that newspapers were being over-looked by the editors and that the material chosen was "too heavy." The Literary Awards Committee and the editors thought to silence these objections by planning another publication utilizing materials submitted for Realities but not included in it. One suggestion was to prepare a "handbook of representative types of materials in the Catholic press" that would be useful to editors and especially to students of journalism. The committee recommended that an experienced newspaper man work with a teacher or representative of a university press to produce a handbook to "include samples of the best of writing in various categories" plus critical commentaries on each.[51] Neither this project nor a second fiction work was ever completed because Holub found little support for the handbook among members of the 1958 Literary Awards Committee, and subsequent committees suggested other activities such as exchange of staff members among CPA publications and studies concentrating on the policies of the Catholic Press.[52]

Pointing out in 1958 that there was an overlapping of the Literary Awards Committee with another CPA committee concerned with journalism awards, Holub suggested that the work of the two might be merged. Finally, the board voted to transfer interest that had accumulated on the Literary Awards Fund to the general fund and to use such money to help finance the journalism awards. This action was repeated the following year, and in 1964 a motion was approved providing that "all income from the Literary Awards fund each year be allocated to defraying the cost of the journalism awards;... "[53]

Journalism Awards had originated much later in the history of the CPA than had those given for literary efforts. In 1936 the Catholic Universe-Bulletin of Cleveland had received a hundred dollar award for "outstanding achievement in Catholic journalism during the year," but this contest was sponsored by the Literary Awards Committee.[54] In December of 1944 CPA President, Father Patrick O'Connor, announced that Special Merit Awards would be given to Catholic newspapers and magazines "for excellence in typography, photography, art, general design and public service,...." Nonetheless, the project was not carried out that year, and Father O'Connor informed the 1946 convention that it had been postponed once again due to "sheer preoccupation with other matters,...."[55]

The Catholic Journalist for January of 1948 carried details concerning the "long-talked-of and earnestly-hoped-for Annual Journalism Awards [to] become a reality" at last. The award system, devised by a committee chaired by Father Thomas McCarthy, promised gold medals to the best-edited Catholic newspaper and the best-edited Catholic magazine and Certificates of Merit in eight categories. The Cleveland Universe-Bulletin and Maryknoll, The Field Afar received the coveted top awards.[56] Father McCarthy was reappointed chairman of the Publications Awards Committee the following year, and The New World and The Sign received the gold medals for 1949. The 1950 contest was conducted along the same lines with the Brooklyn Tablet and the Catholic World the medal winners. By this time certificates of excellence and honorable mention were being awarded in thirteen categories. The judges noted weaknesses in news reporting, poetry, and editorials, but admitted that in some cases judging was extremely close.[57]

In 1951 the awards system was revised with newspapers and magazines placed in separate divisions. Although a point system was continued, scoring sheets were more detailed and were returned to the participants to inform the editors of their own strong points and weaknesses. Secretary Kane told the convention that year that this system constituted a "consulting service" which alone was of greater value than the annual membership dues.[58] There were some objections raised to the new awards system especially by editors of newspapers of smaller circulation who argued that their special problems were ignored under the new method. Nonetheless, the same type judging continued through 1953 and underwent only slight changes the following year. By

1955 the board, heeding the requests of the dissident members, inaugurated a new system based on circulation for the "Newspapers of Distinction" which had been named since 1951. Individual awards also replaced the categorical ones, and for the first time Catholic editors were included among the judges.[59] At its first meeting immediately following the convention, members of the new board expressed their dissatisfaction, and the 1955-1956 Newspaper Awards Committee drew up a revised and simplified system with fewer and more meaningful awards. "Newspapers of Distinction" were eliminated, and only one award, that of the best front page, was based on circulation. A new award for "Outstanding Achievement" was introduced "for an outstanding editorial feat in the public interest which... demonstrates the initiative and resourcefulness of a Catholic newspaper."[60]

There had been so many revisions and adaptations of the Journalism Awards that some members became concerned. Discussing the necessity of consistency at the close of the 1956 convention, the directors determined to continue the present method for the current year but recommended that a long-range study of the awards be conducted. A set of resolutions presented to the board members in September called for an awards system recognizing "superior workmanship" and employing competent judges from an outside institution. Acknowledging that "frequent and drastic changes" had lessened the value of the awards, the resolutions asked for a standard set of procedures and a scoring method to be devised by professionals in the field and "subject to change only by a majority vote of the membership." Finally, a resolution urged that means be found to finance such an improved system.[61] Agreeing that this study and its implementation would take time, the directors approved an interim plan for 1957 based on individual awards and judging by the membership. When this later proved impractical because it would have involved extensive duplicating and mailing of entries, judges were chosen as in the past. The "interim policy" was used again the following year with a few minor changes and with judges from outside the Catholic Press.[62]

One reason for delay in formulating a new system was that during this time the board was involved in a fund-raising campaign, and hoped to obtain money from this source to finance the improved Journalism Awards. The Community Counseling Service report to the officers in March of 1957 showed that the Journalism Awards received almost unanimous support, but that members favored a much improved system. For this reason one of the special committees appointed in connection with the Life Membership drive was a Journalism Awards Committee to devise a permanent system for these awards, recommend professional groups for the judging, and suggest a plan for financing the project.[63] The committee report caused consternation as it advocated returning to the scoring method and estimated that about seven thousand dollars would be necessary to do an adequate job. Even though the directors agreed that there was "tremendous interest" in the awards and that they were "almost entirely responsible" for much of the improvement in Catholic journalism in the past several years, they were not satisfied with the report and named a new committee for further study of the problem. Msgr. John S. Randall, CPA president, discussed Journalism Awards at the regional conferences that fall and found much opposition to allocating such a large portion of Association funds to this project. In December the awards committee was asked to modify its plans drastically so that awards in each division could be presented for approximately one thousand dollars.[64]

The revised awards system was finally announced in February, 1959. The Departments of Journalism at Duquesne and Fordham Universities agreed to handle the judging of the newspapers and magazines respectively. Professors Cornelius S. McCarthy of Duquesne and Edward Walsh of Fordham attended the 1959 convention and spoke at the Journalism Awards Luncheon presenting critiques compiled from evaluations submitted by the judges. The contests continued along similar lines, and by 1961 the board agreed that "complaints [about the Journalism Awards]... were at a minimum."[65]

In 1964 the Journalism Awards Committee initiated National Catholic Book Awards in ten categories asking publishers to nominate books from those appearing in the previous calendar year. Twenty publishers entered ninety-three books in the first contest, CPA members did the preliminary voting, and then the top three in each division were submitted to a board of judges who named the winning selection in each category.[66] The committee recommended that the number of categories be reduced to five for the second competition. By 1968 this had evolved into the five best books published during the past year, the contest was under the direction of a special Book Awards Committee, and the judging was done by a panel of 5 distinguished book-reviewers using a two-phased evaluation system.[67]

Special individual awards have also been sponsored by the Association. In 1956 the Catholic Digest asked to present an annual award "for distinguished service to Catholic publishing" consisting of a citation from the Digest and one thousand dollars from the Decency in Reading Program. The first recipient, chosen by the CPA directors, was Father Patrick O'Connor. Dissatisfaction over the award on the part of both CPA members and Catholic Digest personnel led to further negotiations. In a conference with a representative of the Digest, the officers agreed that the award should be given by the CPA, but in the name of the Digest, at the annual convention banquet.[68] The board unanimously chose Dean Jeremiah O'Sullivan of the College of Journalism at Marquette as the 1957 recipient. Although Father Bussard approved of the recipient, he nonetheless suggested discontinuing the award because "it wasn't working out as he had intended." Part of the difficulty was that about this time controversy concerning the feasibility of the school plans as a means of increasing magazine circulation had begun. Members took sides, and the directors were opposed to mentioning the Decency in Reading Program in connection with the award.[69]

The membership was asked to nominate individuals for the 1958 award which was modified somewhat from the original. Nominees were to be from outside the Catholic Press, and the award was to be for "distinguished service to Christian journalism and publishing." From the suggestions submitted, the board chose John Delaney and Image Books, but again the Digest people were unhappy. Although the board went so far as to agree that the Catholic Digest itself should unilaterally set the standards of the award and name the recipient for 1959, the Digest declined to present its award that year because of the criticism by fellow members regarding the Decency in Reading Program.[70]

About the same time that the Catholic Digest Award was being given, a suggestion was made that the CPA itself establish an appropriate award to be presented annually in conjunction with the convention. Nothing was done until it became evident that the Digest intended to discontinue its award. The 1958-1959 Literary Awards Committee suggested that a yearly award be established recommending that the award be one of honor and prestige rather than a monetary prize. Guidelines determined from suggestions made by the committee stated that the Catholic Press Association Award was to be given for "the most distinguished contribution to Catholic journalism during the calendar year" within the Catholic Press itself. Nominations were to come from the general membership; a special committee would choose the award recipient from these subject to the approval of the directors.[71] The Special Awards Committee notified the members in February that Registered Agents of CPA publications would participate in the balloting once a list of nominees was drawn up and announced that the recipient would receive "a specially designed trophy and a scroll citation" at the Civic Banquet during the annual convention. A noted sculptor, Thomas McGlynn, OP, was commissioned to execute a statuette of St. Francis de Sales to be cast in bronze so that duplicates might be presented each year to the award winner.[72]

To enhance the award, the identity of the winner was not revealed until the actual presentation at the banquet. Because the vote was very close, the Special Awards Committee presented citations to the three runners-up. The 1959 recipient was Dale Francis, columnist for Our Sunday Visitor, who during the previous year had launched "Operation Understanding, a plan to get Catholic literature into the hands of Protestant ministers..." Citations went to Frank Hall of the NC News Service, Msgr. James I. Tucek who headed the Roman Bureau of NC, and John LaFarge, SJ, whose book, An American Amen, had been published that year.[73]

Even before the first CPA Award was presented there were certain misgivings about it. The democratic procedures used to ascertain the recipient, although laudable insofar as they aroused general interest in the award, left much to be desired. Some of the directors feared that the result might be an unworthy candidate or that the entire choice could deteriorate into a "popularity contest," and they questioned the decision to name runners-up. For these reasons, the board instructed the Special Awards Committee to re-study the entire procedure to determine how it might be improved. One revision later adopted was that the directors screen the original nominations leaving only a limited number to be presented to the membership for balloting.[74] Beginning in 1960 six candidates ordinarily appeared on the ballots; winners were cited at the convention and presented with the bronze statuette while "certificates of nomination recognition" were mailed to the other finalists. In 1966 the board decided that nominations could be made by Registered Agents only, and the next year the directors ruled that if no nominee met the requirements of outstanding accomplishment over the past calendar year, no award need be presented.[75]

Despite an undercurrent of dissatisfaction, no overt action was taken by the members until the closing session of the 1968 convention when John Reedy, CSC, charged that the Award "instituted to encourage journalistic excellence and professional pride... [had become] an embarrassment to the Association and its recipients." He attributed this to the method of selection which was too subjective and had been used to frustrate "the original intent" of the award. Demanding that the board abolish the award or "radically revise" the process of selecting the recipient, Reedy added that if neither alternative was followed he would not only "refuse to cooperate in the nomination or voting" but would also "reject publicly the claim that this is a truly professional recognition," would encourage others to do the same, and would boycott future presentations of this award. Although the board entertained a motion to suspend the award, at least temporarily, the directors concluded that it should be retained.[76]

Obviously, promotion, publications, and awards have been of paramount importance to CPA members during the mature years of the Association. Even the organization's Golden Jubilee celebration evidenced this. Whereas the Silver Jubilee Convention had emphasized the past achievements of the group, the 1960 convention program looked to the future and was designed to increase the prestige of the Association. The board of directors began planning the event immediately following the 1959 convention, and throughout the year the national office, President John J. Daly, and the convention committees continued promotional and planning efforts.[77]

As a result the convention was a tremendous success --"by far the best" ever held. Theodore M. Hesburgh, CSC, President of the University of Notre Dame, delivered the keynote address urging the delegates to meet the challenges presented to them in scientific areas, higher education, international affairs, and human rights. His Eminence Gregory Peter XV Cardinal Agagianian, Pro-Prefect of the Sacred Congregation for the Propagation of the Faith, gave the main address at the Civic Banquet. The Armenian Cardinal, in the United States at the invitation of the CPA, also presided at the Golden Jubilee Memorial Mass celebrated at the National Shrine by The Most Reverend Egidio Vagnozzi, the Apostolic Delegate.[78]

At a luncheon meeting Vice President Richard M. Nixon spoke of the "moral and spiritual heritage" of the country asking the Catholic editors to do their part in strengthening this facet of American life. One morning one hundred fifty Senators and Representatives attended a Congressional Breakfast sitting with journalists from their home states. Bishop Albert R. Zuroweste, Episcopal Chairman, spoke and his address was printed in the Congressional Record. The rest of that day was devoted to a tour of Washington with two important meetings scheduled enroute. At the Pan-American Building the delegates heard an address on the progress achieved in inter-American relations. Later, officials of the State Department answered questions concerning disarmament, the Free World, and Communism.[79] The majority of convention-goers were pleased with the program and appreciated the uniqueness of the Jubilee Convention while outsiders were impressed by the display.[80]

In addition to these varied endeavors to bring their organization into greater prominence, the Catholic Press personnel has also remained alert to world problems, national concerns, and social issues. Foremost in the beginning of this period were those touching on war, peace, and post-war adjustments with the conventions of the early 1940's adopting resolutions deploring the war and calling for a just and lasting peace. Once the United Nations was established, it became a focal point for CPA activities related to inter-national affairs. Already at the 1947 convention it was suggested that the Association establish some sort of contact with the UN, but it was not until 1952 that a CPA member became an official consultant at the United Nations headquarters through an appointment made by the International Union of the Catholic Press (IUCP) to which the Association did not belong.[81]

The representative, Charles J. McNeill, noted that both the Vatican and Episcopal Chairman Thomas K. Gorman strongly favored Catholic participation in the various meetings of agencies of the world today. Finding this contact extremely worthwhile, McNeill immediately began advocating that the CPA affiliate with the IUCP. Marc Delforge, a director of the International Union, visited the United States that fall and urged Catholic publishers "to take their rightful place" in the world organization. When McNeill became CPA president in 1954, one of his first official acts was to propose affiliation with the IUCP. Noting that the CPA itself could not qualify for "consultative status with the United Nations," he maintained that such a connection would enable the CPA "to play an active role in the workings of the Economic and Social Council" thereby giving the Association "a more direct and official role in UN affairs...."[82]

President McNeill appointed a Public Affairs Committee to act as liaison between the CPA and the IUCP, to study developments within the UN of matters relating to the Catholic Press or the Church in general, and to serve in an advisory capacity to the delegation already representing the Union in the Economic and Social Council. In February of 1955 members were notified that affiliation had been completed, and the Public Affairs Committee recommended to the annual convention that a full time representative of the International Union be appointed to the UN.[83] That summer the new committee chairman, Father Hugh Morley, traveled to Europe and through meetings with personnel in the IUCP office in Paris effected a "working arrangement" concerning the delegation at the UN. In the fall of 1962 when the IUCP named Morley as its permanent representative to the UN, the CPA provided him with secretarial and telephone service as well as office space.[84] A few years later at the invitation of the IUCP, Doyle and Msgr. R. H. J. Hanley became members of its board.[85]

Because of the affiliation of the CPA with the IUCP, Association members had become interested in the International Congress of the Catholic Press scheduled for the fall of 1957 in Vienna. At this Congress the secretary of the International Union expressed the hope that such a gathering might be held soon on the continent of North America.[86] In his address to the 1962 convention, CPA President, Father Albert J. Nevins, told the members that plans were being made for a Congress to be held in conjunction with a CPA convention in the near future. Father Emile Gabel, executive secretary of the IUCP, attended the 1963 convention, and in meetings between him and the directors it was decided to hold the next Congress in New York City with the 1965 convention of the CPA. Efforts were made to give an "international tone" to the meetings, and the Seventh World Congress proved to be "the outstanding international cooperative effort" in the CPA's history. At this first meeting of a Catholic World Press Congress beyond the continent of

Europe, the delegates, numbering over seven hundred, visited the UN where Secretary General U Thant addressed them.[87] Reporting on the Congress, Doyle commented that not only had it greatly enhanced the status of the CPA and the entire American Catholic Press, but due to it the Association also had "assumed a substantially larger and more important place in world Catholic press circles..."[88]

Although the Public Affairs Committee was concerned primarily with the UN and the IUCP's representation there, it was also very much involved in one other issue during part of the period in which it was active, an effort in the later 1950's to convince the Bureau of the Census that there should be a "religious question" in the 1960 census questionnaire. Despite activities that continued for over two years, the committee reported to the 1958 convention that the question had not been included because of the controversial aspects of the issue as well as for financial reasons.[89]

Perhaps this involvement with the religious question stemmed in part from an over-emphasis on communism during these and earlier years which resulted in an excessive fear that atheism and irreligion were real threats to the American way of life. The theme of the 1948 convention was "The Scourge of Secularism," and Father John S. Kennedy who keynoted the convention the following year gave the delegates one word--"Mindszenty." Striking out against totalitarian regimes, he called on the Catholic Press to imitate the Hungarian Cardinal in diligently defending the right. In 1950 even though Episcopal Chairman Michael J. Ready in the keynote address pointed out that men in public life who had long defended the interests of their country and of their God "deserve the encouragement and notice of our press as well as those who lately and hysterically identify themselves as the defenders of the nation," the majority of the delegates warmly welcomed Senator Joseph McCarthy when he presented the principal convention address. Subdued perhaps by the turn of events in McCarthy's career, the 1954 convention passed a resolution urging "positive as well as negative means of halting and defeating the enemies of God and man."[90]

Positive means were also used to some extent in dealing with social issues of the times. In 1943 Bishop Karl J. Alter, Episcopal Chairman of the NCWC Department of Social Action, addressed a convention session asking that the journalists take an active part not only in promoting peace but also in creating "a better social order based on Christian principles." Over a decade later a private survey of Catholic publications concluded that "never before in its history has the Catholic press in America been doing more to promote the social teachings of the Church and their application to current problems."[91] In the fall of 1961 the board called on the membership to study in detail Pope John XXIII's recent encyclical, Mater et Magistra. Noting that the English translation was "Christianity and Social Progress," the directors asked that the Catholic Press observe 1962 as the "Encyclical Year" and publicize it so thoroughly that a program of social action might emerge as a result.[92]

Particular social issues were also brought to the attention of the editors at various times. A 1948 resolution concerning immigration called for "vigorous action by the President and Congress to restore basic human rights to Displaced Persons." A few years later the Association urged that President Truman veto the McCarran-Walter Act, and the following year it supported President Eisenhower's request for the admission of immigrants on an emergency basis. The 1956 convention not only asked for a revision of the McCarran Act which had been passed over the President's veto, but also urged that the emergency immigration quotas be extended. A year later the CPA called on Congress to "enact long-delayed legislation" regarding immigration.[93]

The editors also met the challenge of racial difficulties within the United States. Delegates attending the 1942 meeting heard Edward F. Murphy, SSJ, who spoke on "The Negro Question, North and South," trace the history of the Negro in America and ask the journalists to instill in their readers a sense of interracial justice. The speaker "was so warmly applauded that he was forced to return," and the CPA endorsed a resolution offering "its support to the Negro in his problems."[94] Resolutions of a general nature continued to be common during the 40's and early 50's, but by the mid-1950's they were describing discrimination and racial segregation as "evil" and calling on the Catholic community to exert leadership in housing, school integration, and other areas.[95] As early as 1952 the Catholic Interracial Council cited the CPA for its work in behalf of racial justice, and it declared a few years later that the Catholic Press had "crusaded militantly, courageously and uncompromisingly" to procure full equality for all American citizens.[96] CPA members also discussed racial problems at their regional conferences, editors spoke to other groups on the subject of racial equality, and various publications carried features and special editorials on racial issues. In the recent past even more concerted action has been taken. Commenting on the coverage by Catholic publications of the assassination of Dr. Martin Luther King, one columnist declared that the Catholic Press had spoken "with one universal cry for racial justice."[97] In addition, several major addresses at the 1968 convention concentrated on Black America and its needs.

Finally, the Association has been solicitous for the well-being of the laboring class. A 1947 convention resolution re-affirmed "that working men have the inalienable right to organize in unions..." In the 1950's much attention was given to the "right-to-work" laws,[98] and a special Association committee made extensive studies of group insurance and retirement plans for its own employees encouraging member publications to provide such benefits.[99]

These various activities, like the business affairs of the Association, are bound to be part of the future history of the CPA. Despite their importance, they are mere adjuncts to the essential concern of such a group--that of striving for professional excellence.

Notes

1. For earlier press month efforts, see above Chapter III and Chapter IV. The poster was discussed in Transcript... 1941, pp. 9-14. CPA. The committee reports are from In Vain, I (October 6, 1941), p. 3 and Proceedings... 1942, p. 20. CPA.

2. "Minutes, Board... October 10, 1947," p. 121. CPA.

3. "Minutes, Board... October 13, 1950," p. 27; James F. Kane, "Report on the Operation of Your CPA National Office" to 1951 Convention, p. 4; and F. A. Fink, "Report of the President" to Annual Convention, June 19, 1952, p. 3. All in CPA.

4. "Catholic Press Month Committee Report" to Board of Directors, November 21-22, 1963. Doyle had rec-

ommended this action in his spring report. "Executive Secretary's Report" to Board of Directors, April 30, 1963. Both in PC. Schools particularly had much earlier found a Catholic Library Association Kit more attractive. This from "Minutes, Board... "February 13-14, 1958," p. 1. CPA.

5. For the report see: CJ, VII (March, 1956), p. 7. The committee was named in "Minutes, Board... May 18, 1956," pp. 1 and 7. CPA.

6. CJ, II (June, 1950), pp. 2-3 reprinted Bussard's address. The decision is in "Report of the Joint Committee on Catholic Press Month" to Board of Directors, May 16, 1951. CPA.

7. Discussions concerning Press Month are recorded in: "Minutes, Officers... August 8, 1957," p. 4; "Minutes, Board... May 26, 1964," p. 2; "Minutes, Business Meeting," May 17, 1968, p. 1; and "Minutes, Board... May 17, 1968," p. 4. All in CPA.

8. "Catholic Press Month Committee Report," to Board of Directors, September 20-21, 1962. PC. "Minutes, Board... May 26, 1964," p. 2. Both in CPA.

9. "Executive Secretary's Report" to Board of Directors, May 17, 1965, p. 2 and ibid., August 17, 1965, p. 2. Both in CPA.

10. For discussion of the Life Membership drive see above, Chapter V. Kane was coordinator of the new committee and Nevelle J. Morgan chairman of a subcommittee on Press Promotion and Publicity. The Mt. Angel project is explained in: "Report of Press Promotion Committee" to Board of Directors, February 25, 1960. The force behind the cooperative attempts was Gerard Sherry who later chaired the committee. See: "Catholic Press Promotion Committee Report" to Board of Directors, May 15, 1962. Combination of the committees is noted in: "Minutes, Officers... June 18, 1964," p. 1. All in CPA.

11. For examples see: CJ, I (April, 1950), p. 1; "Min-

utes, Board... October 18, 1951," p. 5; "Executive Secretary's Report" to Board of Directors, May 10, 1960, p. 2. Both in CPA.

12. Discussion of the Marquette project is from "Minutes, Board... February 13-14, 1958," p. 13. CPA. Interviews with R. N. Hamilton, SJ, University Archivist, and David Host of the Marquette College of Journalism on October 7, 1968, verified the non-existence of such a collection.

13. Doyle's activities can be traced through: "Executive Secretary's Report" to Board of Directors, May 12, 1959, p. 1 (CPA); CJ, X (April, 1959), p. 1; "Minutes, Board... May 13, 1960," p. 2 (CPA); and "Executive Director's Report" to Board of Directors, May 1, 1966, p. 19 (CC).

14. Resumé... 1935, p. 44. CPA. However, a resolution was passed at the 1928 convention to publish a quarterly bulletin following President S. A. Baldus' suggestion for such a publication as a means of acquainting Catholics with "the objects and endeavors of the Catholic Press Association." This from Yearbook... 1928, pp. 17 and 22. CC. No action was taken. Ridder to Hall, January 19, 1939. PDF.

15. Hall to Ridder, January 17, 1939; Ridder to Hall, January 19, 1939; and Hall to Ridder, January 21, 1939. All in PDF.

16. Hall to Humphrey E. Desmond July 12, 1939. PDF.

17. Approval is noted in Resumé... 1940, p. 7. CPA. The reader is reminded that Wynhoven had just been elected president. By the time the second issue appeared, Wynhoven had become editor-in-chief and a member from each region had been named to a Board of Editors. See: In Vain, I (December 30, 1940), p. 2. The material from the initial number of In Vain is from pp. 1-2.

18. Transcript... 1941, pp. 28-33. CPA.

19. Considine was named by the board in "Minutes, Board ... May 30, 1942," p. 3. CPA. All eight issues

of In Vain were included in one volume even though it appeared over a two year business period: September 1940 through May 1942. Considine's plans for the publication are from "Minutes, Board... October 30, 1942," p. 1. WC.

20. Blocker was named in "Minutes, Board... October 18, 1943," p. 2. His suggestions are from Proceedings... 1944, p. 19. Both in CPA.

21. Desmond's appointment is in Proceedings... 1944. p. 41. CPA. For his plans see: C. P. A. Bulletin, IV (December, 1944), p. 1.

22. Shanahan neglected to supply volume and issue numbers in the first three issues of June, July-August and September, but he labeled the November, 1945, issue Volume I, #4. Issues in 1946 were Volume II, but through an error which apparently involved a juxtoposition of Roman and Arabic numbers, the January 1947 issue appeared as Volume 12, #1, and the error was perpetuated to July (#6) of that year after which the numbering system was discontinued. This makes it difficult to determine accurately how many issues were published between that date and August of 1949 when Father Barrett took over and began a new series with Volume I, #1. Examples of Shanahan's recruiting are found in letters from him to Publisher of Central-Blatt and Social Justice Review, July 24, 1945, and to The Bulletin-National Catholic Women's Union, July 30, 1945. Both in CC. The move toward a trade journal is explained in Abbreviated Report... 1946, Foreword. WC. References to the supplementary bulletins were made in CJ, I (November, 1945), p. 9 and II (May-June, 1946), p. 7. The latter issue stated that 28 such "bulletins" had been distributed. This author has been able to locate only five of these circulars.

23. There were nine issues in 1946-1947: Abbreviated Report... 1947, Foreword. WC. Difficulties with the printers were reported in CJ, [no volume given] (February, 1948), p. 2. The organ was published in August and November of 1948 and in February and April of 1949. Mrs. Homan in her report to the board dated June 15, 1949, p. 8 (CPA) stated that she had published only the last two named issues

during her term as secretary. If others appeared in the fall of 1948, they have not been located.

24. CJ, II (June, 1950), p. 2.

25. "Executive Secretary's Report" to Board of Directors, September 15, 1959; Ibid., February 25, 1960; "Report on Catholic Journalist Expansion" to Board of Directors, May 10, 1960. All in CPA.

26. "Minutes, Board... January 5-6, 1961," p. 1. DC. "Executive Secretary's Report" to Board of Directors, October 26, 1961, p. 2. CPA.

27. Doyle's plan was presented in April of 1963: "Executive Secretary's Report" to Board of Directors, April 30, 1963, p. 2. PC. His hopes for monthly issues is noted in: Ibid., November 21-22, 1963, p. 4 and his "revamping" plan in ibid., May 17, 1965, p. 2. Both in CPA. The conversion to eight Newsletters is reported in ibid., May 1, 1966, p. 21. CC. In February, 1970, the Catholic Journalist changed format and became a tabloid newspaper.

28. Shanahan's original plan is in a circular to all Active and Associate Members, February 16, 1946. His estimate of the number needed is from a similar circular dated March 23, 1946. Both in WC. The initial run was reported in CJ, II (May-June, 1946), p. 6.

29. Catholic Press Association of U. S., I am The Catholic Press (n. p., 1946), passim. WC. Shanahan reported in CJ, II (May-June, 1946), p. 7 that he had many difficulties compiling this material since records were scattered or non-existence.

30. Hall's letter concerning the publication appeared in CJ, II (July-August, 1946), p. 6. Shanahan received permission for reprinting in "Minutes, Board... October 17, 1946," p. 91. CPA. The report on the few numbers of reorders is from Abbreviated Report... 1947, p. 10. WC.

31. Copies of all these convention booklets are in CC.

32. Doyle to Floyd Anderson, January 12, 1960, stated his

vision of the 1960 book. Anderson was editor and Doyle business manager of the publication according to a memo from President Daly to Directors, February 4, 1960. Both in DC. Doyle's plan for continuous annuals is in "Appendix to Executive Secretary's Report" to Board of Directors, February 25-26, 1960, p. 3. CPA.

33. Criticisms are referred to in letters from Father Albert J. Nevins to Doyle, April 27, 1960, and Anderson to Daly, May 2, 1960. DC. Progress on the 1961 Annual is reported in "Executive Secretary's Report" to Board of Directors, May 10, 1960, p. 1; Ibid., January 5-6, 1961, p. 2; and ibid., October 26, 1961, pp. 4-5. All in CPA. Doyle's report on the 1962 book is from ibid., May 15, 1962, p. 1. PC.

34. Except for the 1965 annual the remaining issues were not particularly impressive. For this reason and due to losses in advertising revenue Doyle made the suggestion in "Minutes, Board... May 10, 1966," p. 1. CPA.

35. For the earlier history of the Directory, see above Chapter III. The endorsement appeared on p. 4 of J. H. Meier (ed.), Catholic Press Directory (Chicago, 1928). The 1940 venture is from Resumé... 1940, p. 6. CPA.

36. "Minutes, Board... October 17, 1946," p. 92 and ibid., October 10, 1947, p. 121. CPA. The following year Charles Ridder considered publishing the Directory. See: "Minutes, Board... May 19, 1948," p. 124. CPA.

37. CJ, I (August, 1949), p. 1. Barrett and Wagner had been schoolmates. "Report of the Executive Secretary to the Executive Board of the Catholic Press Association," November 11, 1949, p. 2. CPA.

38. Arrangements were discussed in letters from Wey to Barrett, September 8, 1949, and Barrett to Wey, October 3, 1949. WC. See also: CJ, I (October, 1949), p. 1. References to the slow returns from Catholic publishers is from CJ, I (March, 1950), p. 4.

39. Wagner's reaction is from a letter to Father Nevins from Clement J. Wagner dated August 10, 1950. The compromise was reported to Kane by F. A. Fink in a letter dated September 5, 1950. The front cover option was agreed on in "Minutes, Board.. October 13, 1950," p. 28. All in CPA.

40. For reports on the first Directory see: CJ, II (March, 1951), pp. 1-2 and Kane, "Report on the Operation of Your CPA National Office" to 41st Annual Convention, p. 4. CPA.

41. CJ, III (March, 1952), p. 2 reported the lower price. The increase is noted in "Catholic Press Directory Advisory Committee Report" to Board of Directors, May 26, 1964. PC.

42. Above, Chapter IV. Transcript... 1941, pp. 39-44, CPA. In Vain, I (March 5, 1942), p. 3.

43. "Minutes, Board... May 19, 1948," p. 125 reported that thirty life members came in that year. CPA. CJ, III (December, 1951), p. 1 noted the suspension of the contests. Besides the cost, the contests were also "Too limiting in overall benefit,... unduly difficult to administer, nebulous in effect, and productive of very little quality material." This from "Recommendations to the Board from Literary Awards Committee," November 11, 1954. CPA.

44. Constitution and Bylaws [sic] of the Catholic Press Association of the United States, 1942, Article VI, Section 7. CPA. The amendment was approved in "Minutes, Board.. October 18, 1951," p. 2. PDF. Father Kennedy's appointment and decision are from "Minutes, Board.. October 24-25, 1952," p. 6 and ibid., May 6, 1953, p. 3. CPA.

45. Ridder to Kennedy, June 12, 1953. CPA. "CPA by-laws [revised to] May 14, 1954." Printed with CJ, VI (October, 1954). As late as the winter of 1958, however, the directors again discussed this matter. William Holub noted that some of the older members were quite concerned that the original purposes of the Literary Awards Foundation no longer appeared in the by-laws. He was assured that "living tradi-

tion... would always govern the use of [the] fund.." This from "Minutes, Board... February 13-14, 1958," p. 25. CPA.

46. "Recommendations to the Board from Literary Awards Committee," November 11, 1954; "Minutes, Board ... November 11-12, 1954," p. 3. Both in CPA. Hughes' appointment was announced in CJ, VI (April-May, 1955), pp. 1-2.

47. The title was reported in CJ, VI (December, 1955), p. 6. Reports of the book are from "Literary Awards Committee Report" to Opening Business Meeting, May 16, 1956, and William Holub, "Report on the CPA's Literary Awards Committee," Books on Trial, XV (February, 1957), 236.

48. The second printing was announced in CJ, VII (November-December, 1956), p. 7. The total of 10,000 copies had been disposed of by December of 1958. P. J. Kenedy & Sons to Catholic Press Association, December 31, 1958. CPA. The French edition was discussed in "Minutes, Board... May 18, 1956," p. 7, and the Dutch in "Minutes, Officers ... July 12, 1956," p. 4. Both in CPA. The Dublin book was All Kinds of People: Representative Fiction From the American Catholic Press (Clonmore and Reynolds, Dublin, 1958). Copy in CPA Library.

49. For objections from directors see: "Minutes, Board ... May 27, 1955," p. 4 and "Minutes, Officers ... July 12, 1956," p. 6. Both in CPA. Discussion of the 1960 collection is from "Literary Awards Committee Report" to Board of Directors, September 21, 1956. CPA. Holub told the 1957 convention that "Herr and Lane have six large packing cases of raw material from which to make their selections." "Report to CPA Convention, May 15, 1957." CPA. Herr was with the Thomas More Association, and Lane was City Editor of the Chicago Daily News. The theme was reported in CJ, VIII (July-August, 1957), p. 3.

50. NC Release 1/20/58 carried an article on the forthcoming book and explained the title. The sub-title was Significant Writing from the Catholic Press.

Evaluations of the anthology are from "Literary Awards Committee Report" to Board of Directors, May 20, 1958 (CPA) and Library Journal, LXXXIII (April 1, 1958), 1081. This reviewer called Realities "A completely satisfactory collection reflecting Catholic culture in this country, dignified, scholarly and yet popular enough to appeal to the average intelligent reader, Catholic or otherwise." The report on the number sold is from a letter from Doyle to Herr dated July 30, 1958. CPA.

51. "Minutes, Board... May 17, 1957," p. 3 noted the criticism. The handbook was suggested in "CPA Literary Awards Committee" to Board of Directors, September 12-13, 1957. "Minutes, Board... September 12-13, 1957," p. 19 empowered the committee to act. The combination of a newspaperman and a university representative was suggested in "Literary Awards Committee Report" to Board of Directors, May 20, 1958. All in CPA.

52. "Literary Awards Committee Report" to Board of Directors, September 22, 1958, showed lack of interest in continuing the anthologies. However, Dan Herr independently of CPA edited with Paul Cuneo Harvest, 1960 which was a collection of Catholic non-fiction from 1959. Since then he has also published various other anthologies containing selections taken from Catholic publications and authors. Other activities are mentioned in "President's Report" to Board of Directors, May 12, 1959, p. 3 (CPA) and "Literary Awards Committee Report" to Board of Directors, January 5-6, 1961 (DC). None of these projects was carried out in full.

53. "Literary Awards Committee Report" to Board of Directors, May 20, 1958 (CPA); "Minutes, Board... September 20, 1962," p. 2 (PC); Ibid., May 26, 1964, p. 1 (CPA).

54. J. H. Meier to A. J. Wey, June 24, 1936. WC. The entry was a "special bound magazine edition for the 7th National Eucharistic Congress, dated October 18, 1935, and displayed at the World Catholic Press Exhibition in Vatican City in 1936." This note from Mr. Wey to the writer, December 11, 1967.

55. C. P. A. Bulletin, IV (December, 1944), p. 1; "Report of the President of CPA," to Executive Board, October 25, 1945, p. 3 (CPA); and Abbreviated Report... 1946, p. 7 (WC).

56. The announcement of the awards is in CJ, [no volume given] (January, 1948), pp. 4-5. Winners were reported in NC Release 5/24/48. Second and third places were won by the Catholic Herald Citizen and the Catholic Chronicle for newspapers and The Sign and Far East for magazines.

57. The 1949 contest was reported in The Sign, XXIX (August, 1949), p. 4 and the 1950 winners in CJ, I (May, 1950), p. 2.

58. The voting system was explained in CJ, II (January-February, 1951), p. 1. Dean O'Sullivan and professors Robert Kidera and David Host, all of Marquette, devised the scoring system. Kane's evaluation is from "Report on the Operation of Your CPA National Office" to the 41st Annual Convention, p. 5. CPA.

59. For reports on the changes in the awards system consult CJ, III (April, 1952), p. 5; Ibid., IV (December, 1953), p. 1; Ibid., VI (November-December, 1954), pp. 1 and 4 and (January, 1955), p. 2.

60. "Minutes, Board... May 27, 1955," p. 7. CPA. Changes are from CJ, VII (January, 1956), p. 2. The new award was explained in "Report of Newspaper Awards Committee" to Board of Directors, October 17, 1955. PDF.

61. "Minutes, Board... May 18, 1956," p. 2 and ibid., September 12, 1956, pp. 2-5. Both in CPA.

62. Reports on the interim plan appeared in CJ, VII (October, 1956), p. 2; "Minutes, Board... March 15, 1957," p. 6 (CPA); and CJ, IX (February, 1958), p. 1.

63. See above, Chapter V for discussion of the fund-raising project. The support for the Journalism Awards is given in "Catholic Press Association-Survey Report" to Officers Meeting, March 1, 1957, p. A. CPA.

The committees were named in "Minutes, Board ... May 14, 1957," p. 5. Father Hugh Morley (OFM, Cap.) was coordinating chairman. The work of the committees was outlined in CJ, VIII (May-June, 1957), pp. 1-2.

64. Discussion resulting in the new committee is in "Minutes, Board... September 12-13, 1957," pp. 5-7 and 10. "Special Journalism Awards Committee" Report to CPA Board of Directors, May 20, 1958, covers the work of the committee for the year. Both in CPA files.

65. The announcement was in CJ, X (February, 1959), p. 1. Duquesne continued to handle the newspaper awards until 1966 when St. Bonaventure's took over. Fordham judged magazines from 1959 to 1964 and again in 1966 and 1967. St. Bonaventure's handled the 1965 awards, and Marquette judged them in 1968. The critiques of the professors is from CJ, X (April, 1959), p. 3. In the 1960's, critique booklets were published and distributed to the members. The comment on fewer complaints is from "Minutes, Board... May 19, 1961," p. 1. CPA. It is interesting that even though these awards received so much of the attention and finances of the Association, less than half the members publications ordinarily participated in the contests. As late as 1964 a survey showed that during that year only forty-one per cent of the newspapers and forty-three per cent of the magazines entered the competition. This from "Minutes, Board... May 26, 1964," p. 4. CPA.

66. Publishers' Weekly, CLXXXV (March 23, 1964), p. 33 announced the Book Awards. 1964 competition was announced in 'National Catholic Book Awards." Procedures are from "Rules and Procedures Governing National Catholic Book Awards of the Catholic Press Association." Both in PC.

67. Recommendations for the second competition are from "Journalism Awards Committee Report" to Board of Directors, October 7, 1964. PC. The 1968 data is from "National Catholic Book Award Winner," 1968. CPA. There were 113 titles entered by 39 publishers in this contest.

68. The first award was discussed in "Minutes, Board ... May 18, 1956," pp. 5-6. Dissatisfaction and further negotiations is from "CPA-Catholic Digest Award Committee Report" to Board of Directors, October 10, 1956. Both in CPA.

69. See: "Minutes, Board... January 21, 1957," p. 7; Ibid., May 17, 1957, p. 3; and ibid., September 12-13, 1957, p. 19. All in CPA. For details on the school plans, see above, Chapter VI.

70. 1958 modifications are reported in CJ, IX (January, 1958), p. 1. Delaney's selection is in "Minutes, Board... February 13-14, 1958," p. 11. The unilateral action is suggested in a letter from Doyle to Bussard, January 28, 1959, and the withdrawal of the award in a letter from Bussard to Doyle, February 10, 1959. All in CPA.

71. G. Roger Cahaney claimed to have originated the idea of a special CPA award: "Minutes, Board . . . May 27, 1955," p. 6. The suggestion is in "Literary Awards Committee Report" to Board of Directors, September 22, 1958, and the method of selection is in "Minutes, Board... January 15, 1959," p. 2. All in CPA.

72. Memo from Special Awards Committee to Registered Agents, February 7, 1959. PC. Agents were to give their reasons for nominations and to include "exhibits illustrating the reasons." McGlynn's appointment was announced in CJ, X (March, 1959), p. 1.

73. "Special Awards Committee Report" to Board of Directors, May 12, 1959, explained the procedure. CPA. Winners were announced in CJ, X (June, 1959), pp. 1-2.

74. Directors' objections are noted in "Minutes, Board ... May 12, 1959," p. 4. Plans for a re-study are in ibid., May 15, 1959, p. 1. John J. Daly in "Report of the President" to Annual Convention, May 10, 1960, p. 3 reported the limit on nominees. All in CPA.

75. Methods used in the early 60's appear in "Special

Awards Committee Report" to Board of Directors, April 30, 1963. CPA. Recipients were: 1960-Frank Hall; 1961-John Courtney Murray, SJ; 1962-Albert J. Nevins, MM; 1963-Floyd Anderson. There were slight revisions after the 1963 contest. "Special Awards Committee Report" to Board of Directors, May 26, 1964. PC. Recent revisions are recorded in "Minutes, Board... May 13, 1966," p. 2 and _ibid._, May 16, 1967, p. 1. CPA.

76. The Reedy action and the board's decision are in "Minutes Business Meeting," May 17, 1968, p. 1 and "Minutes, Board... May 17, 1968," pp. 4-5. Reedy referred to no nominees by name but pointed out that "one obvious candidate" was being excluded. CPA records show that among the final nominees each year from 1961 to 1968 inclusively was Robert G. Hoyt. Recipients in recent years have been: 1964-Patrick O'Connor, SSC; 1965-John Cogley; 1966-Joseph A. Breig; 1967-John Reedy, CSC; 1968-Bishop James P. Shannon.

77. Golden Jubilee plans are discussed in "Minutes, Board ... May 15, 1959," p. 6; "Minutes, Officers... August 6, 1959," pp. 1-3; "Minutes, Board... September 25, 1959," pp. 5-8; and "Executive Secretary's Report" to Board of Directors, May 10, 1960. All in CPA.

78. Description of the convention is in "Minutes, Board ... May 13, 1960," p. 1. Mention of Hesburgh's speech and the Cardinal's activities are in _CJ_, XI (July, 1960), p. 1.

79. The text of Mr. Nixon's speech was included in _Proceedings... 1960._ CC. Articles on the breakfast were included in _CJ_, XI (July, 1960), p. 5 and (September, 1960), p. 8. Other sessions are listed in _Program... 1960._ CPA.

80. Doyle reported on the success of the convention in "Appendix to Executive Secretary's Report" to Board of Directors, September 8, 1960, p. 1. CPA. An executive of the Associated Church Press who attended the sessions as a guest was very impressed, reported at length on the Golden Jubilee meeting, and told his fellow Protestants of the advantages of

cooperative effort and "editorial unity." See: William B. Lipphard, "Catholic Press Association," Christian Century, LXXVII (June 8, 1960), 708-709.

81. Contact was suggested in Abbreviated Report... 1947, p. 10. WC. McNeill reported his appointment in a letter to F. A. Fink dated October 14, 1952. The IUCP "was established in 1935 as a coordinating agency for Catholic press activity throughout the world." This from a memo from C. J. McNeill to Board of Directors, May 14, 1954. Both in CPA.

82. McNeill advocated affiliation in a letter to CPA President, Reverend T. A. Meehan, October 14, 1952. His action as president is from a memo to the Board of Directors, May 14, 1954. Both in CPA. Delforge's visit is reported in CJ, IV (November, 1952), p. 8.

83. Notice of the committee is in NC Release 7/19/54. Completion of affiliation was reported in CJ, VI (February, 1955), p. 1. "Report on the Public Affairs Committee of the Catholic Press Association, 1954-1955" (CPA), suggested the full time representative.

84. Morley's tour was noted in "Minutes, Board... October 10-11, 1956," p. 3. CPA. His appointment is in "Report on International Cooperation by the Catholic Press Association of the United States, Inc.," 1965. HC

85. An invitation for board membership is noted in "Minutes, Board... May 21, 1965," p. 2. The appointments are in "Report of International Union of the Catholic Press" to Board of Directors, August 17, 1965. CPA. In "Executive Director's Report," May 1, 1966 (CC) Doyle reported that the IUCP had changed its name to the International Catholic Union of the Press in order "to include in its membership and its concerns Catholics in the general press as well as those people and organizations in the specifically Catholic press."

86. See: McNeill, "Report to CPA Convention," May 16, 1956, pp. 2-3 and "Minutes, Officers... October

18, 1957," p. 2. Both in CPA.

87. "President's Opening Statement" to 1962 Convention, p. 1. CPA. "Report on International Cooperation by the Catholic Press Association of the United States, Inc.," 1965. HC.

88. "Executive Director's Report," May 1, 1966, p. 1. CC.

89. For details on this activity see: "CPA Public Affairs Committee Report" to 1957 Convention; "Closing Business Meeting," May 17, 1957, p. 2; "Minutes, Board... September 12-13, 1957," p. 11; "Public Affairs Committee Report" to Board of Directors, May 20, 1958. All in CPA. To include the question would have cost a half million dollars.

90. See: "The Catholic Press--A Necessity," CA, XXX (June, 1948), p. 8; NC Release 6/20/49; NC Release 6/1/50 for Ready's speech; "Prose and Poetry," Commonweal, LII (June 9, 1950), 213 for delegates' reaction; and D. J. Thorman, "Anti-Communist Record of the Catholic Press," America, XCII (February 5, 1955), 473 for resolution. In a study of the general attitudes of the Catholics of this country regarding McCarthy it was found that "only a handful of Catholic newspapers came out against McCarthyism." See: Vincent P. DeSantis, "American Catholics and McCarthyism," Catholic Historical Review, LI (April, 1965), 1-30.

91. Proceedings... 1943, pp. 120-124. CPA. Donald J. Thorman, "The Catholic Press and Catholic Social Action," Catholic Mind, LIV (January, 1956), pp. 1-9.

92. NC Release 10/30/61.

93. This action may be traced through: "The Catholic Press-A Necessity," CA, XXX (June, 1948), p. 8; "Closing General Business Meeting," June 20, 1952, p. 1; Register (Denver), May 17, 1953; "Catholic Press Meets in Texas," America, XCV (June 2, 1956), 239; and CJ, VIII (May-June, 1957), p. 3.

94. The speech is recorded in Proceedings... 1942, pp.

99-107. CPA. The reaction is from "Comment," America, LXVII (June 13, 1942), 257, and the resolution from Proceedings... 1942, p. 23. CPA.

95. The evil was mentioned in "Closing Business Meeting," May 18, 1956, p. 2 and the call for Catholic leadership in ibid., May 17, 1957, p. 4. Both in CPA.

96. CJ, III (March, 1952), p. 2 and "Leadership of the Catholic Press," Interracial Review, XXIX (June, 1956), p. 93.

97. S. J. Adamo, "The Press," America, CXVIII (May 4, 1968), 624.

98. Abbreviated Report... 1947, p. 16. WC. Secretary of Labor James P. Mitchell received "a round of enthusiastic applause" when he spoke out against the right-to-work laws at a Civic Banquet. See: CJ, VIII (May-June, 1957), p. 3. A Jesuit economist, Father Benjamin L. Masse, spoke on the same topic the next year according to CJ, IX (May-June, 1958), p. 6.

99. "President's Opening Statement," May 16, 1962, p. 1 refers to the pension plans. CPA. The central office files also contain numerous reports of the committee and of the executive secretary dating from 1955 to the present.

Chapter VIII

Emphasis on Professionalism

Critics have often singled out lack of professionalism as the most glaring deficiency of the Catholic Press, and the CPA has long endeavored to stimulate improvements in this area. Besides providing special professional services for its member publications and for writers in the field, the Association has maintained ties with the Catholic School Press Association and has interested itself in the education of future journalists. Encouragement and aid have been extended to other Catholic Press groups, especially those of Latin America. In collaboration with the Press Department of NCWC, the CPA has sponsored News Service studies and editors' seminars; it has also sought to improve relationships between editors and publishers. Members have debated the place of truth, censorship, and freedom in their publications and have adopted a Code of Fair Publishing Practices. Since Vatican II they have come to realize the importance of theology as a background for their writing and have participated in theological seminars. Finally, in 1967 the convention theme, "Accent on Professionalism," was chosen because:

> Intellectually as well as physically, this time calls for highly developed skills and for expert judgment in journalism. The post-Vatican Council world more than ever demands information, interpretation, and expression presented professionally.[1]

Attempts to remodel Catholic publications professionally began with content and physical appearance rather than intellectual aspects. The earliest efforts to improve the content and format of Catholic papers were made in the years 1911-1919. But after the establishment of the NCWC Press Department in 1920, Catholic editors tended to rely exclusively on the NC News Service which issued a weekly News Sheet.[2] For well over a decade Catholic newspapers particularly presented a duplication of make-up and content that excluded any great need for originality and professional ability. During these years, too, many of the papers passed to the ownership of dioceses and were frequently edited by priests untrained in the techniques of journalism and unaware of the shortcomings of their publications.[3] But after World War II a number of laymen who had attended schools of journalism and worked on secular publications moved into the field of the Catholic Press. These laymen joined the concerned priest-editors in appealing for professionalism and often took the initiative in doing something about it.[4]

The editors turned first to the physical appearance of their publications. In a 1947 convention session devoted to typographical analysis of both newspapers and magazines, 120 members presented their publications for criticism by a jury of experts who named those exhibiting professional standards. Secretary James A. Shanahan said of the affair: "The criticisms in general, although adverse, should prove invaluable to many member publications, for the betterment of these--typographically--was the principle [sic] objective ..."[5] Shanahan also advocated a "year-round counseling service" to criticize and provide "suggestions and layouts for improvement." During 1949-1950 Father Alfred Barrett, with the donated services of professional advisors, sponsored such a project in the CPA headquarters at Fordham.[6] A special Typographical and Layout Analysis Service was provided by the CPA for its magazine members in the fall of 1952. Four specialists donated their services, but the national office charged a fee to cover handling charges. The response was enthusiastic and the editors found that the service was most beneficial, but by April of 1953 it had to be suspended because the judges had offered their aid on a temporary basis.[7]

The practical problems of professional improvement were discussed in the 1953 convention, and in January, 1954, a special meeting was scheduled for the editors of small Catholic magazines. Twenty-five publications having a circulation of fifteen thousand or less sent representatives to this one-day meeting, and the complete text of the discussions was distributed to those unable to attend. G. Roger Cahaney, who had taken over as secretary, praised this type of cooperation: "With a selective audience discussing equally selective subjects, a better understanding of the techniques of all phases of publishing as they can be utilized and applied within the limitation of the particular group can surely result."[8]

The directors continued to be especially concerned about the smaller members, and the discussion technique was continued in the convention programs of the next few years. In 1956 Information Clinics, conducted as round-table discussions, featured leaders who were recognized authorities and included "all phases of publishing activity." These were so well received that the convention committee of the following year included a substantially increased number of them, and the clinics were repeated in 1958. From 1959 to the present, work shops and work sessions have been included in every convention program and have touched on all phases of newspaper and magazine publishing. In conjunction with the annual Journalism Awards, these have done much to improve the physical appearance of Catholic publications.[9]

The CPA has also made an effort to meet the special needs of those who write for Catholic publications. The Literary Awards program begun in an earlier period was intended to produce better quality writing, and during the years in which Associate Members were actively recruited, it was hoped that this affiliation would encourage Catholic authors to contribute to member publications. In 1946 CPA President Father Patrick O'Connor suggested another service for writers: a "Catholic manuscript market guide" to help writers in selecting likely publications in which to place their material.[10] It was not until 1956, however, that such a guide appeared as a supplement to the Catholic Journalist. Originally the "Catholic Writers' Market Guide" was to appear twice a year, once listing Spring-Summer requirements and again giving Fall-Winter needs. Commenting on the 1959 Spring-Summer issue, a Journalist article presented a composite description of Catholic publications:

> The Catholic press offers competent free lance writers and illustrators an extensive, diversified and responsive market. It demands polished, professional writing and eschews pietistic, preachy material. However, in many cases, purposes are ill-defined and the rate of payment for material is low compared to the secular magazines, although most Catholic magazines do pay on acceptance.

The twice-a-year editions did not materialize, but the "Guide" has continued to appear at irregular intervals over the years as a means of soliciting quality writing for the Catholic Press and encouraging professional practices on the part of both writers and editors.[11]

The CPA has also sought to improve the quality of Catholic writing and to encourage professionalism in the Catholic Press by being actively involved in the education of future Catholic journalists. Through the efforts of Jeremiah O'Sullivan, Dean of the College of Journalism at Marquette University, the Catholic School Press Association (CSPA) was organized in 1931, and by the end of the decade the CPA was considering affiliation of the school group with its own Association. A 1940 convention session discussed this proposal as well as the importance of young Catholic Americans to the future of the CPA. Msgr. Peter M. H. Wynhoven, chairman of the Press Planning Committee, explained that the affiliation would be such that there would be no interference on either side, but that a representative of the CSPA would be on the CPA board to expedite planning and joint endeavors. The constitution as amended by that convention provided that one of the directors be such a representative. This arrangement continued until another change in 1953 provided for a Catholic School Press Committee instead of board representation. Though the 1958 revision eliminated the mention of specific committees, a School Press Committee was named through 1961, and since 1965 there has been a special Education Committee appointed each year.[12]

In 1943 and 1944 sectional meetings of the CSPA were held as part of the annual CPA convention. A survey conducted by the Association in 1947 to determine the amount and the quality of journalism training in Catholic schools of journalism concluded that more attention should be given to this area. Although only fifteen teachers of journalism indicated interest in organizing a professional association of their own, the CPA in 1950 issued an invitation to this group to attend its regular convention sessions and special meetings set up to consider educational problems. The teachers discussed forming an organization, and a permanent organizational committee was named. Although the educators met with the CPA again in 1951 and 1953, they did not form an independent group.[13]

Beginning in 1940 and continuing for many years the CSPA held an annual National Catholic Educational Press Congress. In some years the CPA co-sponsored this event, and each year a number of the members of the Association were on the program of the Congress. From 1955 to the end of the decade and again in 1962 special Youth Sessions were held during the CPA conventions. These sessions, open to high school and college students and directed by Association members, were very effective in improving relations between the CPA and the CSPA.[14]

In the recent past these meetings have been discontinued, and the CPA has labored instead to cooperate with the National Catholic Educational Association and in general to improve relations between the Catholic Press and Catholic educators. The CPA Education Committee early in 1966 noticed that this relationship was deteriorating and suggested the need "to study the attitude of the Catholic press toward Catholic education and vice versa, to explore... common elements of both apostolates and to formulate plans to draw the two fields closer together." The committee recommended a "summit conference" during that summer of a small number of leaders in the two fields. The report was filed, but the following spring the committee arranged instead a luncheon meeting with educators during the NCEA convention. Each group presented its position, and areas of mutual concern were discussed. In the fall of 1967 a second meeting of the two groups was held.[15]

During the 1960's also a Catholic Journalism Scholarship Fund (CJSF) was established by a group of CPA members. This fund, intended to assist both undergraduate and graduate journalism students, was limited to study at Catholic institutions, and stipulated that the recipients were to work for at least two years in the Catholic Press field after completing their training. The fund gradually increased with contributions coming from CPA members as well as from other sources. The initial grants, announced so that recipients could begin their studies during the 1963-1964 academic years, went to two men and a woman chosen from among more than twenty applicants.[16] Again in the spring of 1964 the CJSF presented three scholarships, but by January of 1965 it sent out appeals for additional financial support. Two years later the sponsors of the fund asked that the CPA take it over and that, "in the interest of greater stability and more benefit to the Catholic press," funds be used to assist only graduate students. The board in May of 1967 approved a plan whereby the project would be transferred to the national office.[17]

Besides promoting the education of young people for the American Catholic Press, the CPA has also shown special interest in the Catholic Press of Latin America. During the period that he served as Episcopal Chairman, Bishop John Mark Gannon launched "Noticias Catholicas," a news service in Spanish for use in Latin America. A 1942 convention speaker chided the members of the CPA for the scant attention that their publications directed toward Latin American affairs and called for a "rapidly expanding program of inter-Americanism." Explaining that the Catholic Press of Latin America was extremely weak, he asked his fellow journalists to lend a helping hand.[18] Little was done at that time, but many years later the CPA, at the request of the Bishops of Latin America and of the Vatican's Pontifical Commission for Latin America, initiated and developed a program aimed at improving not only the Catholic Press but also all mass communication media in Latin America.[19]

A Committee for Liaison with the Latin American Catholic Press was named by President John J. Daly in 1959. The convention of the following year passed resolutions calling for "increased editorial attention" to the problems of Latin America and recommending that invitations be extended to journalists from those countries to spend time as observers and trainees in offices of CPA members. John J. Considine, MM, director of the Latin American Bureau of NCWC, after lengthy discussions with leaders in the Latin American Press, reported to the new CPA president, Father Albert J. Nevins, that two proposals had been made. One was that a team of experts in the Catholic Press of the United States spend about five weeks in Latin America studying conditions and planning "a program of coordination for the most effective use of mass media to reach Latin America's millions." The second was that a CPA group do a comprehensive study of mass communications in Peru to serve as a pilot study for similar surveys in other parts of Latin America.[20]

By December a four-phase program of cooperation had been formulated. Father Nevins announced that he himself would direct the project and that regional press seminars in Latin America and on-the-job training for Latin American journalists with publications in the United States and Canada were two important elements of the plan. In May of 1961 the directors appropriated one thousand dollars to help cover expenses of the seminar team. Commenting on the expenditure, Father Nevins reported that publishing techniques in Latin America were "sadly lacking in basic know-how," and he reminded the board that because of the very critical times in Latin America, such help was of vital importance.[21]

A study team under Nevins' direction contacted communications leaders and government officials, interviewed clergy and laity, and examined existing press facilities. The members then compiled a lengthy report on "Mass Communications and the Church in Peru" and presented a second report to the Pontifical Commission. Recommendations made by the team including the establishing of mass media centers in Bogota and Montevideo, Uruguay, training schools for radio broadcasters, and the founding of a national Catholic information bureau for Peru were all implemented. Phase three, on-the-job training, was scheduled for the fall of 1961 for twenty-one Latin American journalists to be selected by Dr. Cesar Luis Aguiar, secretary of the recently organized Union Latinoamerica de Prensa Catolica (ULAPC). Seminars to explain publishing techniques, help solve the problems of Latin American publications, "inculcate a desire for high professionalism and sound editorial and business practices," and attempt to appraise and improve the teaching of journalism in those countries were to be conducted by five specialists in October at three locations: Lima, Peru; Caracas, Venezuela; and Sao Paulo, Brazil.[22]

In February another team made communication studies in Honduras, Nicaragua, and Venezuela, met leaders of ULAPC, and attended the first Central American Catholic Press convention. As a climax to the Latin American project, the CPA chose Miami as its 1963 convention city and devoted special attention to Latin American and to Cuba and the problems of Cuban refugees.[23] Dr. Aguiar praised this action and informed the CPA that ULAPC President, Father Revollo Bravo, would attend. President John F. Kennedy expressed gratitude that the CPA was thus focusing its attention on Latin America and lauded the Association for the aid it had given to the Latin American press.[24] The convention named Father Nevins as permanent chairman of the Latin American Affairs Committee. The following year he reported that individual acts of assistance to local elements of the Catholic Press of Latin America instead of a broad general program had been carried out.[25] The committee was reappointed that year, but since then it has been discontinued.

The Latin American project, although emphasizing the Catholic Press, concerned itself with the mass communications media in general. During the earlier periods of CPA history, little attempt was made to coordinate efforts with other media. It was not until 1951, for example, that a formal CPA session was devoted to the problem of handling radio news. Commenting on that development, Secretary Kane noted that TV was already replacing radio as the major communication medium, and he urged CPA members to begin efforts to utilize it as a means of presenting Catholic news. The 1953 convention scheduled an extra Radio and TV Day arranged by the Catholic Broadcasters Association,[26] but apparently it was not until the second session of Vatican II issued the "Decree on the Instruments of Social Communication" that CPA members fully realized that closer cooperation with other communication groups was imperative if Catholic news was to be presented in a professional and competent manner.[27]

Beginning in 1964, the CPA invited representatives of the Catholic Broadcasters Association to attend the conventions, and a 1967 session discussed the possibility of a federation consisting of the CPA, Broadcasters, and others.[28] An intercommunications committee with Father J. E. Eiselein as chairman was named to serve as liaison with other communications organs. By the time the 1968 convention met, the Communications Media Liaison Committee reported contact with seven other groups.[29] At this meeting, too, Msgr. Francis T. Hurley, assistant general secretary of the United States Catholic Conference explained to the convention the reorganization of the old National Catholic Welfare Conference structure. He noted that press matters would be placed under the Department of Communications which would also oversee the Bureau of Information and radio and television.[30]

Dissatisfaction with the NC Press Department and the News Service persisted over the years. After the disagreements of the 1920's and early 1930's no serious clash occurred, but minor incidents were common.[31] During a 1944 session, Joseph Gelin, managing editor of the Catholic Universe Bulletin, presented a paper on how the Service might be improved. Gelin argued that unless the Catholic editors realized the "primacy of news" in their papers, there was no point in talking about improving the News Service. However, once they accepted "news" as the important ingredient of their papers, the Service became all-important. Since quality had to be paid for, Gelin pinpointed financial support as the crucial issue. In addition, he called for competent correspondents; a better sense of news selection; professional news handling, organizing, and interpreting; and faster distribution of the Service to subscribers. Finally, Gelin recommended a feature service and an "expert opinion staff" for research and in-depth reporting.[32] The convention endorsed his program, and the executive board named a committee, which included Gelin, to discuss the expansion of the News Service with Episcopal Chairman John Gregory Murray.[33]

By October the committee had prepared a report calling for all the improvements mentioned by Gelin plus a photo service, the addition of a business manager for the News Service, and an administrative assistant to the director. Implementation plans called for an increase in subscription rates, new sources of revenue through wider sale of the service, and the creation of an advisory committee made up of CPA members. The board appointed this committee immediately and charged its members with beginning a sales program of the proposal to the clients of the service. NC Director Frank Hall who was present at the meeting directed a memorandum on the matter to Msgr. Michael J. Ready, general secretary of NCWC. Describing the expansion program as "very ambitious," Hall declared that the Service had been expanding during the previous three years, and contended that the whole project was "purely a matter of money." The director expressed surprise over the recommendation for added subscribers. "It seems only yesterday," he noted, that "the Association was violently severing relations with us because we served some papers not members of the C. P. A., ..." Although Hall questioned whether subscribers would voluntarily agree to a considerably increased fee, he suggested that the NC editorial staff be expanded immediately.[34] A report to the membership explained that whereas originally the News Service had been subsidized by the bishops, the subscribers were now supplying the revenue and noted that the entire budget was "not much larger than" it had been when the Service began.[35]

The Committee for Expansion of the News Service continued to function, and Gelin, reporting to the board just before the 1946 convention opened, expressed satisfaction with the progress made.[36] In 1947 a liaison committee replaced this committee. Although expansion had been continuous since the 1944 meeting,[37] the 1951 liaison committee prepared a questionnaire to be circulated among NC subscribers to determine what improvements were still needed. Opinion was divided, but subscribers generally wanted better coverage of national issues and domestic events, found some dissatisfaction with NC's selection of news and features, and requested speedier delivery.[38] In his report to the 1952 convention, Hall made no special mention of the questionnaire but stressed how much had actually been accomplished and listed improvement in domestic coverage as the major goal for the coming year.[39]

In May of 1953, Father Thomas A. Meehan, president, reported to the board that Msgr. Howard J. Carroll, current general secretary of NCWC, had invited subscribers to the News Service to attend a session in Washington to discuss matters concerning the Service with staff members of the Press Department. The directors enthusiastically accepted the invitation, and Bishop Thomas K. Gorman offered to extend it to other eligible CPA members.[40] Hall suggested that the program should consist of discussions and round tables rather than speeches and that efforts be made to acquaint the editors with the general operation of the entire Conference. Bishop Gorman, notifying the editors that the seminar would be a two-day affair in mid-September and that the meeting might well reveal to them "many things previous unknown... as to procedures that have been found necessary or wise," informed them that the NC was interested in learning about their problems. To encourage openness and a frank two-way exchange of ideas, the seminar was closed to outsiders.[41]

Over seventy editors gathered in the NCWC headquarters building on September 17 and 18. Editors met staff members from the various departments and bureaus thereby acquiring a much better knowledge of the scope and workings of the Conference and learned at first hand of some of the difficulties in news gathering and distribution. Conversely, NC personnel gained a deeper appreciation of the needs and problems of the editors. Seminar sessions covered both foreign and domestic news, and the editors were encouraged to aid NC in the latter area by forwarding news stories from their own areas.[42] Bishop Gorman, stressing this last point in an address presented to regional meetings shortly after the seminar, mentioned that the outstanding result of the meetings had been the realization by all involved that "the effective, exact and expeditious gathering, processing and distribution of Catholic news can only be achieved by complete and understanding cooperation between the N. C. staff and all our editors." He held that the seminar had cleared up "misunderstandings of long duration," and he asked the editors to help overcome the "wholly inadequate domestic coverage" by sending in news as it happened.[43]

In the summer of 1954, Father Walter J. Tappe, Chairman of the Liaison Committee, recommended that another seminar be held, but it was not until the fall of 1955 that steps were taken to repeat the meetings because an "overwhelming majority" of the members had shown interest in a second seminar. Msgr. Robert G. Peters who had become committee chairman announced to the 1956 convention that a seminar was scheduled for mid-September in the NC headquarters.[44] Again the meeting was limited to subscribers of the News Service, and members were asked to submit questions they wished to have considered. At this second meeting, representatives of the various bureaus made only brief presentations as the majority of those in attendance had been present at the 1953 gathering. Participants discussed both foreign and domestic coverage once more, examined the feature service, and considered the possibility of obtaining a Wire Service from the AP as a means of covering secular news.[45]

Because there had been a three year interval between the first two seminars, the Liaison Committee considered planning a third for the fall of 1959. The 1960 Golden Jubilee Convention was scheduled to be held in Washington, however, and the committee feared that attendance at it might suffer if such a seminar were held. Rather, it suggested that on one of the convention days editors be invited to visit the Press Department. The opening general session of the newspaper members was set aside for this "telescoped seminar." Descriptions and analyses of the various services were presented by the NC staff, and then members asked their questions and voiced criticisms including the perennial ones that the service did not measure up to their needs and that they would gladly pay more if an improved service would be forthcoming.[46]

Although the Liaison Committee suggested a regular seminar for 1962, the editors voted against it. The next year, however, the response was positive, and a "full-fledged" seminar met in Washington in early October of 1963.[47] These seminars and the regular meetings of the Liaison Committee with representatives of the Press Department have resulted in increased competency and greater professional awareness within both groups.

The open windows of Vatican II brought some new problems into the light. The Liaison Committee and the various seminars had been concerned mainly with technical problems: the quality of photos used, the time lapse in providing the various services, inferior rewriting, incomplete coverage in certain geographical areas, and similar matters. Attention now turned to news concerning the Pope, the Church, and religion in general. Criticism centered not on techniques but rather on policy with some editors accusing NC of controlling and withholding news on these matters. In the spring of 1966 dissatisfaction reached a critical point. The board at its pre-convention meeting considered a report from Msgr. Peters stating that the Liaison Committee had planned to establish sub-committees to do a continuing study of the News Service, but NC Director Floyd Anderson would not give his approval to the project. A CPA board member maintained that News Service subscribers were entitled to examine a product for which they were paying, and another wondered aloud if the News Service might be taken over by the CPA. Finally, Bishop Clarence Issenmann intervened noting that if the editors felt that they could get along without the News Service, they were free to cancel their subscriptions to it. Inferring that there must be a misunderstanding, he offered to talk to Anderson about the matter. At a second meeting following the convention, the directors approved Msgr. Peters' suggestion that his committee go ahead on the study. 48

The same board discussed a resolution drawn up during the convention but not presented to the members for a vote because the Resolutions Committee had shown the draft to Bishop Issenmann as a matter of courtesy, and he had asked that he be allowed to present the problem to the bishops at their November meeting. The resolution, intimating that the News Service was controlled, stated:

> This body of journalists responsible for providing the truth to the people of God ask the board of directors to take effective steps to present a petition to the Administrative Board of the National Catholic Welfare Conference to authorize and encourage the N. C. W. C. News Service to report promptly, forthrightly, and responsibly on all matters of interest and concern within the Church

without regard to the special preferences of individual church officials.

The board accepted Bishop Issenmann's plan that he present the thinking of the CPA on this matter to the Administrative Board of NCWC.[49] At their August meeting, which Bishop Issenmann did not attend, the directors again talked about managed news. Bishop James P. Shannon, Assistant Episcopal Chairman, requested that the CPA present some "documented evidence of the alleged suppression and slanting of news" to support Bishop Issenmann's presentation in November. Msgr. Peters offered to have the Liaison Committee compile this material.[50] In March the chairman reported that his committee had met with the NC staff members and Bishops Issenmann, Shannon, and Paul F. Tanner (general secretary of NCWC). The committee had presented the documentation collected, and Bishop Issenmann then issued a letter stating that in the future the policy of the News Service would be to publish any news that had already been made public by the secular media.

The directors decided that CPA members should receive copies of this letter,[51] but by the time that the convention met, a new incident had occurred. Even though the National Catholic Reporter and several other sources had published the full report of the Birth Control Commission, NC had issued nothing. An enquiry showed that the official policy outlined by Bishop Issenmann's letter had been set aside in this instance. The directors drew up a "strong letter of protest" and sent it off at once to Archbishop John F. Dearden, President of NCCB, and the next day they informed the general convention of their action. Archbishop Dearden replied in June that Bishop Issenmann was in charge of the matter and that reaffirmation of the policy by him would be sufficient to preclude any future incidents.[52] In October of 1967 and again in the following January, Msgr. Peters reported that there was no evidence of news suppression, and that controversial issues were being handled satisfactorily by NC. In a convention report in May the chairman again maintained that since the incident of the year before, "... the Committee had found no trace of an attempt to exercise censorship over NC releases."[53]

Paralleling the movement to obtain full news coverage was the continuing study of the News Service by sub-committees of the Liaison Committee beginning in 1966. This project was expected to "provide a thoughtful and concrete analysis" of the various services distributed by NC and to discover "some creative and enterprising ideas" for the betterment of the Service. The fifteen members of the CPA-NC Liaison Committee were named to five different groups: writing and editing, foreign, domestic, features, and photos.[54] The sub-committees met with Director Anderson and NC personnel in February to discuss the usual letters from News Service subscribers and to examine the detailed analyses of the various services. These reports, totalling seventy-two pages and containing both praise and criticism of the Service, were distributed to NC subscribers who also belonged to CPA and were made available to other Association members on request.[55] Studies by such subcommittees continued, and President William Holub declared in his 1967 report that this project was bound to aid both the Service and its subscribers since it would always be goading the NC to greater efficiency.[56]

CPA editors have also been concerned with other phases of professionalism not directly connected with the News Service or with publishing techniques. These, including such intangible elements as general effectiveness and editorial viability, are measured to some degree by reader interest or lack of it. At the 1943 convention newspaper members devoted an entire day to a re-examination of their papers "provoked by the fact that a large percentage of the Catholic Laity persevere[d] as non-subscribers and non-readers"; the following year magazine members set aside a session for a series of papers explaining how to reach various classes of potential readers.[57] A joint session in 1946 considered "Reader Interest: How to Get It; How to Keep It." Here Joseph Gelin advised the editors to develop "showmanship" by dramatizing a story in such a way as to catch the eye of the reader. To achieve this, an editor had to be interested in the human elements of each story so that he could interest his readers in it. Unfortunately, the editors seemed to overlook Gelin's message. When the Journalism Awards system became effective, absence of the human touch in the columns of the Catholic Press was cited as one of its major deficiencies.[58]

Another reason sometimes given for lack of reader interest in Catholic magazines and newspapers was the paucity of humor in them. Charging that Catholic publications presented a false picture of Catholicism, one writer asked Catholic editors to exhibit Christian joy in their pages before they drove all their readers away. Bishop Robert J. Dwyer, addressing a convention session in 1956, mentioned this void and told the editors: "I only wish, once in a while, that we could dare to take ourselves a little less seriously." And, an assistant editor of America observed that "An aperitif of humor might even whet the palate of the faithful for larger portions of the dish we call the Catholic press."[59]

Just what Catholic publications were to say was also a matter of controversy. Even the fundamental dispensation of "news" was questioned. A member of the 1941 convention expressed doubt that diocesan papers were really "newspapers" at all. Another delegate who had the same reservation pointed out that a weekly organ could hardly compete with secular dailies let alone radio coverage. To overcome this problem, it was suggested in 1943 that Catholic weeklies concentrate on news interpretation, and this theme was repeated frequently thereafter.[60] More recently CPA members have been advised to organize, integrate, and interpret news materials so that their readers can really understand the substance of the Catholic Press. It has also been suggested that diocesan weeklies adopt some of the techniques of magazines and attempt to explain why things occur and what effect current happenings might have on the readers themselves--an approach calculated to provoke interest, result in editorial creativity, and even give a special "tone" to the paper itself.[61]

The predominance of the "official" press complicated such issues. Delegates to the 1942 convention were warned against the dangers of a "pressure press" and the possibility of newspapers becoming "propaganda" organs,[62] but Catholic editors at that time were not in agreement as to whether their publications should be house organs or newspapers in the true sense of the word. In later years Catholic journalists have characterized the Catholic Press as an extension of the teaching function of the Church, "the Catholic mind at work," and a means of unification within the diocese.[63] Although members of the hierarchy have at times re-emphasized the official stance,[64] editors have contested this view. They maintain that the bishop should not consider the diocesan paper as his "personal instrument," complain that Catholic newspapers need "a revitalized sense of pastoral mission," and argue that "Ecclesiastical subsidy... is not the sound base for a vital, relevant press voice in the Church."[65]

Too many editors have remained uncertain about the

chief purpose of their publication. Some have seen their role as an arm of the Church with a mandate to preach the message of Christ while others have maintained that the Catholic Press should treat all aspects of life and be a positive element of good in many areas. As it is all but impossible to follow either path completely, editors have often settled for a "Catholic view" of secular news.[66] A minority has even continued to insist that this "Catholic view" should not be limited to a once-a-week edition but should be available to Catholics every day.

In June of 1942 the Catholic Daily Tribune which had been appearing six days a week since July of 1920 ceased publication.[67] The daily had been losing both money and subscribers for years, and there were many deficiencies in its internal management.[68] Since it had never been able to attract national advertisers, the Tribune had to include a disproportionate amount of local news in order to attract advertisers in Dubuque. In competition not only with a secular daily but also with a diocesan weekly, it had often used its pages to solicit financial assistance. With an out-of-the-way location complicating its distribution problems, the Tribune's "news" was always one to four days old by the time the paper reached its subscribers. There was never a well-defined editorial policy, and the lay editors "aspired to represent the Catholic Church in the United States." In the daily's later years, the expansion of the Register and Visitor systems made it much simpler for a diocese to underwrite its own weekly.[69] Moreover, as one editorial noted, "The sad thing was that the vast majority of American Catholics lived in blissful ignorance that such a thing as the Daily Tribune even existed,..."[70]

Practical journalists who surveyed the field realistically dismissed the idea of a Catholic daily because of insufficient funds and lack of support by the Catholic reading public.[71] But others, imbued with some of the idealism and apostolic zeal that had inspired Nicholas Gonner to expand his paper into a daily in 1920, continued to dream of a daily that would present "an integrated Christian viewpoint on the whole of life."[72] A group of these idealists, all under thirty years of age, set out to establish another Catholic daily in the fall of 1949. They planned to call it The Morning Star and to publish in Chicago; but as preparations were nearing completion, a telephone call from the Chancery ordered the project stopped. The organizers looked for another location, and finally in the spring of 1950 Bishop

Edwin V. O'Hara permitted them to move to Kansas City, Kansas. Because the secular paper there was called the Star, the Catholic journalists re-christianed theirs The Sun Herald. The paper, an eight page tabloid issued five days a week, made its appearance on October 10 and ran almost seven months.

The Herald encountered many of the difficulties experienced by the Tribune. Advertisers were few, delivery was slow, the publishers lacked experience, and their executive talents were mediocre. In addition, the paper was very analytical in tone and there was too much reliance on news services rather than on first-hand reporting. In short, the Sun Herald did not measure up to "professional" standards. This fact, according to editor Robert G. Hoyt, may "have distracted quite a lot of critics from taking a careful and meditative look at what the paper was saying." However that may be, the original circulation of 2,500 never grew to more than 10,000, and the Sun Herald was forced to suspend temporarily for want of funds.[73] Hoping for better success in a larger Catholic center, the promoters of the daily moved to New York City, changed the name of the publication to the New York Banner, and issued several bulletins telling of their plans and soliciting financial backing. They hoped to procure enough funds to enable them to employ a staff of fifty and to increase the paper to sixteen pages with a projected press run of fifty thousand. Financial support did not materialize, and in March of 1952 the general manager announced that the proposed daily had liquidated.[74]

Because of the undesirable geographical locations of the two major attempts to establish a daily, and given their absence of high professional standards, it is difficult to judge whether or not Catholics would patronize such a paper if it were not hindered by such obstacles. Nonetheless, the idea of a Catholic daily has remained alive, at least "argumentively," over the years.[75]

Another reason that a viable Catholic daily has never become an actuality in the United States may be that public confidence has been lacking in the weeklies. The defects of the Catholic Press had been discussed and written about so much by the early 40's that it had become "treasonable to extoll the exploits or even to admit the worth of the Catholic newspaper at a C. P. A. Convention."[76] These criticisms continued. A collection of essays published in 1949 labeled the Catholic Press "immature," accused it of suffering from a "Siege Mentality," and in general found it ineffective. A Press Month article the following February called for less complacency and a more realistic treatment of current topics. Self-criticism became so common that Bishop John Mark Gannon told the 1952 convention that there existed an "all too prevalent disease... [which] causes us to disparage our own work, minimize its worth, hyper-criticize it."[77]

Following the usual Press Month diatribes in 1953, one of the journalists called for less negativism and suggested that future campaigns be given a more constructive orientation. Four years later, however, an article noted that many Catholic Press members were still displaying "a defeatist attitude."[78] Even worse, Vatican II resulted in a polarization of "liberal" and "conservative" editors, and they sometimes became openly abusive of one another. Finally, the 1963 convention adopted a resolution pledging the CPA to continue its efforts "to fortify the public's confidence in the Catholic press as an instrument of man's aspirations to full development by the exercise of responsible freedom."[79]

The same Catholic journalists who have been so outspoken in their criticism of the Catholic Press also insisted on exercising "responsible freedom" in their publications, objected strenuously to outside censorship, and often ignored sanctions approved by the Association.

In the earlier years of this period, stress was laid on the element of truth with the corollary that truth by its very nature leads to freedom. It was presupposed, of course, that the "truth" presented in Catholic publications, and particularly in diocesan weeklies, must be acceptable to ecclesiastical authority.[80] Gradually this emphasis changed, and editors turned toward a less restrictive view of freedom. In the fall of 1963 Robert G. Hoyt, addressing the South Central Regional CPA Conference on "Freedom in the Catholic Press," admitted that real freedom would involve risk, and commented that it might well be the "key element" in diffusing the workings and results of the Council. For, Hoyt declared, "only the week-by-week response of the Catholic [press?] in reporting, discussing, criticizing the life of the Church can show that all the talk about freedom is for real." Catholic Press personnel should be "journalists" rather than "press agents," and Catholic editors need courage and a readiness to endanger their own jobs, Hoyt continued. But they should also recognize the limits of their own competence and the place of restraint in their publications.[81]

In 1963 the CPA established a special Freedom of the Press Committee which co-sponsored with the Marquette University Institute of the Catholic Press a conference on press freedom in February of the following year. Joseph A. Breig, in a paper prepared for the Institute, stated that "the true good of the Church can be served only by fidelity to journalism's nature and principles." Defining the true journalist as "a specialist in communications... a professional," Breig insisted that such specialists must have whatever freedom is necessary to fulfill their duties in accord with the nature of journalism.[82]

The Freedom of the Press Committee was reappointed in 1964, and the next year the CPA met with the World Congress of the Catholic Press in New York City. Following the theme, "Truth in the Pursuit of Liberty," the sessions of the joint meeting examined the broad question of freedom of expression in Catholic publications. Discussing truthful reporting, Breig asserted that "... there is no place in moral and honest journalism for compromise of honesty, for double talk, for covering up, for playing fast and loose with truth, for treating adult readers like infants or like persons mentally retarded."[83] In the keynote address at the same convention, Raimondo Manzini, president of the International Catholic Union of the Press, insisted that "... the right to know requires freedom to approach the sources of the news, to discuss the intrinsic worth of ideas, to put man's conscience to the test of his own reflexion" and contended that such freedom, if properly used, would build--not destroy. Given modern communications systems and the propensity of secular journalists to treat of every happening, the speaker held that the present era was not one in which Catholic journalists should give consideration to "what should not be made known, but only about the way in which it should be made known." Quoting from a reference to public opinion made several years earlier by Pope Pius XII, Manzini asked his audience to avoid the two extremes of "servile silence" and "uncontrolled criticism."[84]

While some journalists feel their freedom is limited by restrictions from the hierarchy,[85] others note that editors sometimes try to "second-guess" their bishops and simply by-pass stories they think might offend the local Ordinary. Thus there is an element of self-censorship present which may spring from nothing more exalted than timidity.[86] Be that as it may, maintaining the delicate balance between "servile silence" and "uncontrolled criticism" has not been easy. In 1951 the CPA board considered Association action against members guilty of unethical practices in their publications and named a committee to study the problem. It was not until May of 1954 that David Host, who had become chairman of the Fair Publishing Practices Committee, presented a draft of a proposed Code of Fair Publishing Practices to the board. Host drew up an introduction to the Code which was published with it in the September Catholic Journalist. He observed that some few CPA members seemed unaware of their obligations and that such a Code would remind them of their duties and give public assurance that the Association as a unit was seriously concerned with its responsibility in these matters. Host explained that sanctions were not included since it was assumed that if the Code were adopted it would also be respected.[87] The Code was adopted in 1955 after considerable discussion and slight revision; it covered standards of reporting, treated matters of practical judgment, criticism, and persuasion, set forth criteria for publication rights and payment, and dealt with promoting, selling, and advertising.[88]

The 1957 Fair Publishing Practices Committee in a follow-up check on the Code found various infractions which it reported to the board along with a recommendation that formal disapproval be shown lest the Code become inoperative. The board agreed but at first limited its response to informing the membership that the committee was being empowered to censure violations.[89] A year later a board member noted that he had received a letter objecting to "a strong willed group of small publishers setting themselves up as both censors and policemen." The discussion which followed questioned whether the CPA was a juridical body with the right of censorship over member publications, but the directors moved on to other matters without taking definite action. The new board at its regular fall meeting engaged in "spirited discussion" of the Code, decided that there was very little to be gained in a positive way by enforcement of it, and rescinded the action taken previously.[90]

The Fair Publishing Practices Committee republished the Code in its original form in 1964. A year later the board recommended revisions and approved calling the attention of violators to their infractions. President William Holub chided the members for violations and told them: "We certainly are at a point in history when we should look at ourselves critically and police ourselves, if necessary."[91] The Code was again republished without changes in 1966, and the following May an interim measure was adopted for use until the entire Code could be revised and provisions made for its enforcement.[92]

The CPA also worked to improve relations with the hierarchy so that bishops as publishers might be less prone to interfere with the editors of the diocesan weeklies. One of the programs suggested by the Special Projects Committee in 1962 was that a bulletin be sent each month to bishops and to superiors of religious communities sponsoring publications to educate them concerning "the principles and practices affecting the Catholic press." Although the board discussed the bulletin and tacitly approved it, it was not implemented.[93] Relationships continued to deteriorate due to the lack of prudence displayed by some Catholic publications in their criticism of the hierarchy and, on the other hand, general denunciations of the Catholic Press by a few bishops. In February of 1965 the CPA issued a statement expressing concern, reaffirming the allegiance of the Catholic Press to the Church, and asking that criticisms "be specific enough to point out the very few and to protect the many."[94]

That May the Freedom of the Press Committee was replaced by a committee to study editor-publisher relations. Speaking to a regional meeting in the fall, Holub noted that "authority and freedom complement each other, but there obviously is misunderstanding as to the balance necessary to bring about the mutual benefits." Calling for less sensationalism and greater prudence and responsibility, the president told the members that the new committee under the direction of John O'Connor was exploring the problem.[95] Ultimately O'Connor's committee distributed a printed report which called for establishing effective guidelines so that editors and publishers might together "move harmoniously toward common destinations" and recommended "that an ongoing dialogue be instituted between publishers and editors of the Catholic press [in order to]... help to clarify aims, refine techniques, and renew the press with which we can reach the world."[96]

During the 40's and 50's, the Catholic Press emphasized greater professionalism in technical matters, but Vatican II presented a very special theological challenge to Catholic editors. As early as 1959 the editors of theology magazines held a symposium in conjunction with the annual convention; they called attention to the "ever-increasing interest of the laity in matters theological" and urged other Catholic editors to be more aware of the theological implications in the current news.[97] John G. Deedy, Jr., suggested in 1961 that the caliber of lay editors might well be improved by theology seminars sponsored by the CPA in cooperation with Catholic universities. The following year Father Nevins, then CPA president, took note of the need for a balance between technological and theological competence and suggested that priest-editors might well seek training in the former field while laymen should study theology. Delegates to the 1964 convention were told by Father George H. Tavard, a peritus at Vatican II, that they had a task of forming as well as informing the minds of the laity through their papers. He remarked that the editors must not only have knowledge but also be committed to a theological position.[98]

Some publications made individual efforts to instruct staff members in theology, and in 1965 Deedy's suggestion that a theology seminar be held was approved by the directors.[99] Delegates to the 1966 convention heard much about theology during the sessions. Keynoter Philip Scharper pointed out that because of the Council there would be an increasing need for "theological judgments" in the Catholic Press, and called on his audience to "restore theology to a position of operative rather than merely nominal importance." The convention also discussed and approved the theology seminars, and preparations began for the first one scheduled for February in Pittsburgh.[100] This initial seminar, attended by about sixty editors, focused on the "Constitution of the Church." An evaluation session described it as a "huge success," and Deedy recommended that others be held.[101] A second seminar in March of 1968 followed the theme of peace and the Christian's role and was co-sponsored by the CPA and the Marquette University Institute of the Catholic Press. About thirty members participated in this seminar and found the sessions most useful.[102]

As of 1968, then, the CPA has concerned itself with many aspects of professionalism. That these endeavors have succeeded, at least partially, is evident not only in the physical appearance of the majority of the publications in the field of the Catholic Press but also in the selection of material presented to the readers. Progress in this area depends on whether or not editors continue to adapt to the needs of the times so that their newspapers and magazines remain relevant and meaningful to Catholics of the future.

Notes

1. From "Convention Guide" for 1967. CPA.

2. For the early years, see above, Chapter II. The News Sheet as first issued was full newspaper size (eight columns). See: "Department of Press and Publicity," Bulletin, III (January, 1922), p. 22. Weeklies of the 20's and 30's sometimes used the News Sheet in full as the front page of the paper. Reference was made to this as late as 1941. See: Transcript... 1941, pp. 68-69. CPA.

3. One Catholic journalist in a 1943 article described the Catholic weeklies as "Neither good nor bad, nor hot nor cold; a mass, or a mess of mediocrity." See: Michael Williams, "Views and Reviews," Commonweal, XXXVII (February 12, 1943), 421. In a later article Donald McDonald, "State of the Local Catholic Press," Commonweal, LI (February 3, 1950), 460 referred to the lack of qualifications of the priest editors.

4. John G. Deedy, Jr., "The Missing Dimension; What is Lacking in the Catholic Press?" America, CIV (February 4, 1961), 591. Deedy charged that the Catholic lay editors of 1961 were not measuring up to their predecessors.

5. Reports on the session are from Abbreviated Report ... 1947, p. 20 (WC) and CJ, XII (June, 1947), p. 3. Shanahan's evaluation is in the latter.

6. Abbreviated Report... 1947, p. 20. WC. CJ, I (January, 1950), p. 5.

7. Articles on the service can be found in CJ, IV (November, 1952), p. 1 (December, 1952), p. 1 (February, 1953), p. 6 and (April, 1953), p. 6. Father Meehan, current president pointed with pride to this

service in his "Report of the President" to the 43rd Annual Meeting of the Catholic Press Association of the U. S., May 7, 1953, pp. 2-3. HC. Father Albert J. Nevins had much to do with this project. Reporting to the board in May, he cited the volume of work which burdened the judges as being the basic cause for its discontinuation: "Minutes, Board. . . May 6, 1953." CPA.

8. The 1953 meeting was discussed in CJ, IV (April, 1953), p. 2. Suggestion for the special meeting was contained in a letter from Donald M. Lynch, M. S. SS. T., to Kane, May 20, 1953. CPA. Preparations for the meeting and discussion of it comes from: "Minutes, Officers . . . June 19, 1953," p. 2 (PDF), Memo from Cahaney to Lynch and Rev. Hugh Morley, August 5, 1953 (CPA), CJ, V (October-November, 1953), p. 6 and (February, 1954), p. 4. Cahaney's comment is from "Report of the Executive Secretary" to Opening General Business Meeting, May 12, 1954, p. 4. CPA.

9. Discussion of such sessions can be found in "Minutes, Board. . . May 14, 1954," p. 4, "Minutes, Officers. . . July 8, 1955," p. 2 (CPA), CJ, VII (January, 1956), p. 1 and ibid., VIII (February, 1957), p. 1. President John J. Daly in his 1960 Press Month Statement reported: "There has been a pronounced improvement in technical skills, with editors using a variety of eye-catching makeups. Content reflects more maturity in editing and selectivity." Copy of Statement in DC.

10. For discussion of these Awards in the earlier periods, see above Chapter III and Chapter VII. The 1942 constitution provided that Associate Members "shall be officially and collectively known as the Catholic Press Association League of Writers." It stated that those associates should form local units and send delegates to the national CPA Conventions. Constitution and Bylaws [sic] of the Catholic Press Association of the United States (n. p., 1942), Art. III, Sec. 4. CPA. Father O'Connor's comment is in Abbreviated Report... 1946, p. 7. WC.

11. The first "Guide" was with CJ, VII (May, 1956), pp.

3-4 and was drawn up by an Associate Member Committee. See above, Chapter V. Jesuit Theological students belonging to St. Peter Canisius Writers' Guild in St. Marys, Kansas, had published The Catholic Writers' Magazine Market in 1943 according to C. P. A. Bulletin, II (March, 1943), p. 3. The 1959 CPA "Guide" was entitled Writers' and Illustrators' Guide to Catholic Magazine Market Requirements and came out under similar titles in the later editions. Some "Guides" were published as separate brochures while others appeared as a section of the CJ. The market description is from CJ, X (July, 1959), p. 1.

12. For the beginnings of the CSPA see above, Chapter IV. Discussion of affiliation is in Transcript... 1940, pp. 24-26. CPA. The 1953 change is noted in "Minutes, Board.. May 6, 1953," p. 5. PDF. The CSPA, in turn, had a positive influence on the CPA. During this period Dean O'Sullivan was involved in both groups and did much to coordinate the efforts of the two organizations.

13. Sectional meetings were reported in C. P. A. Bulletin, II (May, 1943), p. 2 and Program... 1944. WC. CJ, XII (April, 1947), p. 3, (June, 1947), p. 4, and (July, 1947), p. 8 carried articles on the survey. It is interesting to note that a private survey done by St. Bonaventures and reported in 1963 found that "Catholic colleges and universities produce an insignificant number of students with graduate journalism degrees and those are all at one institution (Marquette)." The author also reported that Catholic institutions did little to encourage students to enter Catholic journalism as a career. CJ, XIV (February, 1963), pp. 3-4. Dean O'Sullivan was responsible for the effort to recruit journalism teachers. See: CJ, I (April, 1950), p. 2, ibid., II (June, 1950), p. 6, and David Host, "Catholic Schools as a Source of New Members for the Catholic Press Association," n. d., but appears to be a report of the Catholic Press Committee to the officers. See: "Minutes, Officers... August 1, 1952," last page. CPA.

14. Reports on some of the Congresses are in In Vain, I (September, 1940), p. 4, CJ, III (December, 1951),

p. 8, ibid., V (October-November, 1953), pp. 6 and 8, ibid., VII (November-December, 1956), p. 3, and ibid., IX (September, 1958), p. 3. More than 400 attended the first Youth Session. See: CJ, VI (September, 1955), p. 4.

15. The observation concerning relations is from "Education Committee Report" to Board of Directors, January 20, 1966. The "Summit" was suggested in ibid., May 10, 1966. Relationships between the two groups and means taken are discussed in "Minutes, Board... August 4, 1966," p. 3; "Education Committee Report" to Board of Directors, May 16, 1967; and "Minutes, Board... October 27, 1967," p. 3. All in CPA.

16. The beginning of CJSF was announced in CJ, XII (June, 1961), p. 11. Ibid., XIII (June-July, 1962), p. 2 reported that Cardinal Cushing had promised a $5,000 donation. America made a similar contribution later in the year in memory of Rev. Wilfrid Parsons, SJ, according to CJ, XIII (October, 1962), p. 1. Initial grants were listed in CJ, XIII (October, 1962), pp. 1 and 16. Scholarships were offered only to secular journalism students. Personal interview with Msgr. Randall, May 15, 1968.

17. Transfer of the fund was asked for and approved in "Minutes, Board... March 2, 1967," p. 3 and ibid., May 19, 1967, p. 3. Both in CPA.

18. Catholic News (New York), May 31, 1941, credited Gannon with the Spanish service. Rev. Theophane Maguire, CP, was the convention speaker. See: Proceedings... 1942, pp. 80-84 for his address.

19. CJ, XII (August-September, 1961), pp. 10 and 20-21. This was a comprehensive report of the Latin American program.

20. The 1960 convention action was reported in CJ, XI (June, 1960), p. 14. Considine's suggestions are from a letter to Nevins, September 1, 1960. CPA.

21. CJ, XI (December, 1960), pp. 1-2 explained the program. The other elements were those recommended by Father Considine. See: "Minutes, Board...

January 5-6, 1961," p. 5. DC. Nevins' comments are in "Minutes, Board... May 19, 1961," pp. 2-3. CPA.

22. CJ, XII (August-September, 1961), pp. 10 and 20-21. In addition to Nevins the team was made up of Vice President Floyd Anderson and Joseph Sullivan of Sullivan Brothers, a large printing establishment in Lowell, Mass. It had worked from three centers: Lima, Bogota, and Caracas.

23. The second team was made up of Nevins, Msgr. R. G. Peters, and Douglas Roche. Its activities were reported in "President's Opening Statement" to 1962 Convention, pp. 1-2. CPA. Preparations for the Miami Convention were discussed in "Minutes, Officers... February 20, 1963," pp. 1-2. PC.

24. Aguiar to Anderson, March 29, 1963. CPA. President Kennedy to Anderson, April 23, 1963. PDF.

25. "Minutes Opening Business Meeting," May 1, 1963, p. 2 and "Latin American Affairs Committee Report" to Board of Directors, May 26, 1964. Both in PC.

26. CJ, III (September, 1951), p. 6 and ibid., IV (June-July, 1953), p. 2.

27. Catholic editors did cooperate with other communications groups to some extent. For example, a number of them attended a Communications Seminar sponsored by the NCWC Bureau of Information in August of 1959 according to CJ, X (September, 1959), pp. 1 and 6. The Decree itself, one of the first two passed by the Council, was approved at the second session, December 4, 1963. It was the first time that a Council had treated social communications, and it was especially unfortunate that it was not more relevant and forward looking. See: Walter M. Abbott, SJ (ed.), The Documents of Vatican II (New York, 1966), pp. 317-318. A CPA ad hoc committee chaired by Joseph A. Breig drew up a list of suggestions for use in the pastoral instruction which was to implement the Decree. "Suggestions for a Pastoral Instruction Concerning the Application of the Principles Set Forth in the Second Vatican Council's Decree on the Instruments of Social Com-

munications... " to Board of Directors, August 17, 1965. CPA.

28. CJ, XVI (January, 1965), pp. 2 and 9, NC Release 8/19/65, and "Minutes Annual Business Meeting," May 17, 1967, p. 2. HC.

29. At this time three laymen were named to the committee in addition to the four priests who had originally been appointed. "Minutes, Board... May 14, 1968," p. 1. CPA.

30. "Minutes Opening Business Meeting," May 15, 1968, p. 1. CPA. Msgr. Hurley explained that in the new structuring USCC would provide the mechanism for working with secular, political, economic, and social problems, and NCCB (National Conference of Catholic Bishops) would be concerned with religious affairs.

31. For earlier differences see above, Chapter III and Chapter IV.

32. Joseph A. Gelin, "Improving Our News Service," May 11, 1944. CC.

33. Proceedings... 1944, pp. 42 and 132. CPA. Other committee members were A. J. Wey, Father J. A. O'Connor, and Humphrey Desmond.

34. "Minutes, Board... October 20, 1944," pp. 48-49. CPA. Memo from Hall to Ready, October 26, 1944. PDF.

35. C. P. A. Bulletin, IV (December, 1944), pp. 1 and 3. At the same time that the CPA members were deprecating their Service for being inadequate, a Protestant journalist praised the Service saying in part: "The N. C. W. C. material is being used each year by a larger share of the Catholic papers because it is written by craftsmen who are more competent than those any one paper could command .... The Catholic Press is being fed and it is growing." See: Harold E. Fey, "Catholicism and the Press," Christian Century, LXI (December 13, 1944), 1443.

36. Abbreviated Report... 1946, p. 9. WC.

37. "Statement of the Director of the N. C. W. C. News Service" to 1952 convention, June 18-21, 1952, pp. 1-2. CC. Hall outlined year-by-year what had been done to improve and expand the Service. He commented: "Emergence of NC from a financial straight-jacket began seven years ago with effective C. P. A. collaboration. With a new system of charges devised, we have given papers the improvements the added money has made possible."

38. "Minutes, Board... October 18, 1951," p. 4 (PDF) and "Report of the Liaison Committee," November 27, 1951 (CC).

39. "Statement of the Director... ," op. cit., p. 1. CC.

40. "Minutes, Board... May 6, 1953." CPA.

41. Memo from Hall to Msgr. Carroll, June 3, 1953 (NCCB) and circular letter from Bishop Gorman, July 13, 1953 (CPA). The letter was also signed by the Assistant Episcopal Chairman, Bishop Albert R. Zuroweste.

42. "Catholic Press Seminar," CA, XXXV (October, 1953), p. 3 and CJ, V (October-November, 1953), p. 7.

43. NC Release 12/3/53.

44. CJ, V (June-July, 1954), p. 6; "Minutes, Board... November 3, 1955," p. 9 and "Minutes Opening Business Meeting," May 16, 1956, p. 2. Both in CPA.

45. Plans for the second seminar appear in CJ, VII (September, 1956), p. 1. About 90 attended this meeting. Copies of Transcripts made of the first three seminars are in the Press Department Library. Although a committee was appointed to investigate the wire service, this was not implemented since so few subscribers showed any interest in the project. See: "Report of CPA-NC Wire Service Committee" to Board of Directors, May 14, 1957. CPA.

46. The suggestion for the shorter meeting was made in

"Minutes, Board... May 15, 1959," p. 8. CPA. For the session itself refer to "Transcript of Proceedings, Editors' Seminar," May 10, 1960. Press Department Library.

47. Msgr. Peters announced the seminar in "Opening Business Meeting," May 1, 1963, p. 1. PC. By the time that the meeting convened Floyd Anderson had been named to replace Hall as NC Director. However, Hall was to remain until March when he would celebrate his fortieth anniversary with the News Service. CJN, XIV (August, 1963), p. 1. A fourth seminar was held in the fall of 1968; "... one of the more important topics considered was the possible change in the rates or rate formula to be charged subscribing newspapers by NC." This to the writer from Msgr. Peters under date of February 3, 1969.

48. "Minutes, Board... May 10, 1966," p. 2 and ibid., May 13, 1966, p. 1. Both in CPA.

49. Memorandum from Resolutions Committee to CPA Board of Directors, May 13, 1966, and "Minutes, Board... May 13, 1966," p. 1. Both in CPA.

50. "Minutes, Board... August 4, 1966," p. 3. CPA.

51. Ibid., March 2, 1967, p. 4. CPA.

52. The protest is recorded in "Minutes, Board... May 16, 1967," p. 3 and the Archbishop's reply in "President's Report" to Board of Directors, October 27, 1967. Both in CPA.

53. "Minutes, Board... October 27, 1967," p. 1 and ibid., January 19, 1968, p. 4. CPA. When a CPA editor charged in a column in America in March that NC was not "vigorous and honest," Msgr. Peters replied with a letter to the editor in which he stated that "NC stories are subject to no censorship whatever." See: America, CXVIII (March 2, 1968), 301-303; (March 30, 1968), 391; and (April 6, 1968), 426-427. The convention report is noted in "Minutes Opening Business Meeting," May 15, 1968, p. 2. CPA.

54. Preliminaries were announced in "Executive Director's Report," November 7, 1966 (AMF) and ibid., April, 1967 (CC).

55. "Minutes, Board... March 2, 1967," p. 4. CPA.

56. "President's Report to the Membership," May 16, 1967. CPA.

57. Proceedings... 1943, pp. 28-53 and Proceedings... 1944, 136-158. CPA.

58. Gelin's address was carried in NC Release 6/10/46. The lack of human interest was noted in CJ, IV (September, 1952), p. 4 and ibid., V (September, 1953), p. 2.

59. Herbert A. Kenny, "The Gaiety of Catholicism," Catholic World, CLXIX (April, 1949), 341-343; M. Rev. Robert J. Dwyer, "What Are We About?" Convention address printed in CJ, VII (August, 1956), pp. 3-4; L. C. McHugh, S.J, "Should There Be Humor in the Catholic Press?" America, CI (May 9, 1959), 301-303. Most of the responses to this article (printed in the June 20, 1959 issue, pp. 454-455) agreed with the Jesuit.

60. Transcript... 1941, pp. 50-52 and Proceedings... 1943, pp. 37-42. Both in CPA.

61. CJ, III (September, 1951), pp. 3-4 and ibid., IV (January, 1953), pp. 3-4.

62. Proceedings... 1942, pp. 25-31. CPA.

63. Characterizations are from: Myles Gannon, "The Catholic Press," America, XCVI (January 26, 1957), 478; Robert Hoyt, "Questions for Catholic Papers," America, CII (January 30, 1960), 522; and Rev. Vincent A. Yzermans, The Diocesan Press (St. Paul, 1959), p. 6. CC.

64. For example see: M. Rev. Joseph McShea, "Who Speaks for the Church?" American Catholic Historical Society Records, LXVI (December, 1955), 195-200. This was a copy of an address given to the Eastern Regional CPA Meeting on November 4. Bis-

hop McShea was emphatic in his view that "there can be no such thing as an independent Catholic press... " Likewise, Bishop Zuroweste at the 1960 Editors' Seminar reminded the participants that "the Bishops and your religious superiors have the final voice in everything that we do in behalf of the press... " This from "Transcript of Proceedings, Editors' Seminar," May 10, 1960. Press Department Library.

65. Hoyt, op. cit., 523 makes the reference to "personal instrument," John O'Connor, "A Question of Purpose," Commonweal, LXXVII (February 15, 1963), 540 wrote that generally speaking Catholic newspapers have "remained at the level of the American newspapers of General Washington's time: a government press and a party press. . . . " William Holub, "Address to Regional Convention of CPA," Fall, 1965 (CC) came out against a subsidized press.

66. In 1954 the CPA chose as its Press Month slogan: "Only the Catholic Press gives you the Catholic View." See: "Varied Functions of the Catholic Press," America, XC (February 6, 1954), 470.

67. See above, Chapter III, for the early history of this English Catholic daily.

68. Former editor Anthony J. Beck explained the reasons for the paper's failure in a letter to F. P. Kenkel, July 16, 1942. CC.

69. Father Daniel Francis Gebhardt, OFM, "A History of the Catholic Daily Tribune," (Unpublished MA Thesis, Marquette University, Milwaukee, June, 1953), pp. 117-131.

70. "Alarming. . . ," Commonweal, XXXVI (July 17, 1942), 292.

71. Herbert A. Kenny, "Catholic Daily?" Catholic World, CLXXI (April, 1950), 41-44 wrote in this vein.

72. Robert Hoyt, "The Vocation of a Journalist," Integrity, IV (October, 1949), pp. 31-37.

73. Discussion of the daily is based on Robert G. Hoyt,

"The Sun Herald, Catholic Daily of the '50's," Catholic Press Annual '61, pp. 13-18. CPA. For an interesting brief account by one less involved in the project see: Joe Dever, "Man Who Came To Lunch," Commonweal, LIV (April 13, 1951), p. 6. Dever characterized the Herald as "good-solidly good, and highly readable, but in a hybrid sort of way." See also: John G. Deedy, Jr., "Shattered Dream," Voice of St. Jude, XX (February, 1955), p. 8.

74. CJ, III (November, 1951), p. 7 reported the hopes of the group and (March, 1952), p. 7, the paper's liquidation.

75. David Marshall, "A Professional Press - Ways and Means," America, LXXX (February 26, 1949), 565-566 noted that New York Catholics would support such a venture only if it were a strictly professional product of which they could be proud. An example of a recent discussion of a Catholic daily is Clarence M. Zens, "What Happened to Our U. S. Catholic Daily?", CJ, XI (August, 1960), pp. 5-6. This was reprinted from the May 13 issue of The Catholic Standard (Washington, D. C.). In 1962 Msgr. Salvatore J. Adamo, editor of the Catholic Star-Herald of Camden, N. J., re-stated the case for a Catholic daily. See: CJ, XIII (August-September, 1962), pp. 20 and 22.

76. Proceedings... 1943, p. 34. The speaker was Father J. A. O'Connor.

77. The essays are in: Theodore J. Vittoria, SSP (ed.), The Catholic Voice (Derby, New York, 1949). The Press Month article is: Donald McDonald, "State of the Local Catholic Press," Commonweal, LI (February 3, 1950), 459-461. Bishop Gannon's comment is quoted in: Burke Walsh, "Catholic Press Gets Advice," CA, XXXIV (July-August, 1952), pp. 4-5.

78. The call for a positive approach came from Thomas A. Clemente, "How To Write On Catholic Press Month," CJ, IV (March, 1953), p. 5. Myles Gannon, op. cit., p. 479 spoke of the "defeatist attitude."

79. The abuses were mentioned in J. M. H[eidenry], "The Shaping Vision of the Catholic Press," Social Justice Review, LIV (February, 1962), 346. Commenting on the 1963 resolution, a veteran editor told a Southern Regional Meeting that "self-criticism in the Catholic press has gone far beyond the limits of prudence," charged that public confidence had been "grossly undermined" by unwarranted criticism, and called for a "more circumspect approach." See: CJ, XIV (November, 1963), p. 9.

80. See, for example, references to "truth" in Proceedings ... 1943, pp. 116-124 and Proceedings... 1944, pp. 8-11. Both in CPA. In addition: M. Rev. Richard J. Cushing, "The Catholic Press," The Catholic Virginian (June, 1946), pp. 9 and 42-44 and Bishop Ready's Press Month Message of 1951 reported in CJ, II (March, 1951), p. 5.

81. Robert G. Hoyt, "Freedom in the Catholic Press," printed in CJ, XIV (November, 1963), pp. 2-6 and 8.

82. The conference was announced in NC Release 12/30/63. A copy of Breig's paper, received from him, is in the writer's possession.

83. Breig was quoted in Michigan Catholic (Detroit), May 27, 1965.

84. Raimondo Manzini, "Truth in the Pursuit of Liberty," CJ, XVI (July, 1965), pp. 27-30 and 42. This issue printed all the major speeches given at the Congress.

85. Sometimes the complaint is outright. Ave Maria, CVI (November 4, 1967), p. 4 carried an editorial which said in part: "Even today, in many parts of the country, news of the Church is filtered by the hierarchy and middlearchy before it seeps down to us in the lowerarchy, in order not 'to scandalize the faithful'."

86. See: Rev. Don Ranly, C. P. P. S., "How Free is the Catholic Press?" CJ, XX (January, 1968), pp. 7-9. Father Ranly, a MA in Journalism and a staff member of the Precious Blood Messenger (Carthagena,

Ohio), based his article on interviews with Catholic Press personnel. He concluded that "there are excellent Catholic papers today, and some of them exist in places where the bishop is not overly liberal or permissive."

87. "Minutes, Board... May 16, 1951," p. 29, ibid., May 14, 1954, p. 31. Both in CPA. David Host, "An Introduction to A Code of Fair Publishing Practices for the Member Publications of the Catholic Press Association," CJ, V (September, 1954), insert.

88. CPA, A Code of Fair Publishing Practices (New York, 1955). Copy in CC.

89. Infractions were reported in "Fair Publishing Practices Committee Report" to Board of Directors, September 22, 1958. Board action is in "Minutes, Board... September 22, 1958," p. 4. Both in CPA.

90. "Minutes, Board... May 12, 1959," pp. 6-7 and ibid., September 25, 1959, p. 4. Both in CPA.

91. Holub, "Address to Regional Convention of CPA," Fall, 1965. CC. For the official action regarding the Code see "Minutes, Officers... June 18, 1964," p. 3 (PC) and "Minutes, Board... May 17, 1965," p. 1 (CPA). A mimeographed copy of the 1964 Code is in the PC.

92. A mimeographed copy of the Code, dated March, 1966, is in CC. The committee was waiting to incorporate the findings of an Editor-Publisher Committee which had been named to replace the Freedom of the Press Committee in 1965. See: "Minutes, Board... May 17, 1965," p. 1 and ibid., May 10, 1966, p. 3. Both in CPA. The interim procedure is contained in "Fair Publishing Practices Committee Report" to Board of Directors, May 19, 1967. CPA.

93. The bulletin is suggested in "Special Projects Committee Report" to Board of Directors, May 15, 1962. The board discussed the idea in "Minutes, Board... May 18, 1962," p. 1 and ibid., September 20, 1962, p. 6. All in PC.

94. "Statement by the Officers of the Catholic Press Association," February 25, 1965. Copy with "Minutes, Officers... February 25, 1965." PC. The immediate reason for the statement was a Catholic Press Month letter by Bishop Bernard J. Topel of Spokane in which he referred to 1964 as a "year of shame" for the American Catholic Press because of the attacks made against bishops. Reported in Pittsburgh Catholic, March 4, 1965.

95. The committee was named in "Minutes, Board... May 17, 1965," p. 1. Holub's comments are from his "Address... ", op. cit., CC.

96. "Report of Committee on Editor-Publisher Relations of the Catholic Press Association Presented August, 1966, Chicago, Illinois to The Officers and Board of Directors of the Catholic Press Association." Dinner meetings between groups of editors and bishops were arranged in November of 1966 and in April of 1967 and reported in "Minutes, Board... May 16, 1967," p. 3. Both in CPA. Unfortunately, the committee chairman and his own publisher became involved in a controversy which resulted in O'Connor leaving not only the Delmarva Dialog but also the Catholic Press field. The CPA offered its services as mediator, but the situation had become impossible before that measure was taken. See: "President's Report to Board of Directors," October 27, 1967. Both in CPA. Donald Quinn became the new chairman; the committee continued the dinner sessions and recommended a series of "white papers" on the problems of the press. "Report of Editor-Publisher Relations Committee," October 23, 1968. AMF.

97. "Proceedings of the Symposium for the Theological Magazines held in conjunction with The Forty-Ninth Convention of The Catholic Press Association." Copy in DC.

98. John G. Deedy, Jr., "The Missing Dimension: What is Lacking in the Catholic Press?" America, CIV (February 4, 1961), 590-592; Rev. Albert J. Nevins, MM, "The Catholic Editor: Litterateur or Organizational Man," Catholic Press Annual '62, pp. 4-6; Father George H. Tavard, "The Council, The Press

and Theology." This convention address was printed in CJ, XV (July, 1964), pp. 21-24.

99. "Minutes, Board.. August 17, 1965," p. 3. CPA. Msgr. R. H. J. Hanley, a member of the board, remarked that he had been conducting theology sessions for his staff "on a regular basis."

100. Scharper's address was reported in Long Island Catholic, May 19, 1966. Scharper was editor-in-chief and vice president of Sheed and Ward. Discussion of the seminars is in "Minutes, Opening Business Meeting," May 11, 1966, p. 1. HC. The Pittsburgh meeting was announced in NC Release 12/5/66. Deedy was chairman and David Host, moderator.

101. The seminar was reported in NC Release 2/18/67. Evaluation and recommendation for others is from "Minutes, Board.. March 2, 1967," p. 3. CPA.

102. NC Release 4/3/68 and "President's Report" to Board of Directors, May 14, 1968, p. 1. CPA. Msgr. Terrence McMahon also reported that the theology of the press would be discussed at the Midwest Regional Meeting in October and that the Association planned to co-sponsor with the Thomas More Association another theology symposium at Rosary College in River Forest in January of 1969.

Chapter IX

1968 And Beyond

For their fifty-eighth annual meeting CPA members returned to Columbus, Ohio, where the diocese was observing its centennial. The Catholic Times carried an editorial entitled "Welcome home!" reminding the delegates of the first convention held there in 1911, praising the accomplishments of the Association to date, and urging even greater achievements.[1] In keeping with the convention theme, "The Catholic Press and the City of Man," addresses treated racial issues, civil disorders, and the urban crisis. As customary, editorial, advertising, and circulation sessions occupied much of the convention program, and Journalism and Catholic Book Awards as well as the CPA special St. Francis de Sales award were all presented. No attempt was made to evaluate the successes and failures of the CPA since its beginning nor to compare and contrast the varied interests, goals, and activities of the group during more than half a century. Delegates were absorbed with the problems of the present and the uncertainty of the future, and the majority of them paid scant attention to the Association's past.[2]

Nevertheless, this meeting provides a convenient setting not only for such a recapitulation but also for some observations on the possibilities the future holds for the Catholic Press Association and the American Catholic Press in general. In some respects the problems of Catholic journalists have remained unchanged during the years considered in this study. How to increase circulation and obtain national advertising are problems that have never been solved satisfactorily. Apathy toward the press on the part of the Catholic public continues, and a defeatist attitude is fairly widespread among the editors and publishers. The journalists perennially criticize the means used in gathering and dissemminating news and complain that hierarchical support is lacking. Yet many CPA members remain satisfied with the status quo, and complete cooperation within the organization is a rarity. Internal struggles such as the controversy over the school plans, the differences concerning proposed dues increases, and disagreements regarding awards procedures have absorbed time and energy that might well have been expended on positive programs. Financial drives have been abortive, and inadequate resources have consistently frustrated the CPA's expansion plans. Attempts at self-criticism have generally been ineffective, and an underlying antipathy between clerical and lay members erupts periodically. Frequent turn-over of officers and directors of the Association has resulted in operational inefficiency, and committees have too often existed in name only. Conventions have been apt in "resolving that which is not, and considering it even as done,"[3] and the directors have conveniently tabled controversial and difficult matters thus delaying or averting action.

On the positive side, the Association has brought about a limited but real unification of Catholics in the field of journalism. Despite the criticism levelled against the NC News Service, members are aware of its value and of what it has done for their papers. Isolated activities such as the Circulation Vigilance work of the late 20's and early 30's, cooperation with the bishops in the decency drives, and aid to Latin American journalists have been singularly successful. Though often labeled inadequate or unsuccessful, continuing efforts including Press Month drives, involvement in the education of student journalists, publication endeavors, action regarding newsprint and postal rates, and the like, have been productive of much good. It is difficult to imagine what the American Catholic Press of today might be like had they not been attempted. Furthermore, Catholic publications are at last showing the results of efforts carried on for almost three decades to improve them professionally. Even though the CPA has not fulfilled the hope of its first president, Edward J. Cooney, that it might become "an organization of wonderful strength and influence,"[4] it has been the instrument through which solidarity of interests and major improvements in the Catholic Press have come, and for this it deserves commendation.

Certain general trends are recognizable in the history of the Association. The earliest period found the editors, most of whom were laymen, anxious to meet one another and to unite in a common effort to improve their publications. With the establishment of the NC News Service in 1920 emphasis moved from this nascent professionalism to business concerns. But within a decade interest had lagged, conventions were primarily social gatherings, many papers became diocesan owned, and cooperation with the hierarchy reached a record high. The 40's and 50's witnessed a re-invigoration of the organization and a re-orientation of goals. The group established a national headquarters, set up regional conferences, and renewed efforts along professional lines, especially in the area of technology. The 1960's found the members examining the "Image of the Church in America,"[5] and the effects of Vatican II, fostering Catholic journalism in Latin America, discussing the place of truth and freedom in their publications, and recognizing the importance of professionalism in all its phases. In this period, too, editors were quick to question censorship of news, and critics called for a return to an independent Catholic Press.

What, then, is the situation as we move into the seventies? Is the Catholic Press "obsolete" or "challenged"? Should we be writing its obituary or the story of its rebirth? Is the CPA nearing the end of its history or re-aligning its forces for a long and successful future? These are questions that can not be answered, but observations and speculations concerning them are pertinent to this study and have frequently been considered by CPA members in the recent past.

In a 1965 address Lawrence Cardinal Shehan noted that the Catholic Press still had much progress to make. He held that only by following its true purpose, "the pursuit and worthy representation of truth," and striving to attain its ideal which includes "a sense of reverence, of history, of responsibility, of justice and charity" could it reach maturity.[6] A Catholic Press Annual '66 article charged that the Catholic Press in America remained far behind "the rear guard of those involved in the renewal of the Church" and called for editors and writers who would "dare to be unpopular;... [who would] swim against the tide of apathy and passivism and traditionalism;... [who would] dare to be different."[7] Speaking to the International Catholic Union of the Press, Pope Paul VI expressed satisfaction that religion had become a matter of interest for the press in general but asked that Catholic journalists "refuse to embitter oppositions" and observe discretion in the choice of news items.[8] On a similar note, columnist George Shuster recently characterized the Catholic journalist of the future as "a spokesman for the affectionate community... [one who] will ask questions... [and] be critical" but temper his words with love.[9] The value of open communication has also been discussed, and editors have been urged to broaden their view, to be more aware of temporal matters, to bridge the gap between "religious" and "secular" issues, and to cooperate with the general press.[10]

Reconciliation of these views poses a problem which probably had its origins in the historical growth of the Catholic Press in this country. Catholic journals of the earliest period were more nationalistic than religious, but by the time that the Catholic Press Association was formed their major role was polemically religious. Editors concentrating on the refutation of error and anti-Catholic charges seldom printed criticism of the Church or the hierarchy. Having thus established a "defensive perimeter," many Catholic publications took on the characteristics of a "house organ" or an "official" press. At the same time, however, the tradition of a free press was gaining ascendency in the United States. The Catholic Press, unable to remain immune to this influence, became increasingly aware of its role as a "responsible" press. The practical result is that the American Catholic Press has developed a dual nature and finds itself questioning whether it is a "*Catholic* Press" or a "Catholic *Press*." It seems evident that the latter is finding prominence in this day of tension in the Church, and the future of the Catholic Press may well depend on how well it is able to adapt to this position.[11]

This presumes, of course, that it is still relevant to the world of today and specifically to American Catholics. Critics have charged that the Catholic Press is indeed outmoded, that the general news media have become conscious of the news value of religion, and that since anti-Catholic prejudice has virtually disappeared, Catholic news will be competently handled in the secular journals. Despite these arguments many CPA members hold that it is not yet time to announce the demise of the Catholic Press. A 1966 Press Month article argued that precisely because secular papers were carrying Catholic news, the weekly Catholic paper was needed to "deepen, expand, document, put into perspective, or localize the news that everybody read elsewhere during the week...."[12] In a similar vein, a Catholic editor in a 1967 convention address maintained that "... a professional Catholic press, reporting not only the spectacular but the substantial, is needed more than ever before to help Christians cope with the complex demands of living

Christianity in the modern world."[13] Another editor labeled as "simple" the view that the secular press can adequately cover religious news and pointed out that the general press looks for religious news that will provide "headlines and snappy leads" rather than for stories of "lasting significance." Noting the "mushrooming of news," he speculated that diocesan weeklies will be "even more vital to Catholics" in the years ahead as the dailies will be forced to devote less space to these topics.[14] And columnist Joseph A. Breig who devoted a series of articles to the topic charged that "the handling of 'things Catholic' in the secular press is, at best, generally superficial, and at worst, atrocious," and concluded that even if the general press overcame these deficiencies, the Catholic Press would still be needed to present "spiritual, moral and doctrinal matters."[15] Asked if a Catholic weekly is important in the post-conciliar age, Jeremiah O'Sullivan maintained that "... it's more important today if you have a free Catholic Press that gives the readers the truth about what's going on in the Church..."[16]

In addition to the necessity of continuing the Catholic Press as an essential adjunct to the general press, other arguments are given. One is that when Catholic periodicals fail to serve a function, they will cease of their own accord.[17] This law of nature seems to be operating at present especially in the area of Catholic magazines. A related argument holds that the Catholic reading public is now capable of appreciating better journalism and demands for this will ultimately result in improved publications.[18] Since the number of educated Catholics is on the increase, "... the future may be brighter than now appears to be probable."[19] The diocesan newspaper press is open to greater criticism since it is usually not only "official" but also subsidized. Nonetheless, where attempts have been made to sell such a paper on its own merits rather than through a parish coverage plan, results have been discouraging. In announcing the suspension of the New People, a diocesan newspaper in Kansas City, Missouri, the paper's directors disclosed that circulation had declined from twenty-eight to eleven thousand in a two year period during which voluntary subscriptions replaced a 100% plan. The editor attributed part of the decline to the reorientation of the paper toward "involvement in the community and the life of man."[20] This may well be one of the major problems of the diocesan press because seemingly "Countless Catholics don't want to hear about developments in the Church.... [and] are unsettled about changes, demonstrations, departures and defiance."[21]

Alternatives to the diocesan weeklies have been suggested. Though his plan was shelved because of "prior contractual agreements," Bishop Fulton J. Sheen, considered replacing the Rochester, New York, Courier-Journal with a once-a-week "Catholic page" in the secular daily paper.[22] The Diocese of Brownsville, Texas, sponsors a weekly religious supplement as part of the local newspaper,[23] and most recently the Arizona Register (Tucson) announced a changeover to a tabloid bi-weekly with in-depth articles to be sold on a voluntary subscription plan.[24] Some dioceses are considering mergers, and the national weeklies have been updated. Both the Register and Our Sunday Visitor are moving toward a more involved position. The National Catholic Reporter (established in 1964) maintains a liberal-progressive position which the newest national, Twin Circle (first issue November 12, 1967) counter-balances from the conservative-traditionalist viewpoint.[25]

In order to meet the needs of the times editors must be alerted to possibilities of the future. CPA officials have been orienting the thinking of the membership in this direction. During a recent Mid-West Regional Conference centered on "The Catholic Press and the Knowledge Explosion," the editors listened to a theologian, a social scientist, and a physical scientist outline some of the changes that might be expected in these areas within the next few years.[26] The Association also co-sponsored a seminar: "Toward the Seventies; Issues in Religious Journalism," which was attended by representatives of various Church presses. Discussing religious journalism, a speaker characterized it as a "more effective organ of communication than the pulpit, ... [and] an organ of teaching in the Christian Church."[27] Another speaker reminded the participants that we are in the midst of "a communications revolution," and admonished them to "adapt or die." Asserting that the individual is gaining more control over what communication he wants, he speculated that "... salvation for the printed media may well lie in providing assessment, evaluation and interpretation on a scale they never have before."[28]

Thus, the religious press and even the general press also face some of the same challenges as the Catholic Press. All are looking for ways to attract readers and to compete with TV and other audio-visual media.[29] In 1963 a Catholic editor joined a Protestant and a Jew in authoring The Religious Press in America, a study which showed a surprising similarity of problems and activities. The Protestant editor charged that "The whole thrust [of the Protestant Press] is toward organizational self-enhancement and protectionism." He admitted an absence of humor in his press, acknowledged that there were too many periodicals, and confessed to the presence of "house organs" and "blanket subscription" plans. Emphasizing the language problems, the Jewish editor saw little hope for optimism in the future, and pointed to "slipshod journalistic standards." A disinterested outsider who evaluated the "Secular Uses of the Religious Press," criticized religious journals for their lack of relevancy, their limited scope, and their failure to connect "religious vision to a sufficiently specific series of policies,..."[30]

Not surprisingly, then, the CPA has made overtures toward other press organizations sponsored by Church groups. As early as 1963 the Association was exchanging convention greetings with both the Jewish Press and the Associated Church Press (ACP), a Protestant organization,[31] and two years later CPA Director James A. Doyle attended meetings of the ACP which is structured along lines almost identical with those of the Catholic Press Association.[32] A joint convention of the CPA and the ACP met in Atlanta, Georgia, during May of 1969. Some sessions were shared by the two groups, and the general theme followed was "The Religious Press Faces the Future."[33] Such cooperative efforts might well be the solution to some of the common problems of the religious press and particularly to some of those now facing the CPA. As magazines and newspapers cease publication, both membership and income decline, resulting in decreased finances at a time when more money than ever is needed. This in turn leads to a loss of organizational prestige and influence and could well result in the eventual dissolution of a central office. Carrying the suppositions even farther, if the bishops should withdraw their support from diocesan papers, it is likely that most of them would be unable to survive.[34] In addition, young Catholic lay intellectuals of today are not attracted to the field of Catholic publishing in any large numbers.[35]

All this seems to leave but two viable alternatives. Catholic Press personnel might concede that the Catholic Press as we know it today is really no longer relevant. If this road is chosen, Catholic journalists must then decide whether in this ecumenical age a joint religious press may be the answer. The pooling of the resources of the various religious press associations and the maintenace of a common central office would surely be more economical, and the elimination of numerous publications now competing for readers would be welcomed. Perhaps the entire religious press could cooperate in issuing a national religious supplement comparable to that suggested for the Catholic Press in 1940.[36]

The alternative, which seems more acceptable at present, is that these same Catholic journalists realize the importance of "clarifying or redefining the role and function of Catholic journalism in the contemporary and obviously changing Church,"[37] and implement this realization. This will involve meeting the demands of the revolutions caused by the Council and by the recent developments within the communications industry. Catholic journalists of the future must treat all the concerns of the People of God including those affecting their lives in the world. Tensions between freedom and authority should be minimized. Editors must be aware of the importance of discretion in the exercise of journalistic liberty, and bishops need to be convinced that slanted news is not really "news" at all. Criticism of authority and of fellow editors might be curtailed, and efforts ought to be taken to attract talent into the field. If Catholic journalists can surmount these challenges the Catholic Press may enter a new era, one in which it serves as mediator between bishops, the Christian community, and the world.[38]

Notes

1. Catholic Times, May 12, 1968.

2. Program... 1968. CPA.

3. Miss Conway in her 1892 address to the Apostolate of the Press Convention gave this as the chief outcome of most conventions. The Convention of the Apostolate of the Press held in Columbus Hall New York City, January 6th and 7th, 1892 (New York, n.d.), p. 78. See also above, Chapter I.

4. "An Official Circular to the Members of the Catholic Press Association," n.p., n.d. CC.

5. Program... 1961. CPA.

6. NC Release 5/21/65.

7. Owen J. Murphy, Jr., "The Catholic Press Will Never be the Same," Catholic Press Annual '66, p. 32.

8. The National Catholic Reporter, December 11, 1968.

9. The Courier (Winona, Minnesota), January 9, 1969, carried Shuster's column.

10. Terry F. Brock, "How 'Catholic' Should the Catholic Press Be?" Catholic Press Annual '66, p. 23. See also: Catholic Review (Baltimore), May 31, 1966, and The Courier, May 23, 1968, for news stories on open reporting in the Catholic Press.

11. This discussion is based primarily on Daniel Flaherty, SJ, "Intellectual Freedom in the Catholic Press in the United States," Catholic Library World, XXXVIII (October, 1966), 95-99.

12. Anne Buckley, "Is the Catholic Press Obsolete?" Catholic Layman, LXXX (February, 1966), p. 28.

13. Douglas J. Roche, "The Catholic Press: Golden Era Ahead," Address at the 57th Annual Convention, May 17, 1967. CPA.

14. A. E. P. Wall, "The Diocesan Press," America, CXX (February 22, 1969), 220.

15. Breig's columns appeared in the Catholic Universe Bulletin (Cleveland), November 17, November 24, and December 1, 1967.

16. This from Mr. O'Sullivan in an interview, December 28, 1967.

17. Rev. Albert J. Nevins, "Breast-Beating in the Catholic Press," CJ, XIV (September, 1963), p. 11.

18. Roland E. Wolseley, "Publication Explosion in Catholic Press," Critic XXI (May, 1963), p. 56.

19. George N. Shuster, "Publication Explosion in Catholic Press," Critic XXI (May, 1963), p. 56.

20. CJN, XX (June, 1968), p. 1. The New People was characterized by the CPA board as an "excellent

newspaper produced in the best traditions of responsible journalism, highly esteemed by its professional peers..." This from a copy of a night letter sent by Doyle to Bishop Charles M. Helmsing and diocesan officials under date of May 18, 1968. CPA.

21. Wall, op. cit.

22. S. J. Adamo, "The Press," America, CXVIII (April 13, 1968), 522-523.

23. Joseph A. Breig in a column appearing in The Courier, October 19, 1967. Breig labeled it a "Piggyback Diocesan Paper" and called it "wildly impracticable."

24. CJN, XX (November, 1968), p. 1.

25. S. J. Adamo, "The Press," America, CXVII (December 2, 1967), 693-694.

26. Official Program, "Catholic Press Association Midwest Regional Conference, October 23-25, 1968." CPA.

27. Father Gregory Baum, "Theology." Address delivered to the seminar, September 14, 1968. Copy in AMF.

28. Theodore Peterson, "The Future of the Mass Media." Address delivered to the seminar, September 14, 1968. Copy in AMF.

29. Edwin Emery, The Press and America: an Interpretive History of Journalism (Englewood Cliffs, N. J., 1964) has concluding chapters on radio and TV competition, economic pressures, government relations, and "Challenge of Criticism."

30. Martin E. Marty, et al, The Religious Press in America (New York, 1963), passim. Other authors were John G. Deedy, Jr., David Wolf Silverman, and Robert Lekachman.

31. CJ, XIV (June-July, 1963), p. 13.

32. The ACP in 1966 opened a full-time office in Chicago. It provides typographical and layout services for its

190 members, conducts workshops and seminars, and holds annual conventions. In addition to publishing a press Directory, it issues a quarterly trade publication, represents its membership in government matters such as postal rates, and presents an annual "Award of Merit." Information from a brochure on the Associated Church Press. AMF.

33. Official Program, "Joint Convention, May 21-24, 1969," CPA.

34. Roche, op. cit., speculated that if this happened, "... next year's convention could be held in a phone booth."

35. John G. Deedy, Jr., "The Catholic Press," Commonweal, LXXXI (February 19, 1965), 666-667.

36. Msgr. Vincent Yzermans, editor of Our Sunday Visitor, in a TV interview considering "The Future of the Catholic Press," November 24, 1968, suggested some such approaches. An ecumenical monthly, a tabloid entitled Interchurch, began publication in Indiana in May, 1969.

37. "The Catholic Press and Dissent in the Church," America, CXX (February 22, 1969), 211.

38. Based on Roche, op. cit.

Appendix A

Membership Statistics*

Year	Active	Associate	Life
1911	37		
1916	66		
1921	81		
1926	101		
1931	116	23	137
1936	114		141
1941	173	85	
1946	215	428	
1951	192	136	32
1956	286	183	32
1961	291	161	27
1968	302	70	25

---

*Figures are from various sources; they should be considered as approximations rather than absolutes. Remember that the first drive for life members was in the late 20's and the associate member emphasis in the mid-40's.

Appendix B

Convention Dates And Sites

Pre-CPA

Year	Place	Dates
1889	Baltimore, Maryland	November 10
1890	Cincinnati, Ohio	May 7-8
1891	New York City	May 6-7
1893	Chicago, Illinois	September 6
1908	Cincinnati, Ohio	July 25
	Buffalo, New York	September 12

CPA

1911	Columbus, Ohio	August 24-25
1912	Louisville, Kentucky	August 16-17
1913	Milwaukee, Wisconsin	August 14-15
1914	Detroit, Michigan	September 12-15
1915	Toledo, Ohio	August 19-20
1916	New York City	August 18-19
1917	Washington, D. C.	August 10-11
1918	Chicago, Illinois	August 15-18
1919	CANCELLED	
1920	Washington, D. C.	January 23-24
1921	Washington, D. C.	May 13-14
1922	Cleveland, Ohio	July 28-29
1923	Indianapolis, Indiana	June 29-30
1924	Buffalo, New York	May 23-24
1925	St. Louis, Missouri	May 15-16
1926	Detroit, Michigan	June 17-19
1927	Savannah, Georgia	May 19-21
1928	New York City	May 24-26
1929	Cincinnati, Ohio	May 16-18
1930	Asheville, North Carolina	May 22-24
1931	Baltimore, Maryland	May 21-22
1932	Buffalo, New York	May 19-20
1933	Chicago, Illinois	June 22-24
1934	Cleveland, Ohio	May 24-26
1935	Atlanta, Georgia	May 23-25

Year	Place	Dates
1936	Columbus, Ohio	May 28-30
1937	Rochester, New York	May 20-22
1938	New Orleans, Louisiana	May 19-21
1939	New York City	June 22-24
1940	Detroit, Michigan	May 23-25
1941	Peoria, Illinois	May 21-24
1942	Birmingham, Alabama	May 28-30
1943	Toledo, Ohio	May 20-21
1944	Milwaukee, Wisconsin	May 11-13
1945	CANCELLED	
1946	Boston, Massachusetts	May 23-25
1947	St. Paul, Minnesota	May 21-23
1948	Cleveland, Ohio	May 19-21
1949	Denver, Colorado	June 15-17
1950	Rochester, New York	May 24-27
1951	New York City	May 16-18
1952	Notre Dame, Indiana	June 18-21
1953	Atlantic City, New Jersey	May 6-9
1954	Chicago, Illinois	May 12-14
1955	Buffalo, New York	May 25-27
1956	Dallas, Texas	May 16-18
1957	St. Louis, Missouri	May 14-17
1958	Richmond, Virginia	May 20-23
1959	Omaha, Nebraska	May 12-15
1960	Washington, D. C.	May 10-13
1961	Vancouver, B. C.	May 16-19
1962	Boston, Massachusetts	May 15-18
1963	Miami Beach, Florida	April 30-May 3
1964	Pittsburgh, Pennsylvania	May 26-29
1965	New York City	May 17-21
1966	San Francisco, California	May 10-13
1967	Toronto, Canada	May 16-19
1968	Columbus, Ohio	May 14-17
1969	Atlanta, Georgia	May 21-24
1970	Chicago, Illinois	May 20-23

Appendix C

CPA Officers

Pre-CPA

Year	President	Vice President	Secretary	Treasurer
1889	Rev. F. W. Graham		Condé B. Pallen	
1890	Condé B. Pallen	Rev. J. H. Conroy	James Delaney	Rev. F. W. Graham
1891	"	Rev. Patrick Cronin	"	Patrick Donohoe
1893	Rev. A. P. Doyle, CSP	Rev. D. S. Phelan	Thomas A. Connelly	
1908	Dr. Thomas P. Hart	William H. Hughes	John F. Byrnes	William A. King
CPA				
1911	Edward J. Cooney	William A. King	Claude M. Becker	Charles J. Jaegle, Sr.
1912	"	Rev. J. H. Cotter	"	"
1913	John Paul Chew	Rev. W. P. McIntyre, OP	Rev. Oliver T. Magnell	"
1914	"	Rev. Richard H. Tierney, SJ	"	"
1915	"	"	"	"
1916	"	"	Claude M. Becker	"
1917	Dr. Thomas P. Hart	"	"	"

Year	President	Vice President	Secretary	Treasurer
1918	Dr. Thomas P. Hart	Humphrey J. Desmond	Rev. Oliver T. Magnell	Charles J. Jaegle, Sr.
1919	NO CONVENTION			
1920	Claude M. Becker	Nicholas Gonner, Jr.	James A. M. Richey	"
1921	"	"	"	John Paul Chew
1922	Fred W. Harvey, Jr.	Rev. Charles J. Mullaly, SJ	William A. McKearney	Linus G. Wey
1923	"	Msgr. John F. Noll	Benedict Elder	Patrick F. Scanlan
1924	Patrick F. Scanlan	Rev. Thomas V. Shannon	"	Charles J. Jaegle, Jr.
1925	"	"	"	"
1926	Simon A. Baldus	Rev. Edward J. Ferger	"	"
1927	"	"	Joseph H. Meier	Charles H. Ridder
1928	Anthony J. Beck	"	"	"
1929	"	Rev. Thomas V. Shannon	"	"
1930	Benedict Elder	Rev. Harold Purcell, CP	"	"
1931	"	"	"	"
1932	Richard Reid	Rev. Albert E. Smith	"	"
1933	"	"	"	"

Year	President	Vice President	Secretary	Treasurer
1934	Joseph J. Quinn	Rev. James P. O'Brien	Joseph H. Meier	Charles H. Ridder
1935	"	Rev. Wilfrid Parsons, SJ	"	"
1936	Vincent deP. Fitzpatrick	Rev. J. W. DePencier, OSM	"	"
1937	"	"	"	"
1938	Charles H. Ridder	Msgr. Peter M. H. Wynhoven	"	Rev. Charles J. Mullaly, SJ
1939	"	"	Humphrey E. Desmond	Rev. Theophane MaGuire, CP
1940	Msgr. Peter M. H. Wynhoven	Alexander J. Wey	"	Rev. Edward L. Curran
1941	"	"	"	"
1942	Alexander J. Wey	Rev. John J. Considine, MM	Rev. J. Fred Kriebs	Charles S. Murphy
1943	"	"(Resigned-Wynhoven named)	"	"
1944	Rev. Patrick O'Connor, SSC	Humphrey E. Desmond	Rev. Paul Bussard	Francis A. Fink
1945	NO CONVENTION			
1946	Humphrey E. Desmond	Rev. Paul Bussard	Rev. Andrew L. Weldon, O. Carm.	Joseph A. Gelin
1947	"	"	"	"
1948	Rev. Paul Bussard	Francis A. Fink	Rev. Aloysius F. Coogan	George A. Pflaum, Sr.

Year	Vice President	President	Secretary	Treasurer
1949	Rev. Paul Bussard	Francis A. Fink	Msgr. John S. Randall	George A. Pflaum, Sr.
1950	Francis A. Fink	Rev. Thomas A. Meehan	"	Rev. Albert J. Nevins, MM
1951	"	"	"	"
1952	Msgr. Thomas A. Meehan	Charles J. McNeill	"	Rev. Philip L. Kennedy
1953	"	"	"	"(Resigned)
1954	Charles J. McNeil	Msgr. John S. Randall	Floyd Anderson	Rev. Albert J. Nevins, MM
1955	"	"	"	"
1956	Msgr. John S. Randall	John J. Daly	"	"
1957	"	"	"	"
1958	John J. Daly	Rev. Albert J. Nevins, MM	"	Rev. Hugh Morley, OFM, Cap.
1959	"	"	Martin E. Greven	"
1960	Rev. Albert J. Nevins, MM	Floyd Anderson	"	Rev. Raymond T. Bosler
1961	"	"	"	"
1962	Floyd Anderson	Msgr. Robert G. Peters	Msgr. J. G. Hanley	William Holub
1963	"(Resigned in July)	"	"	"
1964	Msgr. Robert G. Peters	William Holub	John A. O'Connor	Msgr. Terrence McMahon

Year	Vice President	President	Secretary	Treasurer
1965	William Holub	Msgr. Terrence McMahon	Msgr. J. G. Hanley	Dan Herr
1966	"	"	"	Joseph A. Gelin
1967	Msgr. Terrence McMahon	John A. O'Connor (Resigned)	"	Rev. Louis G. Miller, CSSR
1968	"	Joseph A. Gelin	Robert E. Burns	"
1969	Joseph A. Gelin	Rev. Louis G. Miller, CSSR	Msgr. Francis A. Maurovich	John F. Fink
1970	"	"	"	"

Appendix D

Other CPA Officials

Executive Secretaries

1945-1948	James A. Shanahan
1948-1949	Mrs. Helen Walker Homan
1949-1950	Rev. Alfred Barrett, SJ.
1950-1953	James F. Kane
1953-1958	G. Roger Cahaney
1958-	James A. Doyle

General Counsellors

1932-1945	Benedict Elder
1945-1954	Andrew McGivney
1954-1957	Richard Reid
1957-	Thomas A. Brennan

Appendix E

NCWC Officials

<u>Episcopal Chairmen, Press Department</u>

1919-1922	Bishop William T. Russell
1922-1924	Bishop Louis S. Walsh
1924-1930	Bishop Philip R. McDevitt
1930-1936	Bishop Hugh C. Boyle
1936-1943	Bishop John Mark Gannon
1943-1947	Bishop John Gregory Murray
1947-1951	Bishop Michael J. Ready
1951-1957	Bishop Thomas K. Gorman
1957-1962	Bishop Albert R. Zuroweste
1962-1965	Bishop Joseph T. McGucken
1965-	Bishop Clarence G. Issenmann

<u>General Secretaries, NCWC</u>

1919-1936	Rev. John J. Burke, CSP
1936-1944	Msgr. Michael J. Ready
1944-1958	Msgr. Howard J. Carroll
1958-1968	Msgr. Paul F. Tanner (Bishop, December, 1965)
1968-	Bishop J. L. Bernardin

NC Directors

1920-1931	Justin McGrath
1931-1963	Frank A. Hall
1963-1969	Floyd Anderson
1969-	Richard M. Guilderson, Jr.

Selected Bibliography

I. SPECIFIC

Because nothing of any extent has ever been done on the Catholic Press Association and very little has been published on the Catholic Press in this country, the majority of the references used in the present work were from original sources. Of greatest value were the available printed minutes, reports, programs, and proceedings of the Association. These were sparse in the periods 1913-1920, 1924-1927, 1931, and 1936-1938. Fortunately, correspondence and memoranda of the Episcopal Chairmen, Press Department personnel, CPA officers, committee chairmen, and Association members were available for those years. Contemporary Catholic newspapers and periodicals, and especially the NCWC publications from 1920-1953 and the CPA house organ after 1940, were very helpful.

A. ARCHIVAL COLLECTIONS

Hartley Papers in the Archives of the Diocese of Columbus, Ohio, consist chiefly of correspondence both to and from the bishop beginning in 1904 when he became Ordinary of Columbus. Unfortunately, the writer was permitted only limited use of this collection which is in excellent condition, separated into annual volumes, and well indexed.

Gannon Papers concerning the CPA from the Archives of the Diocese of Erie, Pennsylvania, were sent for use in this study. They consisted mainly of correspondence between the Episcopal Chairman and CPA officials. Because Gannon held the post during the period of re-invigoration of the Association and was himself a great promoter of the Catholic Press, his correspondence, though not voluminous, was most useful.

The Kenkel Papers and the Hudson Papers in the Archives of the University of Notre Dame contained little of note. Valuable, however, were the McDevitt Papers which contain extensive correspondence, copies of addresses given by the bishop, and pamphlets, clippings, etc., relating to the Catholic Press. Microfilm collections of the Proceedings, Constitutions, and Bulletins of the American Federation of Catholic Societies and the Social Service Newsletters were useful for the pre-World War I years.

B. OTHER COLLECTIONS (in order of their significance)

CPA Central Office contains the most complete collection for all Association materials from 1950 to the present. There are also collections of convention and board minutes beginning in 1924. All correspondence files were made available. The Library contains a number of published works on journalism, especially those relating to the Catholic Press, anthologies sponsored by the Association, Annuals and Directories, and an almost complete file of the various house organs.

NCWC Press Department correspondence dating from 1920-1942 particularly to and from Justin McGrath and Frank A. Hall was extremely useful in the period between the world wars. There is also a collection of minutes of board meetings and reports especially those concerning the News Service from 1920-1955. These were supplemented by memos from the directors which added interesting details.

Files in the Press Department Library included material on conventions, NC releases concerning the CPA and Catholic Press activities, convention addresses, annual reports of NC Director Hall, and transcripts of the Editors' Seminars held in 1953, 1956, and 1960.

NCCB Files of most use were those containing correspondence of Father John J. Burke (first general secretary of NCWC), materials and memos concerning the News Service sent to Burke, Ready, or Carroll by McGrath and Hall, and communications from the Episcopal Chairmen.

Clark Collection includes the correspondence of Rev. Peter E. Dietz, pamphlets and clippings concerning the general Catholic Press and CPA conventions, various convention programs, addresses, minutes, proceedings, reports, and brochures from 1911 to the present. Almost all issues of the house organ are also in this collection.

Wey Collection is made up of correspondence, minutes, and reports especially during the years Mr. Wey served as vice president and president of the CPA (1940-1944). Recently, Mr. Wey donated his collection to the CPA Central Office.

Daly Collection has correspondence, minutes, and reports especially from 1956-1960 when Mr. Daly served as CPA vice president and president. Also, bound copies of the Catholic Virginian during Daly's editorship (1946-1963) are there.

Hanley Collection dates from 1949 to the present. It is composed principally of printed materials: convention sessions, committee reports, and board minutes.

Pflaum Collection contains convention sessions, committee reports, board minutes, and addresses during the 1960's. These were presented to the author and have been added to the CPA and Clark Collections.

Ave Maria Files contain CPA circulars, letters to and from John Reedy, CSC, concerning committee work, and several files of correspondence on the school plans.

Our Sunday Visitor Files include printed materials, convention addresses, and OSV Dedication Booklet (September, 1961). No personal papers of Bishop Noll were located.

Individual items were received from: Floyd Anderson, Joseph A. Breig, Humphrey E. Desmond, Henry Gonner, Brother Lawrence Gonner, Frank A. Hall, David Host, Mrs. Mary E. Howard, James F. Kane, Father Louis Miller, Father Hugh Morley, Jeremiah O'Sullivan, Msgr. Robert G. Peters, Patrick Scanlan, Edward Walsh, and Father Peter B. Wiethe. About 40 Catholic editors responded to a preliminary survey, and several sent clippings or identified items from their files. Chancery officials reported on materials available in dioceses where the various Episcopal Chairmen had been located.

C. CPA PUBLICATIONS

House Organs

In Vain, 1940-1942.

C. P. A. Bulletin, 1942-1944.

Catholic Journalist, 1945-date.

Catholic Journalist Newsletter, 1963-1969.

Annuals

Buyers' Guide and Convention Annual [Titles vary slightly], 1951-1959.

Catholic Press Annual, 1960-1966.

Catholic Press Directory, 1951-date.

Anthologies

Herr, Dan and Clem Lane (ed.). Realities: Significant Writing from the Catholic Press. Milwaukee: Bruce, 1958.

Hughes, Riley (ed.). All Manner of Men: Representative Fiction from the American Catholic Press. New York: P. J. Kenedy & Sons, 1956.

Miscellaneous

CPA. I am The Catholic Press. n. p., 1946.

CPA. Selected Thought on The Catholic Press. n. p., 1936.

Wynhoven, Rt. Rev. Peter M. H. Swim--or Sink. Marrero, La.: Hope Haven Press, 1939.

D. NEWSPAPERS

The most complete collection of Catholic newspapers is that of the American Catholic Historical Society of Philadelphia at St. Charles Borromeo Seminary. The Catholic Columbian is available at Ohio Dominican College in Columbus. A complete file of the Sun Herald is in the Department of Journalism at Fordham. Both the University of Notre Dame and Catholic University have numerous Catholic papers in microfilm collections, and Marquette University has a smaller collection including the Catholic Citizen.

The following list is of those papers most helpful in

the present study:

Bulletin of the Catholic Laymen's Association of Georgia (Augusta)

Catholic Citizen (Milwaukee)

Catholic Columbian (Columbus, Ohio)

Catholic Herald (St. Louis)

Catholic News (New York)

Catholic Register (Kansas City, Missouri)

Catholic Review (Baltimore)

Catholic Standard and Times (Philadelphia)

Catholic Telegraph (Cincinnati)

Catholic Tribune (St. Joseph, Missouri)

Catholic Universe Bulletin (Cleveland)

Catholic Virginian (Richmond)

Church News (DC)

Church Progress (St. Louis)

Indiana Catholic and Record (Indianapolis)

Michigan Catholic (Detroit)

New World (Chicago)

Pittsburgh Catholic

Providence Visitor

Record (Louisville)

Tablet (Brooklyn)

Catholic

E. PERIODICALS

America

American Catholic Historical Researches

The American Ecclesiastical Review

Ave Maria

Catholic Action

Catholic Mind

Catholic World

Central Blatt and Social Justice (Social Justice Review)

Commonweal

Critic

Extension Magazine

Fortnightly Review

Historical Records and Studies

Josephinum Weekly

National Catholic Welfare Council/Conference Bulletin

N. C. W. C. Review

Records of the American Catholic Historical Society of Philadelphia

The Sign

Other

Christian Century

Editor and Publisher

Library Journal

Literary Digest

The Nation

Publishers' Weekly

F. ARTICLES ON CPA CONVENTIONS (Listed Chronologically)

Egan, Maurice Francis. "The Proposed Convention of Catholic Editors," Ave Maria, XXIX (August 24, 1889), 181-182.

Meehan, Thomas F. "The Press Association Harks Back a Half Century," America, LXI (June 24, 1939), 244-245. [Concerns pre-1911 meetings.]

"Catholic Press Association of America," America, V (September 2, 1911), 497.

Burke, John J., CSP. "The Convention of Catholic Editors," Catholic World, XCIV (October, 1911), 81-86.

"Ten Minutes with the Managing Editor," Extension Magazine, VI (October, 1911), p. 1.

[Griffin, Martin I. J.] "Catholic Press Association," American Catholic Historical Researches, XXIX (January, 1912), 70-71.

__________. "'A Real Catholic Press'," American Catholic Historical Researches, XXIX (January, 1912), 36-39.

"Note and Comment," America, XIII (August 28, 1915), 504.

"The Catholic Press Association," America, XV (September 2, 1916), 499.

Happel, L. F. "Echoes From the Catholic Press Convention," America, XIX (September 7, 1918), 523-525.

"The Eighth Annual Convention of the Catholic Press Association...", Extension Magazine, XIII (October, 1918), pp. 24-25.

"Annual Meeting of Catholic Press Association," Bulletin, III (June, 1921), p. 5.

"Cleveland Meeting of the Catholic Press Association," Bulletin, IV (August, 1922), p. 18.

Scanlan, Patrick F. "The Catholic Press Association Convention," Bulletin, V (August, 1922), pp. 5-6.

"Successful Convention of Catholic Press Association," Bulletin, VI (June, 1924), p. 12.

"St. Louis Meeting of the Catholic Press Association," Bulletin, VII (June, 1925), pp. 7†.

"The C. P. A. Meeting at Detroit," Bulletin, VIII (July, 1926), pp. 7†.

"The Catholic Press Association Meets," America, XXXV (July 17, 1926), 330.

"The C. P. A. Meeting at Savannah," Bulletin, IX (June, 1927), pp. 4-5.

"The Catholic Press Association," America, XXXIX (May 26, 1928), 149.

Hall, Frank A. "Cincinnati Meeting of the C. P. A.," Bulletin, XI (June, 1929), pp. 6-7†.

Elder, Benedict. "The C. P. A. Meeting at Asheville," Review, XII (June, 1930), pp. 4-6.

"C. P. A. Holds Successful Meeting at Baltimore," Review, XIII (June, 1931), p. 20.

"Catholic Press Convention," Catholic World, CXXXV (June, 1932), 367-368.

"The Catholic Press Association Meeting in Chicago," CA, XV (July, 1933), p. 12.

"Catholic Press Convention," Catholic World, CXXXIX (July, 1934), 495.

Walsh, Burke. "Atlanta Meeting of the C. P. A.," CA, XVII (June, 1935), pp. 7-8.

Quinn, Joseph J. "Silver Jubilee of the C. P. A.," CA, XVIII (May, 1936), pp. 17-18.

"Convention of Catholic Editors," America, LV (June 13, 1936), 218.

Walsh, Burke. "The C. P. A. at Columbus," CA, XVIII (July, 1936), pp. 15-16†.

"Voice," Time, XXIX (May 31, 1937), p. 27.

Walsh, Burke. "The C. P. A. Meeting at Rochester," CA, XIX (June, 1937), pp. 10-12†.

________. "The C. P. A. at New Orleans," CA, XX (June, 1938), pp. 7-8†.

"Catholic Press Association Convention," Catholic World, CXLVII (July, 1938), 492-493.

Walsh, Burke. "The C. P. A. at New York," CA, XXI (July, 1939), pp. 11†.

"MacManus' Scheme...," Time, XXXV (June 3, 1940), 48-49.

Walsh, Burke. "Detroit Meeting of Catholic Editors," CA, XXII (June, 1940), pp. 7-8†.

"Catholic Press Association," Catholic World, CLI (July, 1940), 491-492.

McDevitt, E. Francis. "The Catholic Press--Auxiliary of the Church," CA, XXIII (June, 1941), pp. 8-9.

"The Catholic Press Association in Birmingham," CA, XXIV (July, 1942), p. 11.

Walsh, Burke. "C. P. A. Measures Accomplishments," CA, XXV (July, 1943), pp. 6-7.

Flynn, Henry C. "C. P. A. Works for Peace," CA, XXVI (June, 1944), pp. 8-9.

Walsh, Burke. "Editors and Publishers Meet in Convention," CA, XXVIII (July, 1946), p. 5.

________. "Catholic Press Meeting in St. Paul," CA, XXIX (June, 1947), pp. 10-11.

"Catholic Press Convention," Catholic World, CLXV (July,

1947), 371-372.

"Catholic Press Awards," America, LXXIX (June 5, 1948), 216.

Fanning, William H., Jr. "The Catholic Press - A Necessity," CA, XXX (June, 1948), p. 8.

"Prose and Poetry," Commonweal, LII (June 9, 1950), 212-213.

"Gathering of Journalistic Interests of United States," CA, XXXIII (July-August, 1951), pp. 4-5.

Walsh, Burke. "The Catholic Press Gets Advice," CA, XXXIV (July-August, 1952), pp. 4-5.

"The Catholic Press and its Future," CA, XXXV (June, 1953), p. 3.

"Catholic Press on Public Issues," America, XCI (May 29, 1954), 236.

"Catholic Press Convention," Commonweal, LXII (June 17, 1955), 269.

"The Catholic Press," Time, LXVII (May 28, 1956), pp. 73-74.

"The Catholic Press Meets in Texas," America, XCV (June 2, 1956), 238-239.

Davis, Thurston N., SJ. "Some Significant Stands," America, XCVII (June 1, 1957), 276.

"Catholic Press in the 'Old Dominion'," America, XCIX (June 7, 1958), 304.

Lippard, William B. "Catholic Press Association," Christian Century, LXXVII (June 8, 1960), 708-709.

Davis, Thurston N., SJ. "Sad Surfside Soliloquy," America, CVIII (May 18, 1963), 702.

G. MISCELLANEOUS UNPUBLISHED STUDIES

Bray, Richard T. "Another: 'How About a Catholic

Daily?'" Unpublished term paper to Department of Communication Arts. Fordham University, 1955. [Study of the Sun Herald]

Donnelly, Rev. John B. "The Catholic Press in the United States - A Survey of its Beginnings and Present Status." Unpublished term paper to the faculty of School of Journalism in partial fulfillment of requirements for the Bachelor of Journalism. University of Missouri, 1959.

Gebhardt, Daniel Francis, OFM. "A History of the Catholic Daily Tribune." Unpublished master's thesis. Marquette University, 1953.

Hurley, John F. "Problems Now Confronting the Catholic Weekly." Unpublished master's thesis. University of Notre Dame, 1937.

McDonald, Donald. "A Study of Editorials in American Catholic Newspapers." Unpublished master's thesis. Marquette University, 1953.

Staudacher, Lucas G. "An Analysis of the Editorial Content of Four Catholic Newspapers." Unpublished master's thesis. Marquette University, 1947.

Valentiner, Rosemarian. "A History of the Catholic Telegraph Register." Unpublished master's thesis. Marquette University, 1947.

White, James A. "The Era of Good Intentions - A Survey of American Catholics' Writing Between the Years 1880-1915." Unpublished doctoral dissertation. University of Notre Dame, 1956.

II. GENERAL

The materials chosen for the general bibliography are those which the writer believes would be of greatest value in future investigations of the American Catholic Press as well as those most closely related to the topics pursued in this study of the CPA.

A. BIBLIOGRAPHIES, INDICES, ETC.

Collections and Miscellaneous

American Catholic's Who's Who, 1911 and 1934-date. St. Louis: Herder; Detroit and Grosse Points, Michigan: W. Romig & Company.

Catholic Builders of the Nation. Edited by C. E. McGuire. 5 vols. Boston: Continental Press, 1923.

Catholic Encyclopedia. Edited by Charles G. Herbermann, *et al.* 15 vols. New York: Robert Appleton, 1907-1912.

Dictionary of American Biography. Edited by Allen Johnson, *et al.* 20 vols. New York: Scribner's Sons, 1928. [Supplementary vols. in 1935 and 1958].

Dictionary of the American Hierarchy. Edited by Rev. Joseph B. Code. New York: Longmans, Green & Company, 1940.

Documents of American Catholic History. Edited by John Tracy Ellis. Milwaukee: Bruce, 1962.

National Catholic Almanac. Edited by Felician A. Foy, OFM. Paterson, New Jersey: St. Anthony's Guild. Began as *St. Anthony's Almanac* in 1904; then *Franciscan Almanac* until 1940. Continuous publication since 1936.

New Catholic Encyclopedia. Edited by a staff from the Catholic University. 15 vols. New York: McGraw Hill, 1967.

Official Catholic Directory. New York: Sadlier and P. J. Kenedy & Sons; Milwaukee and Chicago: Hoffman & M. H. Wiltius, 1871-date.

Bibliographies and Guides: Religious

Burr, Nelson. *A Critical Bibliography of Religion in America.* Vol. IV, Parts 1 and 2; Vol. IV, Parts 3, 4, and 5, *Religion in American Life*, 4 vols. Edited by James Ward Smith and A. Leland Jamison. Princeton: Princeton University Press, 1961.

Ellis, John Tracy. *Select Bibliography of the History of*

the Catholic Church in the United States. New York: Declan X. McMullen, 1947.

Romig, Walter, et al. The Guide to Catholic Literature. 8 vols. Detroit: Walter Romig & Company; Haverford, Pa.: C. L. A., 1940 ff.

Vollmar, Edward R., SJ. The Catholic Church in America: An Historical Bibliography. 2nd edition. New Brunswick: Scarecrow Press, 1963.

Bibliographies and Guides: Journalistic

Catholic Press Directory. Edited by J. H. Meier. Chicago: 1923, 1925, 1928, 1932, 1942. Edited by Joseph F. Wagner & Company. New York: 1943, 1945. Edited by CPA committee. New York: 1951-date.

Directory of Newspapers and Periodicals. Philadelphia: Ayer & Son's, 1930-date. [Appeared as early as 1880 under various other titles.]

Danielson, Wayne A. (ed.). Journalism Abstracts. Chapel Hill: Association for Education in Journalism, 1963-1968.

Price, Warren. The Literature of Journalism, An Annotated Bibliography. Minneapolis: University of Minnesota Press, 1960.

Willging, Eugene P. and Herta Hatzfeld. Catholic Serials of the Nineteenth Century in the United States. First and Second Series. Washington: Catholic University Press, 1959-1968.

Wolseley, Roland E. The Journalist's Bookshelf, An Annotated and Selected Bibliography of U. S. Journalism. New York: Chilton Company, 1961.

Indices

Catholic Periodical Index: Abundant references to the Catholic Press in general and to the CPA after 1930.

New York Times Index: Many references to Catholic Press and to CPA, but articles are only brief news notices.

Readers' Guide to Periodical Literature: Very few Catholic periodicals were indexed here before 1930. There are a few references to articles concerning the Catholic Press in secular journals.

B. BACKGROUND OF GENERAL CATHOLIC HISTORY AND OF MOVEMENTS TREATED IN THIS STUDY

Articles

Anon. "Bishops Urge Support of Legion of Decency," CA, XVI (December, 1934), pp. 5-6.

________. "Echoes From Catholic Week," Josephinum Weekly, II (September 2, 1916), 434-436.

________. "National Catholic Welfare Conference," Catholic World, CXVIII (November, 1923), 261-263.

________. "New York's 'Catholic Week'," Literary Digest, LIII (September 2, 1916), 562-563.

Browne, Henry J. "American Catholic History: A Progress Report on Research and Study," Church History, XXVI (1957), 372-380.

________. "Catholicism in the United States," in The Shaping of American Religion, Vol. I of Religion in American Life. Edited by J. Smith and A. Jamison. Princeton: Princeton University Press, 1961.

Collins, Michael. "What Next in Hollywood?" Commonweal, XX (August, 1934), 421-423.

Donnelly, Gerard B., SJ. "Catholic Standards for Motion Pictures," America, LI (August 18, 1934), 443-445.

Dowling, M. Rev. Austin. "The National Catholic Welfare Conference," The Ecclesiastical Review, LXXIX (October, 1928), 337-354.

Elder, Benedict. "'N. C. W. C.': The Church in Action," Catholic World, CXI (September, 1920), 721-729.

Ellis, John Tracy. "American Catholicism in 1960: An Historical Perspective," The American Benedictine Review, XI (March-June, 1960), 1-20.

Gleason, J. Philip. "Not German or Irish So Much as Catholic," Social Justice Review, LI (March, 1959), 384-385.

Gorman, Sr. Adele Francis, OSF. "Evolution of Catholic Lay Leadership, 1820-1920," Historical Records and Studies, L (1964), 130-165.

Gorman, Sr. Adele Francis, OSF. "Lay Activity and the Catholic Congresses of 1889 and 1893," Records of the American Catholic Historical Society, LXXIV (March, 1963), 3-23.

Guilday, Peter. "The Church in the United States (1870-1920): A Retrospect of Fifty Years," Catholic Historical Review, VI (January, 1921), 533-547.

[Hecker, Isaac P.] "Shall We Have a Catholic Congress?" Catholic World, VIII (November, 1868), 224-228.

Linehan, Paul H. "The Catholic Encyclopedia," in Vol. IV of Catholic Builders of the Nation. Edited by C. E. McGuire. Boston: Continental Press, 1923.

McAvoy, Thomas T., CSC. "The Background of American Catholic Unity," The American Ecclesiastical Review, CLV (December, 1966), 384-392.

__________. "The Catholic Minority after the Americanist Controversy, 1899-1917: A Survey," Review of Politics, XXI (January, 1959), 53-82.

McMahon, Charles A. "The National Catholic Welfare Council Explained - A Review of its Aims and Purposes, Accomplishments to Date and Plans for the Future," Bulletin, III (January, 1922), pp. 14-30.

McNicholas, M. Rev. John T. "The Episcopal Committee and the Problem of Evil Motion Pictures," The Ecclesiastical Review, XCI (August, 1934), 113-119.

May, Henry F. "The Recovery of American Religious History," American Historical Review, LXX (October, 1964), 79-92.

Mooney, John A. "Our Recent American Catholic Congress," American Catholic Quarterly Review, XV

(January, 1890), 150-169.

Reynaud, Albert. "Organize the Laymen," Catholic World, L (December, 1889), 285-291.

Slattery, Michael J. "Fraternal Societies of the Laity," in Vol. II of Catholic Builders of the Nation. Edited by C. E. McGuire. Boston: Continental Press, 1923.

Sullivan, P. J. "National Catholic Office for Motion Pictures," New Catholic Encyclopedia, X (1967), 222-224.

Books

Abell, Aaron I. American Catholicism and Social Action: A Search for Social Justice, 1865-1950. Notre Dame: University Press, 1963.

Callahan, Daniel. The Mind of the Catholic Layman. New York: Charles Scribner's Sons, 1963.

Cross, Robert D. The Emergence of Liberal Catholicism in America. Cambridge: Harvard University Press, 1958.

Ellis, John Tracy. American Catholicism. 2nd ed. revised. Chicago: University of Chicago Press, 1969.

________. American Catholics and the Intellectual Life. Chicago: Heritage Foundation, Inc., 1956.

Fox, Mary Harrita. Peter E. Dietz, Labor Priest. Notre Dame: University Press, 1953.

Gleason, Philip. The Conservative Reformers: German-American Catholics and the Social Order. Notre Dame: University Press, 1968.

Greeley, Andrew M. The Catholic Experience: An Interpretation of the History of American Catholics. Garden City, New York: Doubleday & Company, Inc., 1967.

Guilday, Peter. A History of the Councils of Baltimore (1791-1884). New York: Macmillan Company, 1932.

________. The National Pastorals of the American Hierarchy (1792-1919). Washington: NCWC, 1923.

McAvoy, Thomas T., CSC. The Great Crisis in American Catholic History: 1895-1900. Chicago: Henry Regnery Company, 1957. Paperback edition: The Americanist Heresy in Roman Catholicism: 1895-1900. Notre Dame: University Press, 1963.

Official Report of the Proceedings of the Catholic Congress held at Baltimore, Md., November 11th and 12th, 1889. Detroit: William H. Hughes, Pub., 1889.

Roemer, Theodore, OFM, Cap. The Catholic Church in the United States. St. Louis: Herder, 1950.

Shaughnessy, Gerald, SM. Has the Immigrant Kept the Faith? New York: Macmillan Company, 1925.

World's Columbian Catholic Congresses... 1893. Chicago: J. S. Hyland & Company, 1893.

C. BACKGROUND ON RELIGIOUS AND GENERAL PRESS

Wolseley, Ronald E. "The Influence of the Religious Press," Religion in Life, XXVI (Winter, 1956-1957), 75-86.

Emery, Edwin. History of the American Newspaper Publishers Association. Minneapolis: University of Minnesota, 1950.

__________. The Press and America: An Interpretive History of Journalism. Englewood Cliffs, New Jersey: Prentice-Hall, 1964.

MacDougall, Curtis D. The Press and Its Problems. Dubuque: William C. Brown Company, 1964.

Marty, Martin E., et al. The Religious Press in America. New York: Holt-Rinehart & Winston, 1963.

Mott, Frank Luther. American Journalism, A History: 1690-1960. 3rd edition. New York: Macmillan, 1962.

Park, Robert E. The Immigrant Press and Its Control. New York: Harper & Bros., 1922.

D. PAMPHLETS AND BOOKS ON THE GENERAL CATHOLIC PRESS

Burke, John J., CSP. Life and Literature: the Need of a Catholic Press. New York: Columbus Press, 1910.

Host, David. Education for Journalism: Notes on the Marquette Concept. Milwaukee: Marquette University Press, 1962.

The N. C. W. C. News Service. Its Value to the Catholic Press of the United States. Washington: N. C. W. C., 1925.

Pursley, Rev. Leo. The Catholic Press in the World Today. Huntington, Indiana: OSV Press, 1944.

Yzermans, Rev. Vincent A. The Diocesan Press. St. Paul: North Central Publishing Company, 1959.

Baumgartner, Apollinaris W., OFM, Cap. Catholic Journalism: A Study of its Development in the United States, 1789-1930. New York: Columbia University Press, 1931.

Bishops' Committee Sponsoring the National Organization for Decent Literature. The Drive for Decency in Print. 2 vols. Huntington, Indiana: OSV Press, 1939 and 1940.

The Catholic Press in the World Today: Addresses at the National Catholic Educational Press Congress... 1940. Milwaukee: Marquette University Press, 1941.

The Convention of the Apostolate of the Press held in Columbus Hall, New York City, January 6th and 7th, 1892. New York: Columbus Press, n. d.

Foik, Paul J., CSC. Pioneer Catholic Journalism. New York: U. S. Catholic Historical Society, 1930.

Ginder, Richard. With Ink and Crozier: A Biography of John Francis Noll, Fifth Bishop of Fort Wayne and Founder of Our Sunday Visitor. n. p., n. d.

Morley, Hugh, OFM, Cap. The Pope and the Press. Notre

Dame: University Press, 1968.

The Press In the Service of Faith and of Reason: Addresses at the National Catholic Educational Press Congress... 1938. Milwaukee: Marquette University Press, 1939.

Vittoria, Theodore J., SSP (ed.). The Catholic Voice. Derby, New York: Society of St. Paul, 1949.

E. ARTICLES ON THE GENERAL CATHOLIC PRESS

Adamo, S. J. "A Catholic Page," America, CXVIII (April 13, 1968), 522-523.

__________. "Dilemma in the Catholic Press," America, CXIII (August 14, 1965), 154-158.

__________. "Measuring Up," America, CXVIII (May 4, 1968), 624.

__________. "The Nationals," America, CXVII (December 2, 1967), 693-694.

__________. "No News Is Good News Is No News," Critic, XXVII (April-May, 1969), pp. 61-65.

Aguiar, Dr. Cesar Luis. "Struggles for Christ and Life: The Catholic Press in Latin America," Catholic Press Annual '62, pp. 9-11†.

Anderson, Floyd. "The Beginnings of the Catholic Press in America," Catholic Press Annual '60, pp. 31-34†.

__________. "The Big Problem of Diocesan Papers," Catholic World, CLXXX (January, 1955), 282-287.

__________. "Diocesan Weeklies: Good Can Be Better," America, LXXI (June 10, 1944), 261-262.

__________. "Union Internationale de la Presse Catholique," Catholic Press Annual '60, pp. 57-59.

Anon. "Alarming...," Commonweal, XXXVI (July 17, 1942), 292.

__________. "Almost a Century," America, XXVIII (November 11, 1922), 88.

Anon. "The Cardinal's Advice," Commonweal, LXIII (December 2, 1955), 228-229.

__________. "A Catholic 'Party Line'?" Commonweal, LXIII (March 23, 1956), 631-632.

__________. "C. P. A. Drive For Life Members," Bulletin, IX (December, 1927), p. 3.

__________. "Catholic Press Association Sponsors New Book Awards," Publishers' Weekly, CLXXXV (March 23, 1964), p. 33.

__________. "Catholic Pressure on the Press," Christian Century, LV (May 11, 1938), 582-583.

__________. "Catholics Launch a Daily Paper," Literary Digest, LXVII (October 23, 1920), p. 36.

__________. "Christian Decency Crusade in Regard to Reading," CA, XVI (March, 1934), p. 6.

__________. "Death Claims Director of N. C. W. C. News Service," Review, XIII (June, 1931), pp. 4-5.

__________. "Department of Press and Publicity," Bulletin, III (January, 1922), pp. 21-23.

__________. "Dissent in the Catholic Press," Commonweal, LXII (July 22, 1955), 387-388.

__________. "Father Burke Memorial Issue," CA, XVIII (December 15, 1936), in toto.

__________. "Is There Really a Catholic 'Line'?" America, XCIV (March 10, 1956), 627.

__________. "Leadership of the Catholic Press," Interracial Review, XXIX (June, 1956), 93.

__________. "A Look at the Catholic Press," Ave Maria, LXXXIX (February 28, 1959), pp. 5-10.

__________. "A National Catholic Press Month," Bulletin, II (October, 1920), pp. 14-15.

Anon. "National Catholic Press Month," Bulletin, II (February, 1921), p. 5.

__________. "National Catholic Press Month," Bulletin, III (January, 1922), p. 13.

__________. "N. C. W. C. News Service Approaches Self-Support Goal," Bulletin, VIII (January, 1927), pp. 4†.

__________. "The New Market," America, LXXXV (April 7, 1951), p. 4. [Catholic Press Directory]

__________. "News in Diocesan Papers," America, XCV (June 30, 1956), 314.

__________. "Notes and Comments," Catholic Historical Review, XXIV (April, 1938), 99-100. [Announcement of theses contest]

__________. "The Post Office and the Catholic Press," Extension Magazine, XLV (May, 1951), p. 22.

__________. "Press Month," Commonweal, LV (February, 1952), 414.

__________. "The Publication Explosion in the Catholic Press," Critic, XXI (April-May, 1963), 52-57.

__________. "Regarding the Short-Lived Cath. G. A. [sic] Press Society," Central Blatt and Social Justice, XXIV (January, 1932), 324.

__________. "The Religious Press in Danger," America, XVI (January 13, 1917), 338. [Postal increases]

__________. "A Short Story Contest," Extension Magazine, XII (April, 1918), p. 1.

__________. "Special Problems of the Catholic Press," America, XCII (February 5, 1955), 470.

__________. "10th Anniversary of the N. C. W. C. News Service," Review, XII (September, 1930), pp. 6-7†.

__________. "Varied Functions of the Catholic Press," America, XC (February, 1954), 470.

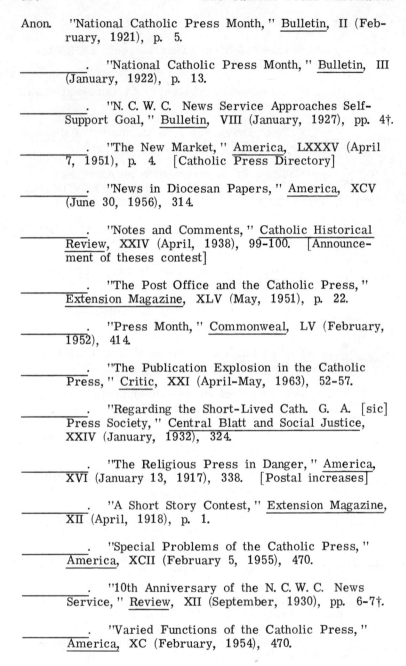

Anon. "We Catholics and Our Country," CA, XXIII (January, 1941), pp. 10-13.

_________. "Why Not ERNS?" America, CXVII (July 22, 1967), 73-74. [Advocates an ecumenical news service]

_________. "World-Wide Catholic Press Day," America, XXIII (May 15, 1920), 95.

Baldus, Simon. "Seventeen Years of the 'C. P. A.'," Bulletin, IX (May, 1928), pp. 7-8.

Barrett, Alfred, SJ. "The Catholic Press Must be Professional," America, LXXX (February 19, 1949), 542-544.

Beard, Eva. "Newsprint is a Weapon," America, LXXXVI (March 15, 1952), 637-639.

Beckman, Joseph. "How You Can Help the Growth of the Catholic Press," Grail, XXXVI (February, 1954), pp. 17-20.

Berding, Andrue H. "The Catholics and the Newspapers," America, XXXIV (January 2, 1926), 275-276.

Bovee, Warren G. "The Professional Needs of the Catholic Press," Social Justice Review, XLIX (February, 1957), 330-333.

Boyle, M. Rev. Hugh C. "A Call to the Laity," CA, XVII (February, 1935), pp. 7-8.

_________. "Catholic Press Month-1932," CA, XIV (February, 1932), p. 4.

Breunig, Jerome, SJ. "Present Position of the Catholic Press," America, XCII (February 19, 1955), 532-535.

Brock, Terry F. "How Catholic Should the Catholic Press Be?" Catholic Press Annual '66, pp. 20-23.

Brophy, Liam. "A Golden Opportunity," Apostle, XXXIX (February, 1961), pp. 2-3†.

Buckley, Anne. "Is the Catholic Press Obsolete?" Catholic Layman, LXXX (February, 1966), pp. 27-28.

Burke, John J., CSP. "How to Improve the Catholic Press," America, XIII (September 4, 1915), 511-512.

Cushing, Richard Cardinal. "'To Dare to be Involved'," Catholic Mind, LVII (July-August, 1959), 336-340.

Davis, Thurston N., SJ. "The Catholic Church on Temporal Affairs," Catholic Mind, LVI (June, 1958), 225-231.

Deedy, John G., Jr. "The Catholic Press," Commonweal, LXXXI (February 19, 1965), pp. 666-667.

________. "The Missing Dimension: What is Lacking in the Catholic Press?" America, CIV (February 4, 1961), 590-592.

________. "Shattered Dream," Voice of St. Jude, XX (February, 1955), pp. 7-9. [Catholic daily]

Desmond, Humphrey E. "Humphrey J. Desmond," Catholic Press Annual '62, pp. 20-21†.

Dever, Joe. "Man Who Came to Lunch," Commonweal, LIV (April 13, 1951), 6. [Sun Herald]

Doyle, James A. "History of the Catholic Press Association," Catholic Press Annual '60, pp. 27-30.

Dwight, Walter, SJ. "Supporting the Catholic Press," Catholic Mind, XIII (January, 1915), 16-20.

Eberhardt, Auleen B. "Women and the Catholic Press," America, LXX (February 5, 1944), 483-484.

Egan, Maurice Francis. "The Need of the Catholic Press," The American Ecclesiastical Review, X (May, 1894), 349-357.

Ellis, John Tracy. "The Catholic Press: Reflections on Past and Present," The American Benedictine Review, XIV (March, 1963), 45-61.

Everett, Millard F. "Blue Pencil Prelate," [Msgr. Matthew

Smith] Catholic Press Annual '61, pp. 41-44.

Fedash, Mayteel. "State of the Catholic Press," Catholic World, CLXVI (February, 1948), 416-423.

Fey, Harold E. "Catholicism and the Press," Christian Century, LXI (December 13, 1944), 1442-1444.

Fink, Francis A. "Our Sunday Visitor," Catholic Press Annual '60, pp. 37-41.

Flick, Lawrence F. "A Catholic Daily Newspaper," America, XII (November 14, 1914), 114-116.

Francis, Dale. "The Catholic Press and the Ecumenical Dialog," Catholic Press Annual '66, pp. 8-11.

Gabel, Rev. Emile, SA. "The Catholic Press of the World," Catholic Press Annual '61, pp. 23-26.

Gannon, M. Rev. John Mark. "Gravity of Times Makes Catholic Press Necessary," CA, XXIV (February, 1942), pp. 3-5.

__________. "Influence of Catholic Press on Post-War Reconstruction," CA, XXV (February, 1943), pp. 4-5.

Gannon, Myles. "The Catholic Press," America, XCVI (January 26, 1957), 477-479.

Garesche, Edward F., SJ. "Catholic Reading in Catholic Homes," Bulletin, V (February, 1924), pp. 7-8†.

Gonner, Brother Lawrence, SM. "The C. P. A. Has Come A Long Way - A Golden Jubilee in the Offing," Social Justice Review, LII (February, 1960), 327-329.

__________. "Facts and Hopes of Our Catholic Press," Social Justice Review, LI (February, 1959), 330-333.

__________. "First English-Language Catholic Daily in U. S.," Catholic Press Annual '61, pp. 35-40.

Gorman, M. Rev. Thomas K. "Saintly Patron of the Catholic Press," Columbia, XXXV (February, 1955), pp. 10-11†.

Graham, Robert A., SJ. "The Catholic Press and the United Nations," America, XC (October 24, 1953), 98-99.

__________. "The Catholic Press on the Eve of Vatican Council II: A Crisis of Confidence?" Catholic Press Annual '61, pp. 10-12.

Hall, Frank A. "Justin McGrath: First Director of NCWC News Service," Catholic Press Annual '62, pp. 38-41 †.

Hallett, Paul H. "The Register," Catholic Press Annual '60, pp. 47-51.

Happel, L. F. "The Catholic Daily Once More," America, XIX (September 14, 1918), 547-549.

__________. "Nationalism and the Catholic Press," America, XXI (August 30, 1919), 516-518.

__________. "One or Twenty?" America, XXI (July 5, 1919), 326-328. [National Catholic newspapers]

__________. "The Responsibility of the Catholic Press," America, XXI (July 26, 1919), 398-400.

H[eidenry], J. M. "The Shaping Vision of the Catholic Press," Social Justice Review, LIV (February, 1962), 345-346.

[Heuser, Rev. H. J.] "The Catholic Press and Episcopal Authority," The American Ecclesiastical Review, X (May, 1894), 358-368.

Holub, William. "Report on the CPA's Literary Awards Committee," Books on Trial, XV (February, 1957), 235-236†.

Holubowicz, William. "A Catholic Press Year," The Catholic School Journal, XLIII (February, 1943), 39-41.

Hoyt, Robert G. "Ads in the Catholic Press," Commonweal, LXIX (February 20, 1959), 538-540.

__________. "The Issue is Greatness," Commonweal, LXXVII (February 15, 1963), 534-538.

Hoyt, Robert G. "Questions for Catholic Papers," America, CII (January 30, 1960), 521-524.

__________. "The Sun Herald, Catholic Daily of the '50's," Catholic Press Annual '61, pp. 13-18.

__________. "The Vocation of a Journalist," Integrity, IV (October, 1949), pp. 31-37.

Hull, Ernest R., SJ. "The Catholic Press," Catholic Mind, XIII (January 8, 1915), 1-8.

Illig, Alvin, CSP. "Magazine Sales in the Vestibule," Priest, XIII (February, 1957), 119-124.

Kanka, Robert J. "Trends in Diocesan Newspapers," Religious Journalism Newsletter, 11 (Spring, 1968), pp. 10-12.

Kenny, Herbert A. "A Catholic Daily?" Catholic World, CLXXI (April, 1950), 41-44.

__________. "The Gaiety of Catholicism," Catholic World, CLXXI (April, 1949), 341-343.

Kerns, Vincent. "Some Notes on the Journalists' Saint," CJ, IV (June-July, 1953), p. 3.

King, Lawrence T. "Why Not a Catholic Daily?" Catholic World, CLXXXII (February, 1956), 352-357.

Kneip, Joseph. "Dr. Hart of Cincinnati," Catholic Press Annual '63, pp. 16-17.

Kramer, George N. "Has the Catholic Press Failed?" Catholic World, CXV (August, 1922), 610-622.

LaFarge, John, SJ. "Thomas Francis Meehan," Catholic Press Annual '61, pp. 19-20†.

Laviolette, Gontran, OMI. "The Catholic Press in Canada: Its Present Status," Catholic Press Annual '61, pp. 30-34.

Linden, Michael. "Musings of a Catholic Journalist," America, XXIX (July 28, 1923), 346-348.

Lucey, W. L., et al. "Catholic Press, World Survey, United States," New Catholic Encyclopedia, III (1967), 314-326.

McAvoy, Thomas T., CSC. "The Catholic Press and American Democracy," Ave Maria, LVII (May 22, 1943), 657-659.

McCabe, Clarence J. "The Press and the Family," Review, XII (January, 1930), pp. 17-18.

McCarthy, Charles. "The Man Who Proposed the Register System," Catholic Press Annual '63, pp. 31†.

McCarthy, John. "The Catholic Magazine Market," The Writer, LXXII (May, 1959), pp. 22-23.

McDevitt, E. Francis. "The Catholic Press Meets the War Emergency," CA, XXV (January, 1943), pp. 5-6†.

McDevitt, M. Rev. Philip R. "Catholic Press Month," Bulletin, VI (February, 1925), p. 2.

McDonald, Donald. "The Catholic Press," Commonweal, LXVII (October 18, 1957), 63-65.

__________. "The Catholic Press on Temporal Affairs," Catholic Mind, LVI (June, 1958), 224, 231-239.

__________. "Dean O'Sullivan," Catholic Press Annual '61, pp. 49-51.

__________. "How to Handle Temporal Issues," CJ, III (February, 1952), p. 3.

__________. "The State of the Local Catholic Press," Commonweal, LI (February 3, 1950), 459-461.

McGrath, Justin. "Catholics and the Catholic Press," Bulletin, X (January, 1929), pp. 5-6.

__________. "The National Catholic Press Bureau," Bulletin, I (June-July, 1920), pp. 7-8.

__________. "Some Considerations on Catholic Journalistic Ideals," in Vol. IV of Catholic Builders of the Nation. Edited by C. E. McGuire. Boston: Continental

Press, 1923.

McHugh, L. C., SJ. "Should There be Humor in the Catholic Press?" America, CI (May 9, 1959), 301-303.

McKune, Msgr. J. William. "Benedict Elder," Catholic Press Annual '61, pp. 61 and 64.

________. "A New Role for Catholic Weeklies," CJ, IV (January, 1953), pp. 3-4.

Markert, Francis, SVD. "How The Catholic Press Month Originated," The Christian Family and Our Missions, XLV (February, 1950), pp. 38-39.

Marshall, David. "A Professional Press — Ways and Means," America, LXXX (February 26, 1949), 565-566.

Martin, Brother David, CSC. "Catholic Periodical History, 1830-1951," Catholic Library World, XXVIII (1956-1957), pp. 74-83; 223-232; 341-349; and 401-405†.

Meehan, Thomas F. "The Catholic Press," in Vol. IV of Catholic Builders of the Nation. Edited by C. E. McGuire. Boston: Continental Press, 1923.

________. "Early Catholic Weeklies," Historical Records and Studies, XXVIII (1937), 237-255.

________. "The First Catholic Daily," America, XXXIX (May 26, 1928), 155-156.

________. "Periodical Literature, Catholic, U. S.," The Catholic Encyclopedia, XI (1911), 692-696.

Meier, J. H. "Notable Growth of the Catholic Press in the United States," CA, XV (February, 1933), p. 15†.

Meyer, J. Louis. "The Catholic Press Directory," Catholic Press Annual '63, pp. 24-25†.

Morley, Hugh, OFM, Cap. "The Catholic Press in the U. S.," Journalistes Catholiques (January-February, 1967), pp. 14-17.

Mundy, Paul. "The Catholic Press Triangle: Editor, Reader, Writer,..." Ave Maria, LXXXIII (February

25, 1956), pp. 15-17.

Murphy, Dr. Frederick V. "U. S. Exhibit at the World Catholic Press Exhibition," CA, XVIII (May, 1936), pp. 19-20.

Murphy, Owen J., Jr. "The Catholic Press Will Never Be the Same," Catholic Press Annual '66, pp. 27-33.

Murphy, William C., Jr. "The Catholic Press," American Mercury, IX (December, 1926), 400-408.

Murray, M. Rev. John Gregory. "The Catholic Church in Action," CA, XXVIII (February, 1946), pp. 3-4.

Myers, Rev. Rawley. "Are Catholic Weeklies Obsolete?" CJ, XIII (October, 1962), pp. 5 and 8.

Nevins, Albert J., MM. "Breast-Beating in the Catholic Press," CJ, XIV (September, 1963), p. 11.

__________. "The Catholic Editor: Litterateur or Organizational Man," Catholic Press Annual '62, pp. 4-6.

__________. "Our Coming of Age," Catholic Press Annual '61, p. 9.

__________. "The Strong Voice of Christ," Catholic Press Annual '63, pp. 14-15. [Latin American project]

Nicholson, Robert C. "Improved Typography in Catholic Papers," CJ, III (October, 1951), pp. 3-4.

O'Brien, M. "What the Catholic Press Most Needs," America, XIX (August 3, 1918), 399-400.

O'Connor, John. "A Question of Purpose," Commonweal, LXXVII (February 15, 1963), 538-541.

O'Grady, Desmond. "Lessons for the Catholic Press from the Council," Catholic Press Annual '66, pp. 3-6.

O'Hayer, Eileen. "Simon A. Baldus," Catholic Press Annual '62, pp. 51 and 59.

O'Sullivan, J. L. "Education for Journalism at Marquette University," Alumni Directory, Marquette (1960-1961), pp. 1-12.

Pallen, Condé. "The Independence of the Catholic Press," The American Ecclesiastical Review, X (May, 1894), 329-342.

[Preuss, Arthur] "The American Catholic Press Forty Years Ago and Now," The Fortnightly Review, XXXIX (October, 1932), 230.

__________. "The Catholic Press, Past and Future," The Fortnightly Review, XX (#15), 442-443.

Ranly, Rev. Don. "How Free is the Catholic Press?" CJ, XX (January, 1968), pp. 7-9.

Reilly, L. W. "The Weak Points of the Catholic Press," The American Ecclesiastical Review, X (February, 1894), 117-125.

Ridder, Charles H. "The United States Catholic Press Exhibit at Vatican City, 1936," Historical Records and Studies, XXVII (1937), 28-51.

Scanlan, Patrick F. "Claude M. Becker, A C. P. A. Founder," Catholic Press Annual '60, pp. 25-26.

Schalk, Adolph. "A Catholic Daily - A Creative Approach," Catholic Mind, XLVIII (April, 1950), 229-232.

Sheehy, Maurice S. "Catholic Press Victory," Commonweal, XXVII (February 4, 1938), 407-408. [Legion of Decency]

Sheerin, John B., CSP. "The Development of the Catholic Magazine in the History of American Journalism," Historical Records and Studies, XLI (1953), 5-13.

Smith, John Talbot. "Partisan Politics in the Catholic Press," The American Ecclesiastical Review, X (May, 1894), 343-349.

Southworth, H. Rutledge. "The Catholic Press," The Nation, CXLIX (December 16, 1939), 675.

Spillane, Edward, SJ. "The Catholic Press," Catholic Mind, IX (August 22, 1911), 259-272.

Stuart, Anne M. "History of the Catholic Press of Iowa," The Iowa Catholic Historical Review, V (October, 1932), pp. 11-38.

Sykora, Lawrence A. "The Student Crusade Plan In Action!" CJ, VI (November-December, 1954), pp. 3-4.

Thorman, Donald J. "Anti-Communist Record of the Catholic Press," America, XCII (February 5, 1955), 473-475.

________. "The Catholic Advertising Dilemma," Catholic World, CLXXVIII (February, 1954), 357-363.

________. "The Catholic Press and Catholic Social Action," Catholic Mind, LIV (January, 1956), 1-9.

VonFeldt, Elmer. "The Press and the Second Session of Vatican Council II," Catholic Press Annual '64, pp. 6-7†.

Wakin, Edward. "The Catholic Press: Parochialism to Professionalism," Journalism Quarterly, XLIII (Spring, 1966), 117-120.

________. "A Sociological View of the U.S. Catholic Press," Catholic Press Annual '65, pp. 46-47.

Wall, A. E. P. "The Diocesan Press," America, CXX (February 22, 1969), 220.

Walsh, Burke. "1939-Banner Year for the Catholic Press," CA, XXII (January, 1940), pp. 8-10.

Walsh, Edward A. "Tips on Feature Writing," CJ, IV (November, 1952), p. 3.

Walsh, J. C. "The Catholic Daily Paper," America, XIX (May 25, 1918), 158-159.

Welzbacher, Robert J. "How We Make the Parish Plan Work!" CJ, VI (February, 1955), pp. 3-4.

Whalen, James W. "The Catholic Digest: Experiment in Courage," Journalism Quarterly, XLI (Summer, 1964), 343-352.

Williams, Michael. "The Basis for a Catholic Daily Paper," America, XIX (October 5, 1918), 619-621.

__________. "The Bishops and Our Press," Catholic World, CXII (March, 1921), 721-732.

__________. "The Growth of the Bishops' Press Bureau," America, XXIV (February 26, 1921), 446-448.

__________. "Sharing Catholic Publicity with the Papers," America, XIX (June 22, 1918), 253-254.

__________. "Views and Reviews," Commonweal, XXXVI (September 18, 1942), 517-518. [Catholic daily]

__________. "Views and Reviews," Commonweal, XXXVII (February 12, 1943), 420-421. [Press promotion]

Wolseley, Roland E. "The Roman Catholic Press," Christian Century, LXVIII (March 14, 1951), 333-334.

Yzermans, Vincent A. "The Press and Vatican Council II," Catholic Press Annual '63, pp. 4-7.

__________. "The Priest and the Press," Chicago Studies, IV (Fall, 1965), 275-283.

Zens, Clarence M. "What Happened to Our U. S. Catholic Daily?" CJ, XI (August, 1960), pp. 5-6.

F. HISTORIES OF OTHER CATHOLIC GROUPS (useful for comparative purposes)

Gavin, Donald P. The National Conference of Catholic Charities, 1910-1960. Milwaukee: Bruce, 1962.

Gleason, J. Philip. "The Central-Verein, 1900-1917: A Chapter in the History of the German-American Catholics." Unpublished doctoral dissertation. University of Notre Dame, 1960.

Gorman, Sister Adele Frances. "Federation of Catholic Societies in the United States, 1870-1920." Unpublished doctoral dissertation. University of Notre Dame, 1962.

Plough, James. "Catholic Colleges and the CEA: the

Foundation and Early Years of the CEA, 1899-1919." Unpublished doctoral dissertation. University of Notre Dame, 1968.

Shanahan, R. J. "The Catholic Hospital Association: Its First 25 Years." Microfilmed doctoral dissertation. St. Louis University, 1961.

INDEX